DOGS BEHAVING BADLY

ALSO BY NICHOLAS H. DODMAN

The Dog Who Loved Too Much

The Cat Who Cried for Help

Dr. Nicholas H. Dodman

DOGS BEHAVING BADLY

An A-to-Z Guide to Understanding and Curing Behavioral Problems in Dogs

BANTAM BOOKS

New York   Toronto   London   Sydney   Auckland

Several different pharmacological agents are mentioned in this book for therapy of behavior problems in dogs. These drugs should only be prescribed by a licensed veterinarian who is familiar with their use. Drug doses vary considerably and side effects and idiosyncratic reactions may occur in some cases. In addition, many of the drugs referred to have not received formal (FDA) approval and a veterinary license. They may therefore only be prescribed when, in the veterinary clinician's opinion, they are truly indicated and when a veterinary label product that has the same action is not available. Also, the low protein diets referred to in the text should not be applied indiscriminately, especially in growing, pregnant, or nursing dogs. Veterinary advice should be sought before instituting such a dietary change.

DOGS BEHAVING BADLY
A Bantam Book / March 1999
All rights reserved.
Copyright © 1999 by Nicholas H. Dodman

Book design by Tanya Pérez-Rock

Library of Congress Cataloging-in-Publication Data
Dodman, Nicholas H.
Dogs behaving badly : an A-to-Z guide to understanding and curing behavioral problems in dogs / Nicholas H. Dodman.
p.   cm.
ISBN 0-553-10873-5
1. Dogs—Behavior.   2. Dogs—Psychology.   3. Animal behavior therapy.   4. Veterinary psychopharmacology.   I. Title.
SF433.D634   1999
636.7′088′7—dc21   98-46042
                                                CIP

Published simultaneously in the United States and Canada

Bantam Books are published by Bantam Books, a division of Random House, Inc. Its trademark, consisting of the words "Bantam Books" and the portrayal of a rooster, is Registered in U.S. Patent and Trademark Office and in other countries. Marca Registrada. Bantam Books, 1540 Broadway, New York, New York 10036.

PRINTED IN THE UNITED STATES OF AMERICA
BVG   10 9 8 7 6 5 4 3 2 1

To my family

CONTENTS

Contents

ACKNOWLEDGMENTS

I would like to thank the staff and faculty of Tufts University School of Veterinary Medicine for their encouragement and support in this, my third book project. I owe special thanks to Ronni Tinker and Vicki Aho for their patience and hard work in preparing the final manuscript. My thanks go also to my excellent editors, Brian Tart and Ryan Stellabotte of Bantam Books, and my agents, Glen Hartley and Lynn Chu of Writers' Representatives in New York City. Also my thanks go to my patients and their owners because their stories are the essence of this book and from them I have learned so much.

INTRODUCTION

Recently a Chihuahua cross with a fear of loud noises and flashing lights was brought to see me at Tufts Behavior Clinic. Among the list of things to which this dog was phobic I read camera flashes. This presented something of a dilemma because I photograph all of my clients and their pets during the initial visit to help me remember them better on follow-up. Naturally concerned about the dog's welfare, I was prepared to waive my photographic option, but the client insisted that I take the picture and witness her dog's reaction. She positioned her dog on top of one of the blue felt chairs in the consulting room and sat right next to him, as if posing for a family portrait. The minute the dog saw the camera his attention became riveted on it, and it was with some trepidation and concern for the dog that I finally raised the camera to my eye and depressed the button. As the flash went off the dog launched himself from his thronely position and attacked me. I wasn't scared, of course. Who would be, with a dog the size of a pocket-handerchief? But I certainly was surprised. After removing her dog, the woman smiled at me and said, "Yes, that's what he does. I just thought you'd like to see it." I thanked her for the opportunity, but I also thanked my lucky stars the dog was not a lot bigger.

The reason for this dog's reaction was most likely fear. Descriptions of other dogs like him and ideas for their treatment will be found in the section entitled "F—Fear-Based Conditions," although this case could easily be covered in "A—Aggression," too. Naturally there are several ways of classifying behavioral conditions and employing the various letters (*H* could stand for *hyperactivity* as well as *humping*), but I have selected a way that provides the greatest coverage of all commonly encountered behavioral problems. How did this alphabetic approach get started? You might well ask . . .

Years ago shortly after I developed an interest in animal behavior I was summoned to deliver my first talk on dog behavior to a group of owners and trainers who were visiting our school. For a while I racked my brains for an appropriate lead-in, doodling on a piece of paper and listing all the conditions I thought worthy of mention. I jotted down *aggression,* the most common and potentially most serious behavior problem of all, added *compulsive behavior,* a subject of considerable personal interest, appended *fears and phobias,* then *hyperactivity, barking,* and so on.

Very early in the process of generating the list I noticed that it lent itself to organization by means of an A-to-Z approach. Completion of the list became something of a challenge. "What could *D* stand for?" I would wonder. Then a couple of alternatives would occur to me—*destructive behavior* or *digging,* perhaps. "And what about *G*?" *Geriatric behavior,* of course.

Progress was rapid. Pretty soon I had a slide of the first ten letters of the alphabet assigned to launch my lecture and illustrate the plethora of potential problems that exist: I had, at this stage, an A-to-J of canine behavior problems, passing off other undesignated letters as "and so on." The list went something like this: A—Aggression, B—Barking, C—Compulsions, D—Destructive Behavior, E—Elimination Problems, F—Fears and Phobias, G—Geriatric Behavior Problems, H—Hyperactivity, I—Imprinting Problems, J—Jumping Up, "and so on." I always intended to complete the A to Z at some point, realizing that letters like *P,* for *predatory behavior,* and *S,* for *sexual behavior,* were just there for the taking. However, the years passed by and my slide became well-worn before I resumed the challenge.

In lectures that followed my initial icebreaker, I found it increasingly necessary to explain to my audience the staggering significance of canine behavior problems in the context of the larger world of canine health and well-being. The reason for this was that some people appeared to me to regard "behaviorism" lightly, viewing it as more of a curiosity, a sideshow, rather than the vital science that I know it to be.

I accomplished my objective by means of two slides. One showed shelter statistics of the millions of dogs (and cats) that come to untimely ends in the nation's shelters and pounds as a result of supposedly untreatable behavior problems. The other depicted a Dracula-ish veterinarian lurking outside his practice, where a brass plaque hung announcing DR. HARLEY GRIM. LICENSED TO PRACTICE BEHAVIOR MODIFICATION AND EUTHANASIA. The points were not lost on the audience. Misunderstood, untreated behavior problems account for some three million unnecessary dog deaths per year, more than all those dying annually from infectious diseases and half of the total annual mortality for dogs.

Many vets have, until recently, ignored behavioral-problem management and have simply punted these cases to trainers to manage as best they can, or have dispensed the ultimate solution, euthanasia. The holocaust, which is still occurring, is not all about bad behavior. Many dogs that are considered to be "behaving badly" are in fact displaying normal species-typical behaviors; it's just that these behaviors—like leg lifting on the couch, for example—are considered out of place in the home. Eric Burdon of the rock group The Animals (how appropriate) sang, "Oh Lord, please don't let me be misunderstood." That could easily be the canine equivalent of the Twenty-third Psalm.

One of the difficulties that behaviorists face is public perception of what they actually do to treat animals. Many people, it seems, are under the false impression that pet-behavior counselors believe themselves to be animal psychologists or psychiatrists that somehow "communicate" with their patients in order to effect a cure. One man, whose dog I successfully treated, commented to *USA Today* that "if you told me two years ago I'd be taking my dog to a shrink, I'd have just put a gun to my head." He called me up after this statement was highlighted center page in a blue box to say how sorry he was to have blurted it out and how well his dog was now doing. I told him I wasn't particularly concerned because I thought the story spoke for itself. Rather I hoped that the success of the treatment might sway others of the John Wayne mentality—"Never apologize (for your animal), mister, it's a sign of weakness"—to seek help. I found two great cartoons to illustrate the ludicrousness of the pet-psychiatrist concept. One depicted a dog sitting next to a dog "psychiatrist's" couch with a bubble coming out of his head saying, "Sixty bucks an hour and I don't even get to lie on the couch." The other showed a man drifting downriver in a torrent of water, hand raised, yelling to his faithful dog, who perched anxiously on the bank. The man was saying, "Lassie, get help." The next scene was of the dog reclining on a couch in a psychiatrist's office, apparently receiving counseling from the good doctor. I hope no one took these images literally. The fact is, we behaviorists do nothing more exotic than ask pertinent questions about dogs' behavioral histories, observe their behavior in the office, and sometimes run a few tests. And the bottom line is, the treatments work when nothing else does.

The purpose of this book, like its forerunner, *The Dog Who Loved Too Much,* is to increase owner awareness of canine behavior problems, both perceived and real, and to help the owner get a handle on his or her dog's behavior. Although dogs are social animals, making them wonderfully compatible with us, there are some areas in which they do not overlap with us and have quite different agendas. A dog is always a dog and never a person, no matter how hard we might try to personalize it, and will always have purely canine behavior traits to prove it. Interspecies dyslexia (as I call it) accounts for many of the misunderstandings that occur, but some other problems are truly dysfunctional in nature. In this book I describe all the main behavior problems that occur and detail their treatment. I focus on understanding what a dog's behavior means about its internal state, what it is trying to communicate by its behavior. Once this is grasped, then treatment options become logical selections rather than something of a crapshoot.

My hope is that *Dogs Behaving Badly* will turn out to be for pet owners what Dr. Spock's book was for generations of new parents—a source of information where there was little before. It is a dog owner's responsibility to make an effort to learn the ABC's of communication with his pet to maximize his understanding of a creature that is now frequently regarded as an additional family member. Such understanding will help head off potential problems at the pass, improve the quality of the psychological bond that exists between owners and their dogs, and should help prevent some of the unnecessary loss of dogs' lives attributable to behavior problems and miscommunication. Even if your dog's behavior is not problematic, but just plain puzzling, this encyclopedic approach to fathoming its behavior and improving your level of understanding should fill the gaps right down to the letter. New understanding has to start somewhere, so what better place than at the beginning, with "A—Aggression."

Nicholas H. Dodman
June 1998

DOGS BEHAVING BADLY

AGGRESSION

What does it mean if a dog bares its teeth at you? Is it warning you to back off or is it simply smiling? Or if a dog snaps at you—is this a failed bite, some other faux pas, or a well-placed warning shot across the bow? (Here's a clue: Dogs can snatch flying insects out of the air with their teeth.) And how about a large dog that stands on its hind legs, puts its forepaws on your shoulders, and stares at you, pupils big as manhole covers, making the hair stand up on the back of your neck? Is this dog checking you out or simply saying hello?

The truth is, these are typically aggressive behaviors, ranging from simple visual warnings to postural and symbolic threats. Most people like to think that they can easily recognize aggressive behavior in a dog when they see it, but from what they tell me in my consulting room, this is certainly not true. Aggression can be enigmatic. It presents in several different forms and its function, though often misunderstood, is not primarily to harm so much as to alter the behavior of another creature. Dogs communicate their aggressive intentions through changes in expression, posturing, and maneuvering, some so subtle as to be easily missed or misconstrued by a passerby, or even an owner. At the other end of the spectrum there's the ultimate form of aggression, the physical kind, which we all immediately recognize and dread.

The trouble people have interpreting aggression in their pets arises from difficulty in interpreting the premonitory signs, which involve a communication system quite different from our own. Physical aggression in the form of biting is only the final step in an elaborate progression of possible aggressive responses. Staring, growling, tensing up, and walking stiffly are just some of the ways that dogs signal aggression. No one, however, would misinterpret the savage attack of a child by, say, a pit bull, as anything other than aggression, and most people would be quite comfortable ascribing the term *vicious* to such a dog. Also, the causes and context of aggression differ considerably from what we might anticipate, and our pets' motives can be difficult for us to grasp. Few intuitively understand the intrinsic value of bathroom tissue to a dog, or the high price placed on garbage-can contents or a pair of socks. The progressive unfolding of aggression as a dog matures can be another point of confusion. Aggression may develop gradually in a pup as it matures, and because of this, owners can become immune to its occurrence until a serious incident takes place. Play growling and nipping by puppies may seem innocuous, but they often represent the tip of the iceberg.

Let's consider "mouthy" puppies first. These are puppies that won't take no for an answer and just keep chomping on people's hands with their needle-sharp teeth. Is this a normal behavior that should be tolerated and allowed to work itself out, or should the pup be firmly disciplined and stopped in its tracks? To understand what nipping means to a puppy, it helps to put yourself in the puppy's shoes (paws?). At a certain age, let's say about six to nine weeks, a pup finds itself a reasonably confident navigator of its environment and has a rambling mind that just won't quit, at least until naptime. It explores everything it can, using whatever means are at its disposal. Since the pup's feet are not really designed for this kind of work (no opposable thumb), it has only one respectable tool with which to investigate its environment—its mouth. To a puppy, its mouth is like a hand, an appendage for exploration.

Puppies direct their initial oral attentions to their mother's soft underbelly—the milk bar. If a pup bites its mom too hard during suckling she will rebuke the little tyke in no uncertain terms by means of a well-directed *contrecoup* of her own. The pup quickly learns lesson number one—Always listen to Mama. As the pups mature, their oral attentions turn more and more to extraneous targets, including their own littermates. It doesn't take long for the youngsters to discover that firmly grasping a littermate during play will often cause the other pup to complain vociferously and withdraw. Thus the game ends. Both the biter and the recipient learn something from this exchange. The biter learns to take it a little easier if the fun and games are to continue; that is, it develops bite inhibition, while the pup that is bitten learns to avoid the circumstances that lead to the painful consequence and that withdrawal is a good deterrent strategy.

Almost every pup finds itself in a new home without Mom and its former littermates. Instead, the pup now has doting human owners who must serve as parents and sibs rolled into one. What happens if a puppy wants to play, can't find its littermates, and nips a human? The answer depends on the temperament of the one assailed. A person knowledgeable about puppy matters might react like the mother dog or a littermate, with a sharp rebuke (perhaps the words "Stop it" or "Ouch") or a light tap on the nose with a finger, and/or immediate withdrawal of attention. Those less experienced might simply flail their hands around in vain attempts at avoidance. The result of the latter approach is that the puppy gets a large human squeaky toy, which is tremendous fun for the puppy, but, alas, irksome for the owner. The louder the owner complains and the more frantically the person waves around, the more entertaining the game becomes for the puppy. If there are no repercussions from overly rough play, as Rodney Danger-field so often says, "You just can't get no respect." And remember, some ten-pound puppies turn into humongous dogs—not that a fully grown land shark of any size is much fun to live with.

So when should you start to suppress nipping by puppies? Right from the get-go or later on? The most logical solution is to allow young pups some free rein at first, but once they start to nip with more force and confidence the brakes should be applied. You can, for example, make a loud noise and put your hands behind your back or in your pockets each time the pup's nipping exceeds your tolerance level. This advice is along the lines of the well-trodden path of nature—teaching puppies that humans are fun to play with, like Mom and littermates, but there are limits. Essentially, what you are teaching is bite inhibition. Pups that never nip in play do not learn this lesson. Unfortunately, when such standoffish youngsters grow up they often deliver a harder-than-necessary bite to make their point. Oriental breeds (such as the Akita and the chow) seem particularly reticent as youngsters and have to be drawn out of themselves if they are to learn this important lesson.

But beware, rehearsal of aggressive roles by puppies is not confined to nipping. There are other insubordinations that pups practice on unsuspecting owners as they push the envelope of tolerance through play. Growling, face licking, and humping, especially by males, make up the trinity of this one-upmanship. Puppies, like children, will never be perfect (except to look at), and a certain amount of tolerance is called for, but it is well to understand the messages being delivered so that you know how to react to reshape the behavior when limits are exceeded.

Let's deal with growling here (face licking and humping are dealt with in sections K—Kissing and S—Sexual Behavior, respectively). Growling is, by any manner of means, an aggressive act, a voluble warning or threat. A human equivalent would be a child cursing at or verbally threatening his parents. The child, like the growling puppy, is likely to incorporate this obnoxious form of communication into its behavioral portfolio (and even build on it) *if* the behavior goes unchecked. The best way out of this unfortunate loop is by avoidance, both with children and dogs. If watching the Power Rangers makes children start to speak and act aggressively, they shouldn't be allowed to watch the show. Likewise, stop whatever you are doing that makes your pup growl. For example, if tug-of-war causes growling, don't play with your dog in that way. Choose a more benign game, like fetch or hide-and-seek. If unchecked, growling will progress to nipping, nipping to biting, and so on. This is not to say that rough games like tug-of-war are always totally forbidden. There is a time and place for everything. Top sporting-dog trainers often use tug-of-war to increase a pup's confidence to a point, after which they know to put a lid on it. I sometimes use tug-of-war to increase a subordinate dog's self-esteem. It's like playing a board game with an underconfident child and allowing the child to win every time. This builds confidence, but if you already have an overconfident and pushy pup on your hands, such interactions are inadvisable.

Aggressive pups often first use their newly honed aggressive skills to make a serious demand when they are six to eight months of age. Some owners recognize the sudden change in attitude for what it is and scurry off to the nearest dog trainer. Others find an excuse for their dog's bad behavior and continue on until the next time. Typically, the first really troubling incident occurs when the dog is ten or eleven months old. By this time the problem may have escalated to one of a full bite. Next comes a limbo period, in which still-committed owners bounce around from trainer to behaviorist, trying to understand and fix the problem. The truth is that getting a handle on aggression once it has progressed to a biting stage is not always easy but, with patience and understanding, some inroads can be made with the consistent application of dominance-control strategies (see Appendix). The outlook is bleak, however, for repeat offenders, very large dogs, dogs that have bitten hard, and dogs that have bitten children.

Dominance Aggression Toward People

Dominance, the driving force behind virtually all canine aggression, can be difficult to fathom. Without it, dogs would not be able to stand up for themselves. Even dogs supposedly submissive by nature have at least a smidgen of dominance—for example, enough to warn usurpers off a favorite food morsel when circumstances dictate. Protection of valued assets is the hallmark of dominance and it can be virtually the only sign. An aggressive response by a dominant dog may also occur when the dog is prevented from doing something it wants to do, like napping or eating; in response to manipulations, particularly around the head and neck; or when the dog is admonished or disciplined. Different dogs have different priorities with regard to this list of potentially troublesome interventions. Some care less about food but will practically kill for a Kleenex tissue. Others are incensed by being stared at or disturbed while resting. For yet others, a hand placed over the head (as in petting) is the ultimate insubordination, to be repelled using all means available. It's literally and metaphorically different strokes for different dogs.

Not only do events that stimulate dominance-aggressive responses differ, but also the time of day is a factor when it comes to a given intervention. Happy times are usually safe times and earlier in the day is better than later in the day in this respect. Changing levels of the neurotransmitter serotonin may be responsible for this diurnal variation. The place of the challenge and the person doing the challenging are other important considerations. Crates and other "personal" spaces are often vehemently guarded by dominant dogs, though certain individuals may be able to get away with flagrant incursions into a dominant dog's inner sanctum, as if they have diplomatic immunity. Whomever the dog perceives as its leader is least likely to be subject to its aggressive advances. Family members are the usual targets of dominance aggression. It is as if their familiarity with the dog breeds contempt. But those who have weakened their social standing with the dog by, for example, indiscriminate petting and by spoiling of the dog are, as we often say in England, on a sticky wicket.

Adding all this together, you will see that dominance aggression is something of a moving target, its expression altering depending on time, place, and circumstance, though being relatively consistent under defined circumstances. A further complication is that extremely dominant dogs, like people who are in charge, are aggressive less often. This is because they know they can have their way if they want. To explain this to my clients, I sometimes use the analogy of the dean of a school, who is almost always a confident, smiling yet assertive and "in-charge" type of individual. Dominant? Yes. Aggressive? No. Not usually. However, if you were to walk straight into a dean's office uninvited, staring directly at him, and start patting him on the head, that might well elicit some verbal, if not symbolic, threat. Once I was going through this diatribe with a client when he burst into fits of laughter until tears ran down his cheeks. When I inquired what had prompted this sudden outburst, he said, "I am a retired dean and I know exactly what you mean. It's all so true."

The most dominant dog I ever saw was a three-year-old uncastrated male Labrador. He practically swaggered when he walked. The reason he was brought to me was because he would occasionally launch himself at his owner, an experienced dog trainer, from behind while they were out jogging together. No one else was bothered by the dog (though they knew not to cross him). The trainer was the only one worthy of competition. The trainer dealt with the problem using some well-timed karate kicks but wanted to know if there was any way the dog could be further rehabilitated (the effects of the kicks were only transient). Well, there are ways, but this owner didn't want to bother with them and decided instead on refining his karate-kick technique. What stands out in my mind, though, was this dog's arrogant behavior with regard to people and other dogs. As he exited our clinic that day, a medium-sized mixed-breed dog in the waiting room lunged at him amid much barking and threat behavior, only to be apprehended by his owner's lightning-fast reactions. Our hero did not even flinch. He just walked on by, looking straight ahead, not even giving his challenger the time of day. I believe he could have broken the other dog's neck if he had chosen, but fortunately an accident of this nature was averted by the quick response of the other dog's owner. And as the challenger resigned himself to a thorough scolding from his rattled owner, the Labrador walked stiffly past them through the swinging doors and on to a grass strip, where he proceeded to urinate, and then began powerful, slowish but intentional scratching of the ground with his hind feet. He was just strutting his stuff, marking his turf to make his point. We all understood perfectly, even the humans.

Dominance aggression is sudden and, to owners, often seems unprovoked. The enigmatic nature of this form of aggression and the sheer speed of the dog's reaction make for an intimidating response. The dog delivers its assault at whatever level it considers appropriate (growl, snap, or bite) and the whole affair is over almost as soon as it begins. Following an attack, dominant dogs are often contrite, remorseful, or seemingly unaware of what has occurred. But they'll do it again later if incited in the same way.

Dominance aggression, symbolic or otherwise, is the primary way dogs establish their hierarchical structure and relationships with one another. It's not that every dog has to be the top dog, just that each pack member needs to know where it stands in the hierarchy. This whole gestalt is what is referred to as the pack mentality. Once dominant dogs have successfully transmitted their leadership signals to subordinates and a mutual understanding has been reached, peace reigns and the dogs will eat and play together amicably. However, an astute observer will notice that there is a definite order to things. Dyadic dominance-deference relationships fashioned in this way form the backbone of pack structure.

Owners seeking to reverse dominance aggression need to transmit a clear signal of their leadership to the dog concerned. A nonconfrontational, no yelling, no hitting approach to achieving this mastery makes most sense and is safest for the owner (dominant dogs resist discipline and usually become more aggressive when admonished) as well as more humane for the dog. The program, described in detail in the Appendix, is often referred to as a "Nothing in life is free" program, though it has also been referred to as "Working for a living" and "No free lunch." This program is designed to make the dog obey a command to get things it previously took for granted. Owners sometimes need to be reminded of their dog's dependence on them for life's necessities and luxuries, including food, toys, attention, praise, petting, exercise, and even entertainment. To ration these commodities carefully by means of what has been termed a "tough love" approach certainly lets a would-be dominant dog know who is in charge. This relatively simple program reduces dominance aggression within a two-month period in about ninety percent of cases.

Interdog Dominance Aggression

A dog that constantly picks fights with other dogs is a concern for its owners. Let's face it, it can be awkward and embarrassing, if not downright dangerous to other people's dogs, to have a loose cannon of this variety attached to you by means of a collar and lead. Walks can cease to be fun and turn into a form of Russian roulette for passing dogs. Dominant dogs don't beat up on everyone, and very dominant characters are usually above having street brawls with any Tom, Dick, or Harry. A subordinate defers to a dominant dog by averting his eyes and by assuming subtle submissive postures: head held low, body hunkered down, tail tucked or held low and wagging a friendly greeting, which is the canine equivalent of waving a white flag. Naturally, the more dominant a dog appears to other dogs, the more they will defer in this way. Middle rankers get into more trouble than very dominant dogs because their status is in flux and they encounter more dogs willing to fling down or pick up the gauntlet. Treatment of aggression between dogs is not easy. You will never be able to persuade an adult would-be dominant dog that he is anything other than what he is with respect to his peers. What you can do, however, is employ a dominance control program and keep him on lead when he is likely to be confronted by other dogs.

Fear Aggression

Fearful and insecure dogs, fueled by a modicum of dominance, feel obliged to repel borders whenever they feel threatened, which is quite often. Their philosophy is that a good offense is the best defense. Some of them get so confident at driving the enemy away that, in the final analysis, it is hard to imagine the behavior as originating in fear. With hindsight, though, it is often possible to identify a point in these dogs' lives when they were exposed to some unpleasant experience involving a person or another dog. The earlier part of a dog's life, when it is most sensitive to learning about people and its peers, is a particularly vulnerable time, but lasting impressions can occur at any time if the incident is sufficiently traumatic—a form of post-traumatic stress syndrome, if you will. In post-traumatic stress syndrome a single catastrophic incident has effects that are usually lifelong. Bursts of epinephrine released during the traumatic incident are instrumental in making the memory indelible.

One case of fear aggression that I saw recently involved a giant schnauzer that had been friendly with other dogs until the age of eighteen months, when he suddenly turned "dog aggressive." So bad a player was this dog that he couldn't be brought through the waiting room lest he attack the other dogs. He had to enter the behavior room through an emergency side door. I was about to inquire about what had happened to the dog at the age of eighteen months when the owner volunteered the relevant facts herself. Apparently this formerly trusting dog was bitten in the ear by another dog around this time and subsequently decided that other dogs were not for him—and he was large enough to make his point very effectively. Although this dog was never entirely comfortable in the presence of other dogs, after treatment he became much less antagonistic. Rehabilitation was achieved by means of a comprehensive behavior modification, obedience training, and desensitization.

Similar scenarios are reported for dogs that develop fear aggression directed toward people. Men and children—almost invariably strangers—are the usual targets of this aggression, probably because they are most likely to cause the dog grief. I did, however, learn of one dog that showed fear aggression toward its master after some brutal treatment involving an electric shock collar. Treatment for this condition involves preventing or avoiding whatever is causing the dog's fear, followed by systematic reexposure to previously fear-inducing strangers, under pleasant circumstances and in an incremental manner (see Appendix).

Territorial Aggression

Some dogs' aggressiveness to strangers and other dogs occurs when they are approached while on their home turf. This turf, or territory, includes the owner's home and property, the surrounding streets, sometimes part of the neighbor's yard, and the mobile territory of the car. Dominant dogs guard these areas because they believe it is their job, and to some extent, it is. They will bark and otherwise attempt to intimidate any intruders until such time as it is clear that the visitor is welcome or has made appropriate conciliatory gestures. After the sometimes rude welcome, these dogs usually seem pleased and interested to have the stranger around. More anxious or fearful dogs are, however, a different kettle of fish. These dogs do not want company around and will do whatever is necessary to drive the bogeyman (or dog) away. They never really settle down and are always liable to erupt again whenever a guest makes a sudden move. I call this composite behavior territorial/fear aggression. Some dogs that react this way are only aggressive when they have the added confidence that the home turf provides. Others may also be aggressive away from home and exhibit a more classical form of fear aggression.

For dogs territorial through dominance, an owner's masterly control goes a long way toward preventing any unfortunate accidents. For more anxious dogs, desensitization and counterconditioning can help (see Appendix) but these dogs are loose cannons and need to be properly restrained in the interest of public safety.

Alternative Classifications of Aggression

Dr. Valerie O'Farrell, a Ph.D. behaviorist in Britain, once classified aggression into only two types, dominance aggression and predatory aggression (see "P—Predatory Behavior"). She included classical dominance aggression and fear aggression together as different affective manifestations of the same underlying phenomenon—control. By this classification, maternal aggression, pain-induced aggression, irritable aggression, and sexual aggression—other types of aggression recognized by behaviorists today—all fall into the category of dominance aggression, in the broadest sense of the word. In all instances the dog uses aggression to alter the behavior of another living creature, whether in defense of itself, its young, or to assist in procuring or protecting a mate. Conceptualizing aggression in this way makes sense from a basic science standpoint.

One other extremely useful classification of aggression, mirroring O'Farrell's classification, is into "affective" and "predatory" types. Affective aggression, like O'Farrell's "dominance," describes any assertive type of aggression that is associated with significant mood change and arousal of the fight-or-flight system. In affective-aggressive states, dogs show emotional arousal both in terms of their posturing, agonistic behavior and by virtue of associated physiological changes. Note that both dominant and fearful dogs show similar autonomic changes. The pupils of dominant and fear-aggressive dogs dilate during conflict; owners usually report that the dog's eyes glaze over or flash green or red, the color of the layer at the backs of the eyes (which is more evident when the pupils are wide open). Owners also sometimes note piloerection (hair standing on end) along the dog's spine, salivation, or elimination of urine or feces in extreme situations. Okay, so fearful dogs are often more demonstrative than more confident ones, and purely dominant dogs exhibit subtly different postures (body stiff, erect tail, fixed gaze), but the only substantive distinction between the different types of affective aggression is the dog's motivation.

The Upside of Aggression

Although I have harped on about aggression as something to watch for and avoid, let me renege a tad and admit that aggression is sometimes a desirable feature—depending on where you stand (literally and metaphorically). In days of yore when dog breeds were being created, aggressiveness was one of the features selected for in some breeds, notably Rottweilers, Dalmatians, Chesapeake Bay retrievers, bull breeds, terriers, and various Oriental breeds. Rottweilers, for example, primarily cattle-herding dogs, were highly prized if they intimidated bandits who were after the herders' money on return trips from the cattle markets of Rottweil. These dogs had the herders' money purses hung around their necks and were lauded (and were subsequently bred) when they successfully defended the spoils. Dalmatians were bred to guard carriages while the voyagers took sustenance at local hostelries. Chessies guarded fishing boats on Chesapeake Bay, and so on.

Even today, when dogs bark aggressively at unwelcome intruders, we might encourage them by saying, "Good dog. See 'em off." When you're not around, a barking dog can be a valuable asset. A good guard dog is better than any alarm system. A house with a dog is far less likely to get burglarized than one without one. What burglar in his right mind would want to tangle with a dog when there are dogless houses for the taking? Many times the house with the dog remains unmolested while neighboring homes are repeatedly pillaged.

Some people feel, and actually are, safer walking in dangerous neighborhoods when accompanied by a dog, whether or not it has been protection trained. Just having a dog with you is a deterrent for many would-be attackers. One of my clients, a Boston University professor, was saved by his pit bull, who drove off some malevolent thugs. The young men had drunk a skinful of the cocktail du jour from the neighboring Margaritaville before lumbering across the road to his yard and urinating on his hedge. From a vantage point by his front door, he yelled at them to stop it, whereupon they turned and walked up the path toward him. One of them knocked him to the ground, breaking his teeth, and as he rolled around on the ground his dog launched itself at one of the marauders and bit him once in the stomach. The young men all fled, only to sic a lawyer on the professor, seeking compensation for the incident and citing his dog as vicious. In the proceedings that followed I went to bat for the professor and what I considered to be his relatively restrained dog. After examining the dog and noting its benign disposition, I wrote a letter to whom it may concern explaining my take on the incident. Armed with this statement, the professor was able to snatch judicial victory from the jaws of defeat. Let's face it, there's a time and a place for everything and this dog got both parts of the equation right.

BARKING

Of all the negative qualities attributed to dogs, barking is right up there along with biting and fouling the sidewalk. But it isn't casual barking, a woof here and a woof there, that causes the angst, it's incessant barking, especially in densely populated urban areas, that puts up the hackles of the anti-dog lobby. These folk will be delighted to know that there *is* an answer to barking in almost all instances—but it isn't always the same one. Dogs bark for a variety of reasons, most of them extremely urgent from the dog's perspective. Once you figure out what is causing the dog to bark, the problem can usually be addressed in fairly short order.

To help us better understand why dogs bark we need to cast a retrospective glance into our dim and distant past, to the flickering campfires of early man some twelve thousand years ago (or, more controversially, some one hundred thousand years ago). At that time primitive man and the domestic dog's canid ancestors merely coexisted rather than shared the intimate relationship we enjoy today with their descendants. The intervening time brought with it domestication as some of our dogs' ancestors were progressively socialized if they showed a modicum of friendliness, playfulness, and yes, even alarm barking.

The relationship that dogs had with man in the early stages of their developing association may have been more commensal than symbiotic, with the dogs simply scavenging the remains of leftover meals from the periphery of the human encampments. But the intricate web of the bond between humans and companion animals was woven progressively over time as humans began to appreciate the dogs' presence. One of the attributes these early dog ancestors would have had to bring to the table (so to speak) was friendliness. No group would have appreciated a malicious predator cruising the borders of their terrain. Adolescent wolves are more playful and friendly than adults, so Peter Pan-type adults retaining their youthful characteristics would have been more welcome and thus more likely to enter into the liaison. Artificial-selection pressures would then have come to bear, furthering this genotype.

Of more relevance to this discussion, young wolves tend to bark rather than howl, providing another possible advantage for the man-dog union. Barking, fueled by territoriality, may have served an alarm function for early encampments in days when (arguably) it was even more important than it is today to know when someone or something was encroaching on your turf. Put it this way: If a caveman wanted to befriend some creature at the dawn of civilization, a wolf showing juvenile characteristics would probably have been the best candidate for such an alliance. Wolves (and possibly other canids) presumably would have sought out people, too, drawn in by the food, with the younger at heart being bolder, more curious, and more venturesome than their more cagey adult counterparts.

Another advantage these neotenized wolves would have had going for them would have been their appearance. They would have been, in a word, cute, having a physiognomical edge over their more pointy-nosed peers. This more superficial allure would have been attributable to their more infantile facial features, which, theoretically, would have stimulated human parenting instincts, providing additional cement for the interspecific bonding process. Thus, young wolves or jackals (depending on whom you read) that retained certain aspects of their youthful joie de vivre, alarm-barking potential, and juvenile physiognomy into adulthood would have had greater survival opportunities in the company of man because of the human selection process. Artificial-selection pressures, operating over the years in their own inimitable, incremental way, would have fashioned the dogs we know today from the raw material of their wild ancestors.

All domestic dogs bark, except for the basenji, which sort of huffs. Barking has evolved to become a diverse though elementary communication system. The long-distance communication function of barking as a howling precursor remains. Domestic dogs don't need to engage in dawn and dusk vocalizations to establish the presence and whereabouts of neighboring packs, as wolves do. They are generally restricted to the same locale and most have little social contact with their neighbors. But once a chorus starts, it's a different matter. As we all know, if one dog starts barking at something on a lazy, erstwhile peaceful summer afternoon, every dog within earshot in the neighborhood will respond and pretty soon you have total mayhem, a cacophony of barking. And there's a ripple effect, too, with the barking spreading to neighborhoods that the first dog's voice couldn't possibly reach. I call the phenomenon the me-too effect. It's as if they're communicating, "Hey, I'm over here. There's something going on and I want to be part of it."

Howling, per se, is not out of the question either. As mentioned, many adult dogs can and do occasionally howl, presumably delving deep into their innate past to fulfill a primordial urge. The stimulus for howling is certain tones and frequencies of sound that seem to act as a releaser, a key unlocking an underlying drive to perform this behavior. In my town, one sound that invariably triggers dogs' howling across the entire valley is that of a World War II–style fire-alarm siren at the fire station. I never have figured out why they don't get the firemen pagers instead of periodically blasting the townfolk out of their beds with this ungodly sound, but I write it off as one of the many idiosyncrasies of small-town life. Anyway, Grafton dogs do howl up a storm whenever this siren goes off, as 1940's technology and prehistory combine to make sure that there is no peace for the just, let alone the wicked.

I once knew a dog that would "sing" (howl) whenever certain high notes were struck on the piano. This tuned-in dog, called Djelias (pronounced *je-lus*; Gaelic for "faithful") was taught to jump on the piano stool and hammer its paws on the keys, creating a discordant medley of sounds. Some of the notes triggered Djelias to howl, producing a spectacular party trick with Djelias sitting at the piano, striking the keys, and accompanying herself in song. (Incidentally, Djelias always seemed to be smiling endearingly between arias.) These performances might have appeared attributable to some creative thought processes but, in reality, they were most likely a product of learning, attention seeking, and reward.

Back to barking. My days in the trenches of veterinary anesthesia had me learning by rote the "signs and stages" of various levels of unconsciousness. I learned, for example, that as you slowly facemask an animal to sleep with an inhalational anesthetic, each species goes through a stage of supposedly unconscious involuntary excitement. In this stage (deemed Stage 2), all creatures great and small exhibit species-typical disinhibition of reflex behavior. Most paddle with their limbs as if running away from something, and superimposed on this hyperkinetic background, all species vocalize. Cows moo, horses neigh, cats swear, and dogs whimper and bark. The point is that if dogs vocalize when disinhibited, when excitatory systems discharge unchecked, barking must be a reflexive behavior triggered by excitement, even in the awake, fully conscious state.

This is not to say that dogs can't initiate barking voluntarily, only that barking may, under some circumstances, be an almost subliminal product of excitement. People get disinhibited by excitement, too, emitting all kinds of sounds at extreme moments, as family members of any sports fan will testify (particularly during the play-off weeks). Dogs may love trucks but many of them really get their juices flowing when they have cornered a squirrel up a tree. And what do they do then? They bark. This would appear to be the wrong strategy for a wily wolf descendant in pursuit of prey. Why let the adversary know of your whereabouts when stealth would appear to be the order of the day? Apparently excitement prevails over good sense in such situations and the dog blurts out a tirade of barks, sublimating its pent-up energy and enthusiasm. A similar response is elicited indoors from dogs in pursuit of stray tennis balls that roll under the couch.

Learning can affect barking either way. Some dogs can have their barking reinforced when it produces the desired effect, whereas they learn to bark less when their cries are unanswered or consistently result in negative consequences. Although conditioned barkers can be a bane or a blessing (depending on the circumstances and your tolerance for noise), dogs that don't bark at all are rather pitiful. A somewhat sad case I recently encountered involved a dog that had been adopted from an abusive situation. The dog was brought to me because of an anxiety-based compulsive-licking problem. As the owner completed this dog's behavioral history she commented that her dog didn't bark at all for quite a while after adoption and appeared extremely shy, nervous, and withdrawn. As the months went by, with consistent kind treatment, the dog's confidence level grew and he ventured his first few utterances.

Barking seemed to be the barometer of his psychological well-being. His benevolent new owners encouraged this dog's barking. The strategy worked well because at the time of the consultation this little dog was in fine voice, barking in appropriate situations to communicate his wants and needs. I figured that prior lack of attention, and perhaps even punishment, had knocked the stuffing out of him, leaving him little reason to display any emotion or attempt to communicate about anything. He was, in retrospect, depressed and resigned to his fate at the time of his adoption. Careful nurturing brought him back and barking heralded his recovery. Dogs that don't bark following psychological trauma are analogous to those tearless famine-victim children you sometimes see on TV. Both are in a state of learned helplessness and are in urgent need of care and attention.

An intermediate and perhaps healthy level of barking is represented by the dog who is happy to bark when anything exciting or demanding attention crops up, but who will respond to a command such as "No-bark" (said smartly as one word) or "Quiet" when enough is enough. I am intimately acquainted with one such dog, Fletch, who belongs to my neighbor. Each summer I spend many hours throwing a tennis ball for Fletch in my backyard (she lets herself in via a gap in the stone wall—no invitation necessary). A collie cross, Fletch's herding instincts impel her toward retrieval games and her focus on such activities borders on compulsive. So enamored of such games is she that her enthusiasm sometimes gets the better of her and translates into impatience. If I am a little slow at delivering the five hundredth pitch, or perhaps engrossed in conversation, she will stand and bark at me until I am forced to acknowledge her. Her meaning is painfully obvious to me: "Throw the darn ball. What's the matter with you?"

Often I respond as she wills and then all is well. Sometimes, however, there is good reason to want to quit the game and at these times it *is* possible to shut Fletch up. "Be quiet, Fletch" or "Go lie down" signals the end of the fun and she usually responds promptly, although not without attempts to manipulate the ball thrower's emotions with a well-cultivated hangdog look. Many scientists would explain her expression as submissive posturing indicating deference to a more dominant authority, but then they haven't seen Fletch. Though obeying, she never takes her eyes off you and her wishes remain abundantly clear. Obedience, yes; submission, not on your life. Her looks continue to talk while she remains silent. You can almost feel her thinking, willing you to throw the ball "just one more time." Eventually she can cause such a guilt trip that she gets her own way again. Some might call this conditioning. I call it manipulation.

The real problem barkers are those who won't take no for an answer and have learned that barking, though not solving all their problems, is a pretty fun thing to do while whatever it is takes its course. In addition, as a bonus and encouragement, barking animates their owners to run around like turkeys in crisis, making loud noises themselves. "Cut that out," "Shut the heck up," or "No! No! No!" are choice owner responses. These sounds are probably regarded by the dog as rather pathetic attempts at barking.

One problem barker, a terrier, was brought to my clinic a few weeks ago by its exasperated owners. The little terror barked for his food, barked at any sound or event, barked when anyone walked by the house, barked when his owners went to leave, and barked continuously in the car when his owners took him with them. These poor people had tried everything to silence the tyke; everything, that is, except for ignoring him.

Masterly inactivity, as it turned out, was the key to resolving the problem. Every time the dog barked thereafter his owners simply ignored him, striking up conversations between themselves about the weather and other trivia. It worked, though it took a few weeks of consistently ignoring the barking to pull it off. Of course, if you are going to ignore unwanted behavior as part of a treatment program it is important to reward desired behavior when it occurs. In the case of barking, this means rewarding silence.

Another type of barking is territorially driven. This is rarely problematic in dominant dogs, who simply raise the alarm when trespassers approach too close. Most people regard this type of intruder-alarm barking as a highly desirable trait. This type of dog will bark at strangers and even your friends as they approach the house and ring the doorbell, but will be immediately silenced by the introduction of a welcome guest. One way of quieting such dogs is to acknowledge the fact that they are barking. Their barking is intended to warn off strangers. Imagine their frustration when their owner says, "No, no. Be quiet," when the dog knows perfectly well that what he has sensed is real. If instead of "No, no," the owner first says "Good dog!", acknowledging the dog's detection of the interloper, this simple measure can be enough to check the barking.

If the barking persists, an "Enough" command should be issued, praising the dog immediately for obeying. The next plan of attack regarding this problem necessitates arranging some negative consequence if the "Enough" command is not heeded. Shake cans (empty soda cans filled with pennies and shaken), air horns, and halter control systems, like the Gentle Leader, work well in this situation. No one really knows what it is about shake cans that gets the job done but it could be that ultrasounds are generated by this arrangement, inducing a startling effect. Certainly shake cans work better in more nervous, sound-sensitive dogs.

The solution is not so simple with a dog that barks through fear and insecurity. The initial reaction of this dog to an approaching stranger is almost identical, but it is not usually silenced by the owner's acknowledgment or acceptance of that person. The dog will either continue to bark or slink away furtively if subdued, seemingly waiting for the next opportunity to deliver a salvo of threatening barks. Opportunity knocks when the guest makes a sudden movement or stands up to move around or leave. These dogs have learned that their barking can intimidate and drive an unwanted person away. They rehearse this behavior with delivery people from the time they are puppies. The one thing that's guaranteed about a delivery person is that he will leave shortly after he has arrived. A dog that barks at such a person in the hopes that he will go away has his behavior reinforced by this pleasing consequence. The dog erroneously attributes the delivery person's departure to his own intimidating behavior, a form of superstitious learning. Treatment of this problem centers around counterconditioning and desensitization to the visitors' approach (see Appendix).

An owner may contribute to a barking problem by praising the dog's vociferous response to strangers when it is young. Men are frequently the guilty parties when it comes to reinforcing aggressive barking in response to approaching strangers. Sadly, however, they forget that the youngster will grow up and may become difficult to train out of the behavior, or even dangerous if aggression is reinforced, too. Many people think that dogs bark at strangers to warn family members of impending danger and that it is an altruistic response, but as you may have gleaned by now, this interpretation needs some modification. Barking may not, and usually does not, have any altruistic function. Dominant dogs are probably delivering a sort of "Halt, who goes there?" message, whereas anxious or fearful dogs seem to be saying, "If you come any closer you'll be in big trouble" (while they are secretly hoping whoever it is will go away).

Barking at people or other dogs is not confined to situations involving territoriality. When it occurs off one's property, and away from familiar streets, it most often involves fear. This can be difficult to appreciate if you are on the receiving end of a barking volley that is designed to intimidate. A dog that is more fearful than dominant will bark at you when approached, particularly if escape routes are blocked: for example, when the dog is on a lead, tied up, or in the car. Careful observation of a dog's behavior will provide clues as to its underlying fearfulness. Furtive sideways glances, diminutive body postures, slight backing, and a tucked tail are the kinds of clues to look for. Make no bones about it, such dogs will bite if pressed but would prefer you to move away and are doing everything within their power to make that happen.

A slightly different scenario: A dog that is more dominant than fearful is a different proposition and far more perilous. It will be harder to intimidate and more proactive in its fear-based response. Such a dog may stand its ground or walk toward you barking ferociously while displaying ambivalent body postures. It could even be wagging its tail. Such dogs are extremely dangerous if they take a dislike to you. In situations where you find yourself the subject of these dogs' unwanted attentions, discretion is always the better part of valor. Vault the nearest fence and run like heck.

Not all barking relates to excitement, attention seeking, or aggression. There are other forms relating to adversity and suffering. A particularly pathetic form of barking occurs as a component of the separation-anxiety syndrome (see "F—Fear-Based Conditions"). Dogs that engage in this form of barking often have dysfunctional or otherwise abusive backgrounds and bond like Velcro to caring owners. They make wonderful pets, but problems arise when they have to be left alone. These dogs almost literally love too much and one of the ways they express their misery is by whining and barking, perhaps in vain attempts to reunite themselves with their owners. The sound they make can be pitiful, even to uneducated human ears, though that is not always the response it generates in neighbors.

Curiously, many owners are unaware of their dog's or neighbors' suffering. This was the case with a veterinary resident in training, Mary Hondalus, who lived in an apartment I once had. Because she worked long hours, her dog was often confined in a crate in my garage. And it barked . . . incessantly. When I informed Mary of the dilemma she was aghast and at first in denial. It took the irrefutable honesty of my children to persuade her that a problem really existed. Once convinced of her dog's plight, she worked to reduce the negative impact of her departures by adopting a more formal, matter-of-fact attitude and, with some juggling of her schedule and alternative kenneling arrangements, managed to get things turned around. The barking was a problem for us but indicated an even more unpleasant experience for the dog, and we were all pleased Mary was able to work things out.

There are many different responses of anxious dogs to being left alone, but barking is probably the most common. After months or years of unanswered cries for help, however, the urgency of this form of barking can give way to futility and the character of barking changes to one of slow, monotonous repetition of a single tone or phrase. At this stage, barking serves no useful function except perhaps to mindlessly dissipate inner tensions. Dogs exhibiting this form of barking have basically given up on help arriving and are even beyond the stage of consciously occupying themselves to divert their misery and frustration. Their barking is merely a behavioral artifact, an indicator of chronic duress, a vestige of the suffering that they have been forced to endure. It's no wonder psychologists consider learned helplessness in its various forms a good model for human depression, because that's exactly how it appears.

An article in the *Smithsonian* magazine a few years back revisited a number of theories regarding the development and presumed function of barking in domestic dogs and their wild ancestors. It was a wonderful article but, after much erudite discussion, the authors concluded that nobody really knows why dogs bark. I believe they suggested that maybe dogs bark simply because they can. If they had studied beagles it is possible to understand how they might come to such a conclusion, because that is the impression that many of these dogs create. These little guys can really bark. It is part of their genetic legacy and a component of a syndrome sometimes referred to as high reactivity (see later under "R—Reactivity").

Gary Larson of *The Far Side* cartoon fame humorized the apparent futility of barking for those disillusioned about its meaning or value in a sketch depicting some nutty scientists who had finally invented a way of interpreting what dogs were saying when they bark by using a phonograph look-alike machine. After years of trials the *Back to the Future* type of device revealed all. And the answer was: "Yo, yo, yo, yo, yo." Very enlightening.

I didn't mean to pick on beagles. Other breeds can be equally voluble, if not more so on occasion. But, just for the record, remember that genetics plays a significant role in which dogs bark a lot and which ones tend to hold their tongues better. It is wise to check into this if you are noise sensitive yourself or live in a confined neighborhood. A little research goes a long way when you have fourteen years or more of (hopefully) stress-free companionship to look forward to. Remember, too, barking is not always an undesirable trait and can sometimes be a blessing. It was one of the reasons man and dog got together in the first place. It also serves as a vocal means of communication between dog and man in dogs that are properly trained. Like it or not, useful or not, barking is here to stay. Most dog owners, even if they don't appreciate it, come to accept it. You have to, really. The only other alternative is to get a cat.

COMPULSIVE BEHAVIOR

Only a few years ago conditions such as lick granuloma and continuous tail chasing, which we now speak about as compulsive behaviors, were referred to as stereotypies. Literally translated, a stereotypy is a "pointless, mindless, repetitive behavior," and one that "serves no useful function." But lick granuloma and other compulsive behaviors *do* appear to serve some kind of function. Arising out of stress and conflict, they seem to have some subtle mollifying effects on mood. Prevention of dogs from engaging in their particular compulsions will create anxiety in its own right. The same tensions occur in people with obsessive-compulsive disorder (OCD) who are prevented from engaging in their rituals.

Two factors seem to be necessary for the development of compulsive behaviors in dogs. One is a genetic predisposition, and the other is a level of environmental stress that will trigger the expression of the behavior. The stress can either be acute high-grade stress or a less severe long-standing pressure, causing a sudden or gradual onset of the condition, respectively. The behavior pattern that emerges depends on the breed in question, but even with a particular breed the behavior expressed is something of a crapshoot. In general, longhaired large breeds of dogs overgroom, herding breeds chase or hoard, and pure predatory breeds bite, mouth, or chase objects. There may even be compulsive behaviors related to sexual behavior and aggression, though this is a little controversial.

All of the behaviors performed by compulsive canines are essentially normal behaviors—it's just that they are performed repetitively and out of context. It's the same with human OCD. There's nothing wrong with washing your hands or checking to see whether the gas stove is turned off, but if you engage in several hundred repetitions of such behavior daily you have a problem. Of course, with humans and with dogs there is always a gray zone where the behavior is performed noticeably more than usual but not quite to the level of being able to label it compulsive. Psychiatrists refer to such conditions as subthreshold or shadow syndromes and treat the problems on a case-by-case basis, but veterinarians remain divided regarding the significance of such overly expressed behaviors.

The big breakthrough in the understanding of these conditions came with the fairly wide acceptance in human medicine of the obsessive-compulsive spectrum disorders. These are disorders of a compulsive nature that, though superficially discrepant, have certain causal and physiological features in common. Basically, the narrower definition of OCD relating to concerns over personal safety has been dropped in favor of a more general description involving other repetitive behaviors as well. In short, you no longer have to be a hand washer, hoarder, or checker to have OCD; compulsive (binge) eaters, people with body dysmorphic disorder (persistent concerns relating to personal image), pyromaniacs, paraphiliacs (those with sexual compulsions), compulsive gamblers (and other chronic risk-takers), trichotillomaniacs (hair pullers), and onychophagiacs (nail biters) are also included, to name but a few. As dogs and other animals cannot stand up at the sink to wash their hands and have no concerns about gas stoves they were written off as potential OCD sufferers, but the new classification has opened up all sorts of possibilities.

If susceptible humans under various forms of stress react by engaging in various compulsive behaviors related to their own species-typical orientations of grooming, exercising caution, gathering, and (arguably) hunting, why not dogs, too? Dogs are self-groomers, predators, and imbibers (to name but a few of their naturalistic behaviors). Even from the drawing board one might expect some dogs to groom themselves compulsively when stressed: and they do. And you might expect others to compulsively chase things that either are or are not there: they do this too. Or to drink water excessively when there is no known medical cause: they do. There are other conditions in dogs and across other domestic species that appear to confirm the view that compulsive behaviors are not unique to human beings but are also exhibited by animals.

Lick granuloma is the quintessential canine (obsessive) compulsive disorder. At least, it was the first touted as such. The reason for its recognition as a compulsive behavior was because it bore a striking behavioral resemblance to compulsive hand washing in people. Affected dogs lick their wrists or hocks excessively, apparently over-cleaning themselves, until the skin in these regions is ulcerated and granulating (forming a base of scar tissue). For years no one knew why dogs engage in this apparently pointless, mindless behavior. Veterinary treatments ranged from physical prevention using Elizabethan medical collars or leg wraps to applying a myriad of palliative balms. Basically, nothing worked. But now, with the OCD link, it is possible to understand and treat the condition much more effectively. As with human OCD, it is now thought that genetic factors are involved in the propagation of lick granuloma, indicated by the fact that it primarily affects certain large breeds of dogs, such as Labradors, golden retrievers, Great Danes, and Dobermans. Besides breed factors, individual susceptibility and environmental influences are also required for the full expression of the behavior. Affected individuals are usually anxious, sensitive, and high-strung. Some give the impression of having a generalized anxiety disorder. Environmental factors promoting lick granuloma include various stresses and conflict situations, including separation anxiety or boredom.

The condition of lick granuloma often arises when a susceptible dog is left home alone. In the early stages of this condition the dog's lonely licking might well be described as displacement behavior that provides some self-comfort and defuses tensions. Later, however, the behavior becomes ingrained and will occur even when there is little stress and even in the owner's presence. This is the stage of compulsion and, in many cases, resistance to treatment, unless medications are employed. Of course, it makes good sense to adjust all the factors that have led to the development of the condition, including making life fuller and more interesting for the dog and ensuring adequate exercise and an appropriate diet. I sometimes call the program for enriching a dog's life the Get a Job program because it involves going with the flow of nature and providing breed-specific occupational therapy. For example, herding dogs should be encouraged to chase and round up almost anything that moves; retrieving dogs should be given the opportunity to retrieve and swim; and predatory dogs should be allowed to "see the rabbit," literally, by taking them on long country walks.

Providing dogs with something to do while you are absent is another important component of rehabilitation therapy for dogs exhibiting obsessive-compulsive behavior, and this is where owners must be creative. My list of things to provide to entertain your dog while you are away includes: Boomer balls, Busta cubes, Kong chew toys, real bones (uncooked), and nylon toy bones (drilled out and with peanut butter squished into the holes). In addition to this, you can make sure your dog has a room with a view and you can provide background noise to neutralize the unnerving sound of silence. I prefer a tape recording of household clamor at a mealtime to fill the auditory void. Finally, most dogs feel better with a buddy to interact with, but you have to be careful about choosing a canine companion for your dog. Not all dogs get on well and you could wind up producing exactly the opposite effect.

Antiobsessional drugs have found a place in the management of this stubborn condition. The first to be tested was Anafranil (clomipramine), a tricyclic antidepressant with preferential serotonin-enhancing activity. Serotonin is a modulator of central nervous system transmission and seems to have an effect on a tormented psyche like oil on the proverbial troubled waters. Of course, Prozac and its first cousins are the best-known antiobsessionals and they also can be used to treat dogs with lick granuloma. It doesn't much matter which of these selective serotonin-enhancing drugs is employed first, though curiously one may be more effective than another in the clinical situation, even though they work in a practically identical way.

One drawback of antiobsessionals is that they take about three weeks to start working, so time and patience are necessary if the optimal effect is to be achieved. Typically there is about a fifty-percent improvement after four weeks, a seventy-five-percent improvement after eight weeks, and ninety-percent improvement after twelve to sixteen weeks. One-hundred-percent cure is unlikely but the improvement made is often sufficient for the healing process to catch up with the damage so that the lesions resolve. Desultory licking, however, usually persists at a low level.

Recently I tried a new strategy on a dog whose woman owner was opposed to "drug" treatment. The dog, a Great Dane, indulged in self-licking mainly when the woman was away, so I decided to try to get it to go to sleep during her absence by treating it with melatonin. Melatonin is a natural sleep inducer and is available over the counter in health food stores at minimal cost. The owner was delighted at my suggestion and decided to give melatonin a try. The result was phenomenal. The lick lesions healed in a few weeks and that was the end of that. One swallow does not a summer make, and more trials are necessary before I can claim reproducible effects, but the success has definitely spurred me to further efforts in this direction.

Not all dogs display compulsive licking when they are stressed. Some pace to and fro like lions or bears in the zoo, whereas others perambulate in massive circles or figure eights or chase their tails. Once again, genetics and circumstances seem to dictate the form of the behavior. Among dogs, German shepherds are most likely to display simple ambulatory compulsions, possibly because of their herding heritage and because the circumstances leading to the disorder often involve thwarted locomotor goals. Typically, an impounded German shepherd will begin to pace the width of its enclosure. After a period of time this behavior becomes ingrained, and it will persist in the same form even when the dog is no longer confined. One German shepherd I saw, which had been rescued after a long while in a pound, paced to and fro taking five paces in each direction. It was no coincidence that its former enclosure was exactly five paces wide.

Running in huge circles or figure eights is another manifestation of a locomotor compulsion, presumably arising in a larger enclosure and one from which there is no obvious escape. One German shepherd I heard of started to run in circles when its police handler gave it the command "Attack" as a robber stumbled toward the handler with malicious intent, brandishing a chair over his head. What confused and stressed the dog was that the signal of raised hands meant "Do not attack," while the policeman had ordered "Attack." The resulting conflict sent the dog circling while the policeman tried to defend himself. The sad ending to this story was that the dog did not stop spinning and had to be retired from police work. This onset was unusually rapid for a compulsive behavior, but the fact that it occurred makes the point that compulsions can arise acutely if the stress or conflict is sufficiently intense.

Another ambulatory compulsive behavior involves dogs spinning in tight circles, apparently trying to catch their tails. Again, specific breeds are involved. The overwhelming number of dogs affected with this compulsive behavior are bull terriers (and related breeds) and German shepherds. Cocker spaniels also spin, but their spinning takes the form of running in circles rather than tail chasing. What do bull terriers and German shepherds have in common? The answer: high prey drive. Freud and the early ethologists used a water-tank analogy to explain the buildup and subsequent release of innate tensions. Water (representing the drive) accumulating in a header tank, if not periodically flushed, would eventually develop a head of pressure sufficiently great to cause spontaneous discharge of the water in the tank. Freud thought that this meant all behaviors required some kind of outlet and that they could not be indefinitely suppressed. The ethologists used the analogy to explain "vacuum behaviors" that occur without the normal cues and for no apparent reason.

The water-tank analogy certainly does help to explain why a predatory dog with no proper outlet for this behavior may displace into chasing prey facsimiles—in some cases their own tails. Presumably the behavior is somewhat rewarding, so once learned, a tail-chasing routine is likely to be repeated. A small amount of tail chasing could even be construed as normal in predatory breeds. Problems arise when tail chasing becomes frequent and intense, occupying a substantial proportion of the dog's day.

The line between "normal" and abnormal, however, is entirely arbitrary, as it is in human OCD. For scientific purposes I have classified compulsive tail chasing as that occupying at least one hour per day, but the whole spectrum of affliction ranges from borderline cases that are not quite diagnosable to others that chase their tails so relentlessly that they only pause to eat or sleep. For these latter characters, *compulsive* is the only word to describe their behavior, and now, at last, the term has scientific validity. The behavioral progression in tail chasing is normally from displaced predatory behavior to that of compulsion, at least in stress-primed individuals. It seems that the reward or release from stress is so great in these dogs that they just keep going. People who drink alcohol to excess may do so for an analogous reason. Alcoholism is now thought to have a behavioral as well as a chemically addictive component and qualifies by modern standards as a compulsion. And as with tail-chasing dogs, people and experimental animals (primates) who are most likely to succumb to alcohol addiction are those most stressed and toting heavy psychological baggage.

Another thing you might expect of tail-chasing dogs is that their compulsion might in some instances be displaceable onto some other target. This is indeed the case. I have encountered several bull terriers that will desert their tails for an object, say a tennis ball or a piece of wood, but their behavior with the object is no less compulsive. Take away the object and they immediately start tail chasing again. Working on the same principle, recovering alcoholics should benefit from channeling their oral/ingestive compulsions along less destructive lines—although coffee and cigarettes, both common substitutes, do not really qualify as super healthful alternatives. The bottom line is that if a dog (or person) has a compulsive ("addictive") personality, it's there to stay, but redirecting the tendencies or placating the urge can go some of the way toward preventing potentially harmful consequences. Do compulsive tail-chasing dogs respond to human antiobsessional medication such as Prozac? Of course they do.

Two other behaviors that represent redirection of the prey drive include light chasing and snapping at imaginary flies. To identify the breeds likely to be affected it's as the policeman said in *Casablanca* whenever there was any crime: "Round up the usual suspects." The suspects are bull terriers, German shepherds, Old English sheepdogs,

Rottweilers, wirehaired fox terriers, and springer spaniels. All have high prey drive, but only susceptible, high-strung individuals are affected. As usual, genetic and environmental factors combine to create the susceptibility. An excitable, anxious, and almost hyperactive temperament seems to typify the character of dogs affected with these disorders. Stressful or deprived circumstances (from the dog's point of view) superimposed upon this nervous personality type seem to be the basic ingredients for compulsive light chasing and snapping at imaginary flies.

One other factor, however, may be necessary for the initiation of the behavior, and that is experience. I often find that dogs that chase lights were played with using a flashlight when they were young. At first it was just fun, but then, like the tail chasers, they just couldn't help themselves and chased everything that moved, from reflections off oven doors and aluminum foil to sunlight and shadows. A surprisingly large proportion of compulsive shadow chasers are deaf. I don't know why this is but I guess that being deaf can be stressful for a dog, especially if the owner has not worked out some way of communicating with it. I imagine that deafness heightens the visual senses and predisposes toward visual fixations. With compulsive "fly biters" it's pretty much the same story. It probably takes a real fly to start the behavioral pendulum swinging, but after such humble beginnings the behavior can develop a life of its own. Internal reinforcement, plus a bit of encouragement from the peanut galley, appears to exacerbate fly biting as a predatory instinct-satisfying, attention-seeking behavior of compulsive proportions.

In the course of being chased by a dog, small prey sometimes go to earth. You don't have to be a rocket scientist to know what happens next: frantic digging to unearth the hapless creature. It's almost a classical cartoon scene to portray a varmint-seeking dog with its head and half its torso buried in a mound of soil with great scads of dirt flying out behind it. Some terriers are particularly good at this mode of pursuit, which has been enhanced by years of selective breeding. As well as digging to unearth prey, dogs also dig to cache food remains (notoriously bones), and may dig to circumvent obstacles or for shelter. Because of the immense utility and survival value of digging it would

be surprising if it were not relatively well hardwired and thus potentially expressible as a compulsive behavior, which of course it is.

So how do compulsive diggers present and what is the driving
force, if any, behind their compulsion? The usual presentation is that
of multiple dog-sized holes in the backyard, though some dogs present
a more complex picture.

Take Hogan, for example. Hogan, a castrated male deaf Dalmatian,
was three and a half years old when I first met him. He was adopted
from the Connecticut Humane Society at the age of eighteen months by
an exceptional and dedicated woman, Connie Bombaci. Apparently
Hogan had a terrible life prior to his adoption by Connie, being rescued from an abusive home by someone at the Humane Society because of a situation involving insufferable neglect. Luckily for Hogan,
Connie was determined to help him in whatever way she could. She
started by bringing him into her family "circle of love," introducing
him to her husband, Jim; their daughter; their other Dalmatian, Indy;
and a wonderful environment full of opportunities for interaction, exercise, and fun. Connie even started to teach him American Sign Language so that she could communicate with him more intimately.

Hogan adapted quickly to this new bountiful lifestyle, building in
self-confidence and increasing his vocabulary. All was well for about a
year and a half when suddenly, one March morning, he woke up and
started pawing everything in sight, and just wouldn't stop. He pawed
rugs and blankets, hardwood floors and linoleum, grass and dirt surfaces. There didn't seem to be any rhyme or reason to this bizarre
behavior, though Connie did notice that the digging was associated
with frantic sniffing and rationalized that a mouse or cat might have
materialized overnight. On encountering an upturned blanket, sofa
cover, or bedsheet Hogan would pause, sniff even more enthusiastically, and then bury his head in it as if searching for something. The
similarity between what he was doing and prey-seeking behavior was
remarkable. Whatever the function of the behavior, it went on day and
night. Finally, the situation became so intense that Connie took to
tethering him to her at night so that he would lie down and sleep.

I am still not sure what triggered Hogan's compulsive digging. It
might have been the hypothetical mouse provoking a predatory re-

sponse or it might have been a flashback to his days of incarceration at the pound, spurring well-worn patterns of digging to escape. I will never know. I do believe, though, that Hogan was under some kind of psychological pressure at the time the compulsive pawing behavior developed. Careful examination of his history, temperament, and circumstances provide the clues. First, he was a shelter dog and one with an inauspicious history of abuse and neglect. Such dogs are usually somewhat dysfunctional, though they can make very fine pets. Second, he was by nature a sensitive, almost overly intelligent, dog whose experiences had made him chronically anxious and overly dependent on people. Add to this the fact that Connie and Jim were compelled to leave him for some eight hours a day while they went to work and you have a recipe for disaster. The pendulum was set and ready to swing. The actual compulsion that develops under such circumstances is less relevant than the fact that one *does* develop. If he had been a bull terrier he might have started to chase his tail. An anxious retriever might have begun work on a lick granuloma, and a wirehaired fox terrier might have started to chase shadows. With his own particular expression of compulsivity, digging, Hogan joined the club.

Theorizing aside, something had to be done about Hogan's situation. Being in unfamiliar territory, I worked from first principles, as I do with other unusual compulsive behaviors. The "three R's" of rehabilitation are exercise, nutrition, and communication. First, I advised Connie to step up Hogan's exercise to a minimum of thirty minutes of aerobic activity daily. In addition, I advised that Hogan should be fed a low-protein, preservative-free diet. Completing the rehabilitation wish list, I exhorted Connie to work even harder with the sign language and instructed her on a new sign to use when Hogan started digging. The sign was a piece of card with the letter *H* written on it in thick black pen. Connie was to show Hogan this sign as soon as possible after he engaged in a bout of pawing and then leave the room. The idea was to let him know that the behavior was not wanted by signaling to him that Connie was about to leave the room. Of course, if he stopped pawing, even by chance, the sign was to disappear and Connie would stay. Another goal of treatment was to occupy Hogan's time better and more thoroughly so that he would not become bored or anxious in the first place. This was to be achieved by so-called environmental enrichment and by attempting to increase the number of positive interactions with Hogan each day.

Designing environmental enrichment can be a creative and imagination-stretching process, but the Bombacis were up to the task. Jim constructed an agility course in the backyard and this proved to be a great success. But the improvements didn't stop there. Hogan had more toys, more ball playing, more visitors, more freedom, and lots of fun. Call me a coward, but I didn't think that alone would cut it because of previous experiences with canine compulsive disorders so, employing a belt-and-suspenders strategy, I also advised medicating Hogan with the tricyclic antidepressant Elavil. Theoretically, Elavil wouldn't be that good in obsessive-compulsive behavior but, limited for reasons of expense, and bearing in mind the possible contribution of separation anxiety, Elavil was my best shot.

Early follow-up reports from Connie two or three weeks after were not particularly encouraging. The only difference she noticed at this stage was that Hogan could now be distracted from pawing, but only when he was indoors. The card had worked well in this respect but Connie gave up using it because she said it made him sad. Whenever she produced the *H* card Hogan stopped pawing for a while but slumped down on the ground, head on paws, and looked at her with very sad eyes. This was too much for Connie, so the card trick disappeared. A month after Connie's first report she called back again to say that Hogan was back to playing and doing many of the things he "used to do," but was still pawing excessively quite a bit of the time. He was sniffing a lot less, though. I prayed that this might be the beginning of a turnaround, as antidepressants often take weeks to kick in.

My prayers were answered—but not immediately. It took six months before Hogan was over the hump of treatment success; six months before I started to feel enthusiastic about what we had done for him. But it was worth the wait. At this time Hogan only engaged in occasional pawing of significantly reduced intensity, and the pawing only occurred in moments of stress. Connie reported that stresses particularly likely to induce pawing included being unable to find her and sensing that he was about to be left alone. She tried disguising the clues she was giving him before leaving but he always figured out what she was up to so she gave up on this ploy, remarking that he was too intelligent for his own good. Another time he was guaranteed to paw was if Connie left him in her Jeep while she went into a store. On such occasions he would paw with a vengeance and even pull at the carpet with his teeth.

Hogan continued to improve and reached a point at which he was almost pawing-free—but not quite. That seems to be the way with compulsive disorders in man and beast. They can be reduced to the level of permitting affectees to lead relatively normal lives, but there are occasional relapses. Connie and I learned a lot by our experience of working with Hogan. We learned that behavior modification plus medication is a valid approach to dealing with compulsive pawing, in some dogs at least. We learned that Hogan could remember forty-three words of American Sign Language. And we learned that Hogan was not alone in his problem. We found out the latter fact from an E-mail chat group for the owners of deaf dogs. One correspondent reported as follows:

> I would like to open up a discussion about strange or unusual behaviors in deaf dogs. Several people have mentioned that their dogs exhibit such behaviors. What my dog Amos does is chase things that we cannot see. I presume it is his shadow but sometimes I wonder because there is no shadow. In the yard he will run around the perimeter stopping at certain points and looking at the ground then moving on to the next spot and so on. In the house he does almost the same thing, running from room to room to different corners or running around and around the dining room table stopping periodically to look, tilt his head, and then move on. Sometimes he will scratch at the spot and bark. If he does this he cannot be distracted from this behavior and will not come when I signal to him. He will also ignore his brother Andy if he interrupts him to play. I used to be worried about him but am not so concerned now. I just think his world is so quiet and free from distractions that it is easy for him to focus on something only he can see.

It does seem that visual compulsions are more prevalent in deaf dogs, though not unique to them. I have discussed this in my book *The*

Dog Who Loved Too Much (chapter: "Shadow of a Doubt"), though there is obviously still much room for additional comment and inter-pretation of this phenomenon. Interestingly, the first dog I saw with what I am now calling predatory compulsive behavior was deaf and chased shadows *and* stared and pawed at the spot where the shadow had "gone to ground." The coexistence and interchange between shadow chasing and compulsive digging is perfectly understandable, based on a predatory theory of origin. Some dogs chase more than they dig—the light/shadow chasers, whereas other dogs dig more than they chase—the compulsive diggers.

Connie continues the good work with Hogan and has since been asked to make numerous media appearances with his nibs to demon-strate his amazing vocabulary. Her message: Deaf dogs aren't stupid, they are adoptable, adorable, and fun. Hogan even met Jack Hanna in connection with his TV show, *Animal Adventures*. Jack's comment: "Oh wow, cool!" I think that says it all.

So, back to compulsive behaviors in general for a final word. We now have a fairly good idea why they occur and, as often is the case with animal behaviors, that nature and nurture are both involved in their inception. We also know that the individual expression of com-pulsive behaviors depends on the species and breed of the animal concerned. Not surprisingly, dogs do doggy things, horses do horsey things (like cribbing), and people do their own thing, developing ex-cessive concerns for their personal safety and all sorts of other human stuff. In dogs there are breed differences in the propensity to develop compulsions to the point that some breeds have almost cornered the market for some of these neurotic behaviors. Doberman pinschers, for example, are the main culprits when it comes to nursing behavior in the form of blanket sucking or flank sucking, whereas miniature schnauzers have the monopoly on a peculiar whirling, falling, sniffing compulsion derived from predatory or social behavioral roots. It's all pretty strange, but predictable. Find me a new species under psycho-logical pressure and I'll be able to predict what compulsions it might develop, working from first principles. And I would probably have a pretty fair chance of treating the creature successfully too, particularly if I were permitted to use medication in conjunction with environmen-tal enrichment and behavior modification techniques.

DESTRUCTIVE BEHAVIOR

(Featuring Separation Anxiety)

When a prospective client calls our clinic and reports destructive behavior as the main problem he is having with his dog, I ask the $64,000 question: "Does your dog engage in this destructive behavior at any particular time?" Almost invariably the answer comes back that the dog is destructive *only* in the owner's absence. This leaves little room for doubt that the diagnosis is one of separation anxiety.

Okay, I may be oversimplifying a little. In one veterinary examination I took, candidates were asked to discuss *four* possible causes of a dog engaging in destructive behavior in the owner's absence. And it is possible to come up with three other explanations for such behavior—but to find them one has to delve deep and wide.

First, the offender *could* be a teething puppy that had been scolded for chewing things in the owner's presence. To avoid the unpleasantness, the pup might decide to continue its gingival massage "in camera" for fear of unpleasant repercussions.

Second, the mystery chewer could be any punishment-wary, owner-shy, occupationally challenged dog that has nothing better to do with its copious spare time than to whittle on a piece of furniture. I'm saying it *is* possible. My dad had a name for such mindless behavior. He called it mooching. The term *mooching,* applied to human behavior, includes any pointless activity like hanging around, kicking rocks, peeling the labels off bottles, carving one's name on desks or trees and, yes, chewing on pencils. Perhaps some destructive dogs also just "mooch" when left alone, displacing their boredom into various mindless activities that often involve destructiveness.

A third and final alternative explanation for destructive behavior occurring only in the owner's absence is thunderstorm phobia. Such a dog usually seeks its owner's company for reassurance during a storm, but if the owner is absent it may panic and attempt to escape. I have yet to encounter a storm-phobic dog that destroys property in its owner's absence that does not also have separation anxiety. These two conditions often coexist. Which brings us back to separation anxiety, with or without associated thunderstorm phobia, as the leading cause of household destruction by dogs in their owners' absence.

The actual destruction engaged in by dogs with separation anxiety involves doors, moldings, rugs in front of doors, windows, blinds, an owner's most recently handled personal effects, or random targets, such as pillows and shoes. The impetus for destruction around doors and windows, termed barrier frustration, represents futile attempts to escape. One dog repeatedly damaged the outside of a house, ripping off vinyl siding, if it was left out when its owners were inside the home—an unusual variation on the theme of barrier frustration.

Many people attempt to prevent destructive behavior by confining their dog in the cellar, behind a kiddie gate, or in a crate. The result is to focus the dog's attention on the barrier immediately in front of it, and that becomes the place where the damage is directed. In many cases, confinement only worsens the dog's panic and hysteria, with results bordering on the inhumane. I have encountered several dogs incarcerated in this way that have ripped their faces wide open in their attempts to escape from wire enclosures. Others have worn their toenails down until they bleed by attempting to burrow through concrete cellar floors, and still others have broken off teeth trying to chew their way out of crates. I grant that many dogs might be more comfortable in a crate, which some say serves as a denlike retreat, but owners should know that impounding dogs can result in disastrous consequences for some dogs, both physically and psychologically.

If I advise a client to use a crate to contain his dog, which I sometimes do, I make sure that the dog has first been trained to regard the crate as a safe haven. Initially, I advise leaving the door of the crate open at all times, allowing the dog to come and go as it pleases. After such a period of acclimation, and only when the dog moves into the crate of its own free will, I request that the door of the crate be closed for brief periods while the owner is present, and I ask them to monitor the consequences. Only when the dog is comfortable—that is, nonstressed—in the crate is it reasonable to progress to the stage of brief departures, leaving the dog confined to the crate for perhaps five minutes at a time.

Some dogs familiarized in this way do quite well in the security of their crates, but beware, occasionally an owner thinks that the dog's problem has been resolved by the use of a crate when in fact it has not. The owner's problem may have been resolved because the dog is no longer damaging property, but he may have done nothing to alleviate the dog's anxiety and might have even made it worse. The only way to find out for sure is to tape-record or film the dog while you are away. Some dogs throw in the towel when they realize they cannot escape from the crate and collapse in a state of depression known as learned helplessness. Others spend time trying to get out by pawing and chewing the bars of the cage, but fail. Neither is a particularly inspiring solution to the problem.

Ideally, dogs with separation anxiety should never be left alone until retraining has been accomplished, but this is often difficult to arrange. Ways in which this can be achieved are by leaving the dog with neighbors or relatives or at a doggy day-care center. Confidence building and the maintenance of a stress-free environment are extremely beneficial to any retraining program. Continued reexposure to the fear of being left alone will simply reinforce the problem. Destructive behavior directed at objects bearing the owner's scent or random shredding of objects in the owner's absence probably represents lesser degrees of separation anxiety. Such dogs might well cope adequately if simply confined in a smallish, snug area, providing there is an ample supply of chew toys to distract them should the mood so take them.

Again, this is not a solution to the problem but it can provide a satisfactory interim arrangement while confidence-building measures are engaged. (See Appendix)

Other behavioral aberrations that occur in separation anxiety include vocalization, house soiling, loss of appetite, self-directed behaviors, and depression. Vocalization takes the form of whining, barking, and even howling (depending on the type of dog) and is one of the cardinal signs of separation anxiety. It usually occurs minutes after the owner leaves and is either intermittent, being interspersed with periods of apparently pointless wandering, or may be almost continuous. Some owners don't even know this is going on unless they tape-record their dogs' activities in their absence. As with BO, it's often friends or neighbors who report the problem first.

House soiling occurring only in the owners' absence is another reasonably good sign of separation anxiety, though it is often not recognized as such by owners who either fail to appreciate the pattern of the behavior or believe that the dog is being malicious or vindictive. Some owners think that in doing this their dogs are trying to get even with them for leaving. This is an incorrect interpretation. Separation-anxiety-related problems may be pathetic, but malicious they are not.

Self-destructive behavior is another occasional sequel to separation distress and results from the dog's attempts to comfort or otherwise occupy itself by engaging in some self-directed activity. The classic example is that of lick granuloma, in which dogs repetitively lick the lower extremities of their limbs. Lick granuloma, however, does not only arise as a result of separation anxiety. Other anxiety-promoting circumstances may cause it, too. Tail chasing, sometimes leading to tail biting, is another compulsive, self-directed behavior, like lick granuloma, that may start as a separation-related problem, though once again any type of stress can precipitate it.

Finally, some dogs with separation anxiety don't do much at all when left alone, even though they're extremely anxious. They simply internalize their feelings and become depressed. It takes an observant owner to spot this problem, with only pre- and postdeparture cues to go on. Affected dogs simply slope away when they realize that their owner's departure is inevitable and spend many lonely hours inactive and despondent.

So what causes separation anxiety? Is it something genetic or is the condition acquired as a result of unfortunate life experiences? The answer is probably a bit of both, but I believe that adverse experiences during an early period of development, the first three months of life or so, are responsible for precipitating most cases of this condition.

The optimal way for puppies to be raised is for them to spend their early weeks with their mother and siblings in an atmosphere of care and positive experience. The transition from this Norman Rockwell-type situation to the new home and family when the dog is placed should be as seamless and psychologically atraumatic as possible. The goal is rapid redirection of loyalties and affection to a new and secure base, the new owners. Attention to detail is important during this transition and, improperly performed, the experience can produce long-lasting detrimental effects relating to insecurity.

I believe that a pup should be transported to its new home in the arms of the new owner, not in a crate. A collar and lead or blanket-wrap will provide some safety measures to ensure that the pup doesn't end up under the brake pedal of the vehicle. Once in the new home, at least until any initial separation problems have disappeared, the new puppy should have constant access to family members, including being allowed in the bedroom at night. Properly arranged X-Pens, the puppy equivalent of children's playpens, can provide some physical restriction without incarceration when direct supervision of the puppy is not possible.

Bearing in mind how critical it is to ensure stress-free relocation of puppies, it is hardly surprising to find that pet-store and puppy-mill pups that have frequently been early-weaned and transported miles across the United States as freight often arrive as, and continue to develop as, psychologically damaged goods. A spell in a shelter or pound can have the same effect. A test that has been developed in Europe predicts the potential for separation anxiety with one-hundred-percent accuracy in shelter dogs.

This is not to say that every dog from the pound develops separation anxiety, but some do. Neither should we ignore these needy animals. They, most of all, need to be rescued and, when all is said and done, probably make some of the finest pets around because of their extreme attachment to their new owners. A mite of separation anxiety could even be viewed as a desirable trait, but severe separation anxiety with major destructive components can cause owners huge expense and heartrending conflict. The direction a dog's separation anxiety goes after adoption depends a lot on the owner's attitude. A loving owner who provides structure and fun things for the dog to do in his absence will likely see the problem melt away before his very eyes. On the other hand, a dog's separation anxiety can be exacerbated in the hands of an overly considerate, undisciplined, emotionally needy individual.

Dogs with separation anxiety always follow their owners around the home, some more so than others. I refer to them as Velcro dogs—because it is hard to peel them off their owners. Given the choice, they will lie next to their owners in the evening as they watch television, will accompany them to bed, watch them get up in the morning, follow them downstairs, and will want to go everywhere with them, including the car. Some are okay in the car if left for a short period while the owner goes into a store, but others are not. Some severely affected dogs will rip up the inside of the car in very short order, resulting in thousands of dollars' worth of damage, if the owner disappears from view for a while or is delayed by more than a few minutes. Dogs with separation anxiety anticipate your every move. They know that car keys, coats, and shoes mean departure, and their anxiety starts at the first indication that the owner is leaving. Even if an owner scrambles the so-called predeparture cues to confuse the dog, the dog will quickly cotton on to the new routine, making it impossible for the owner to slip out unnoticed.

Another cardinal feature of separation anxiety is loss of appetite (anorexia) when the owner is away. All but the most mildly affected dogs refuse to eat in this situation because they are too concerned about their owner being away to show any interest in food. Some dogs will not eat for days if kenneled and come back weighing pounds less than when they went away. The pain of separation is mirrored in the joy of the reunion. Dogs with separation anxiety greet their owners exuberantly when they return to the home, sometimes taking five or ten minutes to settle down. Of course, this greeting ritual is a great compliment, and one that most owners enjoy immensely, but it's really just the flip side of the problem.

You would think with all these signs that separation anxiety would be easy to diagnose. And for the most part, you would be right, but occasionally behaviorists are dealt a curveball by an owner's interpretation of the problem. Such was the case with Sierra, an eighteen-month-old spayed female German shorthaired pointer. Sierra's owners, John and Jerry Maniscalco, were beside themselves because of her behavior and sought my help through our remote consulting service. But they did not start by telling me about an anxiety problem; neither did they report overattachment or neediness. They started by telling me of the problem as they saw it, and I must admit I was initially thrown off course by their revelations.

The report went something like this: "Sierra is an extremely active dog. She seems to be very smart and is easily bored. If she wants something or wants to do something, she will find a way. Her run has a wire fence over the top of it because she has climbed out previously, but she still climbs to the top of the fence looking for an escape. She runs with abandon, jumps over anything in her way, or just goes straight through things, using her strength. She often hurts herself and has been taken to emergency clinics for stitching and X rays on several occasions. She stays in her run in the middle of the day and has the backyard to run in from early afternoon onward. She chews everything. She has many chew toys and rawhides and she has chewed up all the garden hoses, even the propane hose to the barbecue, and frequently chews on rocks. We only have to take our eyes off her for a couple of minutes and she will destroy something."

There were a couple of other comments—she was very bright and intelligent, fast to learn, self-confident, and so on—and the owners concluded that she acted a lot like an intelligent but mischievous child who was very sneaky at times. The vet who was involved in treating this dog had another interpretation and diagnosed hyperkinesis (a form of hyperactivity) or some kind of generalized anxiety disorder. I tended to agree with this diagnosis at first and started typing my response. When I had finished, and having run through the importance of exercise, healthy diet, obedience training, confidence building, and various anxiety medications, I went back and reviewed the original report.

On rereading the owners' words, I found a couple of little sentences that had escaped my attention. One of them was, "We cannot leave her alone for any length of time," which appeared somewhere in the body of the text. The other one was, "When my husband comes home at night, she goes into a frenzy and grabs anything she can get hold of, jumping around like a lunatic (she will eventually settle down if we ignore her)." Further research with the owners elucidated that destruction of property was one of the main problems and that she focused particularly on things that they had recently handled, like car keys, clothing, the wife's pillow, books, and pens. They reported that Sierra demanded attention constantly, that she never left their sides, pulling at their sleeves or shoes.

I had to change my diagnosis. In light of these additional findings, the picture began to come together as one of separation anxiety. I never did find out where they got Sierra from but I can make an educated guess about her background. She was clearly a very needy dog and missed them badly when they went out, doing all the usual things that dogs with separation anxiety do, including her Houdini-like escape acts and well-targeted destruction.

Sierra's treatment included independence training to restructure her overly dependent relationship with her owners and also counter-conditioning (see Appendix). The basic requirement of her independence training was to train her not to follow her owners around the house and to be comfortable about spending time apart from them . . . to stand on her own four feet, so to speak. Sierra's owners also elected for a concomitant medical treatment with the old chestnut antidepressant drug, Elavil. Time will tell how she fares with this treatment, but the outlook for improvement is, well, rosy.

As far as other causes of destructive behavior are concerned, you don't need a Ph.D. in psychology to figure out that puppies need to chew on things and that grown dogs need something to do with their lives. The puppy dilemma is a fairly straightforward one to fix. Treatment involves removing inappropriate chewies and replacing them with pet-store-bought, purpose-made chewable objects onto which they can direct their chewing behavior. Nylon bones, rope bones, and rubber Kong toys make fine substitutes, though sometimes they must be rendered attractive by the addition of smearable food or a few food drops of essence of vanilla or anisette. Trainers sometimes recommend that when a pup is caught in the act of gnawing on a forbidden object it should be instructed to let go with a command such as "Out" or "Drop," following which the item is removed and replaced with an acceptable alternative. The next words out of the owner's mouth should be "Good dog" to affirm the acceptability of chewing on the new object. Thus, redirection, and not correction, is the answer to this chewing problem. To go any other way is to fail to understand the pup's needs and attempt the impossible, to go against the flow of nature.

For older dogs that are chewing out of boredom, the solution is equally intuitive. The dog should be provided with ample opportunity to engage in purposeful, absorbing activities. In other words, to have a job. It is the owner's responsibility to make sure that this happens, and as usual, the fundamentals include plenty of exercise, an appropriate diet, good communication (ensured by nonconfrontational schooling), and breed-specific behavioral outlets.

EATING DISORDERS

Appetite is a peculiar phenomenon. It is one of those things, like sleeping and breathing, that we tend to take for granted until a problem arises. Between meals, dogs, like people, probably hardly give food a second thought, but there comes a time when, like Pooh Bear, they begin to feel a little eleven o'clockish. A time when they feel like a little something. This is the time they gravitate toward the feeding area and assume various postures or behaviors that are likely to remind the owner that food is now due. And some dogs are very good at this. One of my patients would paw open a kitchen cupboard door, take his food bowl in his mouth, and deposit it in precisely the usual feeding location at exactly six o'clock each night. Who says dogs aren't aware of the passage of time?

Both internal and external factors operate to create the motivation to eat, which we call appetite. Internal factors include such things as "stomach fill" and blood glucose concentration, whereas outside factors include the odor and taste of food. As the dog eats, the balance of the scales of appetite readjust because of changes in the internal environment; satiation occurs, and eating ceases. After a suitable interval, the cycle is repeated and by this mechanism the correct intake is maintained within a fairly precise range. If body weight creeps up, appetite is reduced, and if body weight falls, the reverse occurs. At least this is the normal arrangement.

One of the most common reasons for disturbances in this happy homeostatic state of affairs occurs in illness, when appetite is usually suppressed. In fact, appetite is such a good monitor of a dog's well-being that "How is he eating?" is one of the leading questions that veterinarians ask when assessing the health of an animal, or when making the decision about whether to prolong a terminally ill animal's life. It is usually assumed that if an animal has a healthy appetite it can't be too sick or suffering too badly. Obviously, it makes sense to have your dog checked by a veterinarian if its appetite does dip for some mysterious reason, but there are nonmedical causes of anorexia that must be taken into account, too, some of them purely psychological.

It is fairly simple to demonstrate how fickle appetite can be by offering a dog a food treat while it is on the veterinarian's examination table and just about to be vaccinated. All but the most stoic gourmands will turn their noses up at a normally irresistible food treat in this situation, only to gobble it up a minute or two later as they are about to leave the premises. The comedian Shelly Berman captured the essence of the conflict between stress and appetite in one of his stories about a pending airplane disaster. As the plane hurtled out of control, a desensitized and indifferent flight attendant continued to offer "coffee, tea, or milk" to a bug-eyed, terrified passenger. "But you don't seem to understand," the passenger responded to the attendant. "We're going to die." "Well, how about a martini, then?" came the reply.

Acute stresses cause acute changes in our desire for appetitive satisfaction. Urgent matters assume priority over less-compelling drives and continue to take priority until the emergency is resolved or until the desire for food becomes overwhelming. Perhaps the most common reason for dogs to stop eating for a prolonged period is separation anxiety. The panic that ensues when these needy dogs are left alone causes a profound reduction in appetite, often to the point of complete anorexia. "Does your dog eat while you are away?" is one of the key questions that I ask when diagnosing this condition. Of course, separation anxiety, like other psychological conditions, is not a black-and-white situation. It is not a question of whether the dog has it or does not, it is a matter of degree. Some dogs that are only mildly affected may be tempted to chew on a raw bone or peanut-butter-stuffed chew toy in the owner's absence, but others are so severely affected that they want nothing to do with food at all. Owners may not even notice their dog's anorexia if they only leave it for a few hours each day during the middle of the day, feeding it in the evening when they come home. In such cases, the opportunity to assess their dog's appetite during their absence is lacking. However, if they go away for a few days and leave their dog in a kennel, they may return to find out that it has refused food for the entire duration of their absence. Not all kennel owners will admit to this apparent failing on their part, but the bathroom scales never lie. According to principles of physiology, a dog that has not eaten because of separation stress will have an increased appetite for a few days following the owner's return, to get back to its normal set point. But what happens if you do not return for weeks or months—does the dog die of starvation? The answer to this is usually no, because the motivation to eat gradually increases and ultimately assumes irresistible proportions. First it's a nibble, then a mouthful, and finally some regular intake, albeit at a reduced level. I did hear of one case in which a dog refused to eat while its owners were away and accordingly died of starvation. This dog was a gun dog and had been shut in a pantry by mistake while the owners went on vacation. It was surrounded by hanging game and apparently had water to drink but eventually died of hunger. The owners put this down to the dog's loyalty and training but I feel sure that separation-anxiety-induced anorexia was at the root of this dog's untimely demise.

Of course, the longest period of separation that occurs for dogs and people alike is the infinite one following bereavement. As many of you already know, dogs become depressed after the loss of a loved one and often show typical signs of depression, including eating disturbances. The most severe effects of bereavement occur immediately after a loss, and passing time is one of the most valuable factors assisting in recovery.

Returning from the American Veterinary Medical Association meeting in Reno last summer, I found myself sitting next to a dedicated dog owner who told me several stories about dogs she had known and lived with. I found one of her stories, about a dog bereaved of its canine companion, particularly compelling. The woman owned just two dogs at the time when one became terminally ill and had to be put to sleep. To spare the other dog the psychological trauma of the event, she took it to a friend's house while the vet came and swiftly dispatched her other dog. Once the vet had departed, the woman dug a deep grave in her back garden and placed the dead dog's body in the grave, which she then filled with soil and covered with gravel. When her remaining dog was returned to the house, it immediately began searching for its buddy. It ran from level to level in the house but it couldn't find him, so it went out to the garden and looked around, finally honing in on the stony grave. When it finally came to the spot, it lay down, resting its head upon crossed paws, and stared off into the distance, not moving from the spot for two days and refusing to eat. The owner brought it water to drink, which it lapped, but food did not interest it. At the end of this period, the dog ceased its vigil and slowly got back into a relatively normal lifestyle but it obviously suffered terribly at the loss of its companion. Its appetite alone served as the barometer of its internal feelings.

If undereating is the yin, then overeating is the yang. It is a sad fact of life that approximately twenty-five percent of all dogs in the United States are overweight, and some are obese (obesity is defined as a body weight more than twenty-five percent above ideal body weight for that age, breed, and sex of dog), mirroring a similar problem in the human population. So what is overeating all about? Is it just plain gluttony or are there other factors operating? Before we start accusing dogs of being pigs, it is probably wise to take a closer look at the whole syndrome of being overweight.

Returning to our physiological model, and all things being even, a dog's body weight should be maintained within fairly narrow limits by automatic adjustment of its caloric intake to match its energy expenditure. Despite this check and balance, gaining weight still can result from eating too much. If a dog eats puppy food while it is growing and exercising vigorously and is maintained on the same type and quantity of ration once it has achieved its full adult size, it will gain weight. You would think that the internal mechanism designed to maintain a set body weight would kick in to save it from itself, but the extremely palatable nature of modern rations increases the dog's motivation sufficiently to guarantee those extra few mouthfuls each meal.

I am reminded of what Mr. Micawber said to David Copperfield regarding his finances: "Income six pence week, expenditure five pence—result happiness." When the same logic is applied to slightly excessive intake of food, the result is gradual weight gain to a new set point. Of course, this cannot happen if owners don't allow their dogs to eat too much, so it is important to read the instructions on the package and feed accordingly. If a dog has difficulty interpreting its internal signals as to when to stop eating, owners can arrange for a clear signal of their own—an empty bowl. That and a set of bathroom scales should solve most of the problems.

One food dogs find irresistibly attractive is table food. Barbecue foods like hamburgers and hot dogs are high on their list of priorities, cooked or uncooked. Many owners don't think there is any harm in giving a little "people food" from time to time, and perhaps as long as it really is from time to time, it isn't such a crime. But dogs are so good at begging. Some sit by the table with big, sad eyes; some scratch at the owner's lap and whimper or bark, practically asking to be fed. Others take a more proactive approach by stealing the food. I knew one dog recently that stole and ate a whole loaf of bread, and another beat the family to the Thanksgiving turkey. Permitted or not, "people food" on top of normal dog rations may well have the "Mr. Micawber" effect on your dog. Not only that, but if sufficient food is engulfed in this way, your dog's appetite for its own food may well suffer. Because dog foods are so well balanced to meet dogs' needs, this is an unhealthy sequel.

There is a question about feeding human food to dogs in the national board exam that all vets are required to take. The question is that an owner asks the vet whether it is okay to feed a dog human food. The answer is either: (a) Yes, it is okay sometimes; (b) Human food is even better for dogs than dog food; (c) A mixture of dog food and human food is ideal; or (d) Human food should never be fed at all. From what I have said, you will gather that answer *d* is correct. You might consider that this is rather a hard-line approach, but it is a correct one from the lifespan and healthspan point of view.

Aside from food palatability and owner factors, there are other reasons why some dogs eat more than they need. One of these, I believe, is low-grade stress or boredom, often coupled with inactivity. Dogs, like people, are social creatures that thrive on companionship and an active lifestyle. When dogs are unattended for extended periods they have to find something to do to pass the time, however mindless that something may be. The result is what is called displacement behavior, such as pacing, barking, or excessive grooming. Along these lines, some dogs seem to occupy themselves with frequent trips to the food bowl when there's nothing better to do. In such cases, eating replaces some other behavior that would have been performed in a more fulfilling environment.

One way to solve weight gain arising from boredom and inactivity is to restrict the dog's food intake to the recommended amount—but this does nothing to address the dog's psychological dilemma and could lead to other, even less desirable, habits. The correct approach is an all-embracing one in which the dog's lifestyle is enriched and adjusted in every way possible. This involves increasing its level of exercise, feeding it a sensible diet, increasing communication between the owner and dog (by employing positive training methods), increasing fun interactions with the dog, minimizing the time the dog spends alone, and providing an assortment of toys and other distractions to occupy the dog in your absence.

It is not fair to give dogs and owners all the blame for overeating when in fact medical conditions underlie some causes of inappropriate weight gain in dogs. Hypothyroidism is by far the most prevalent and salient condition in this respect. Hypothyroidism is now ranked the number-one problem in six of the seven different breed groups recognized by the American Kennel Club. Fortunately, every vet worth his salt should be able to diagnose classical hypothyroidism from the top of a double-decker bus with a telescope turned around the wrong way, because the signs are so obvious. They include weight gain, lethargy, excessive shedding, symmetrical hair loss, thin skin, slow heartbeat, low body temperature, and so on. Diagnosis is by means of a simple blood test, and treatment is by replacement of the deficient thyroid hormones.

Some other medical conditions make dogs look fat when they actually aren't. Dogs with overactive adrenal glands (Cushing's disease or syndrome) often have a pendulous abdomen, but an enlarged liver accounts for their rotund appearance. Also, dogs with fluid in their abdomen as a result of heart failure or liver failure may appear overweight. When dogs become "fat" for whatever reason it is wise to make an appointment with your vet.

So, you would think that with the yin and yang of eating disorders under our belts (so to speak), there would be very little else to say in this department. But there's still one other issue remaining. I refer to the sometimes unpalatable problem of the ingestion of nonfood items by dogs. First on the list is coprophagia, the habit that some dogs develop of eating their own or other dogs' stool. What on earth would drive a dog to engage in such foul behavior? Genetics provides some of the answers.

Most canine behaviors that trouble owners have their foundations in innate tendencies, and coprophagia is no exception. Like human babies, pups have no control over where or when they eliminate. It is normal behavior for a bitch to ingest her pups' feces in order to keep the nest clean. Whether by learning from observing Mom or because of some internal drive of their own, it is common for older pups to ingest feces, too. However, this disgusting behavior normally peters out after a few months as pups lose interest in this less palatable food facsimile.

There is tremendous variation in the drive to engage in coprophagia. Some pups never eat stool at all, whereas others are incorrigible, relentless in their quest for fecal matter in any shape or form. These critters become experts in the location and rapid ingestion of the forbidden fruit despite their owners' close chaperoning and constant protests.

Although you can argue that dietary deprivation and a craving for undigested protein is a driving force behind coprophagia, I believe that there are environmental and lifestyle-induced changes that contribute to the obsession some dogs have with feces. A potential strike against this theory is that stool produced by dogs on performance rations or puppy chow is much more attractive than that produced by dogs fed high-fiber diets. I have discouraged dogs from eating their own or other dogs' feces by switching them to a proprietary, high-fiber, weight-reducing diet. But here is the other side of that coin. By changing dogs to a high-fiber diet, owners wind up feeding their dogs a larger volume of food, perhaps enough to satiate their oral craving. The compulsion may not be eliminated at all by feeding high-fiber rations—it may simply be displaced onto a more acceptable alternative. If free-choice feeding is introduced, too, then the dog always has the choice between food and feces and, in this situation, food seems to win the preference test.

I don't have much faith in so-called aversive treatments for coprophagia, such as feeding your dog breath mints or meat tenderizer, or running around with a bottle of Tabasco, trying to spike every fecal pile in sight. The most successful approach to dealing with coprophagia is to adjust the dog's diet (as indicated) and then to supervise it when it has to defecate, removing unnecessary temptation immediately with a pooper-scooper.

Last but not least, some dogs seem compelled to eat inedible objects they find around the house. This so-called pica, the iterative ingestion of inedible objects, is almost certainly pathological and I have only seen it in dogs that are behaviorally abnormal in other ways. I first came across it in bull terriers, the ones that spun in tight circles or chased imaginary shadows. I picked it up as an ancillary finding but got suspicious that it might be linked with the primary problem when I found that the behavior was overrepresented in dogs with predatory compulsions.

One theory as to why pica occurs is that it is just another compulsion in a compulsion-prone dog. The curious thing is that the craving for inedible objects does not respond to antiobsessional medication in the same way that other compulsive behaviors do. This treatment resistance remains something of an enigma.

My most memorable example of the stubbornness of pica to treatment occurred in a wirehaired fox terrier. This dog's presenting problem was light chasing (otherwise known as shadow chasing). It chased shadows for hours on end, even excavating through plasterboard walls to pursue its will-o'-the-wisp illusions. The dog, Bumbley, appeared on the television show *20/20* with me and its distraught owners. The one thing that didn't come across clearly in the show was that Bumbley ate everything in sight and the house had to be "Bumbley-proofed" against his relentless ingestion of anything his owners left around. Although Bumbley's light chasing was substantially improved when he was treated with the human antiobsessional drug Prozac, his ingestive fetish never faltered. He had already had surgery to relieve intestinal obstructions resulting from his habit and, each day, his owners reentered their house with trepidation after work, fearing that Bumbley might have eaten something else.

One day their worst fears were realized when they found Bumbley vomiting bile in a corridor on their return. They knew what this meant and quickly took him to the vet's office. Bear in mind that Bumbley's owners had already paid a one-thousand-dollar vet bill for similar surgery a year earlier, spent a fortune elucidating and treating his compulsive-behavior problem, and lived in fear of other ingestive incidents. To top it all, the woman was expecting her second baby. The combination of financial and psychological factors finally took their toll when the vet announced another one-thousand-dollar bill for surgery, and their formerly steadfast resolve buckled. They elected euthanasia this time as the final solution.

When the TV show aired again some nine months later, Hugh Downs, on the anchor desk, quizzed Bob Brown, the correspondent, "So how are Dr. Dodman's patients today?" Bob Brown, who was heavy with a cold and not thinking too swiftly, said, "Most of them are doing very well, but Bumbley died." When I got back to my office, I had a slew of phone calls and E-mail messages waiting for me from people whose dogs had been treated with this antiobsessional medication. "Bumbley didn't die from the medication, did he, Dr. Dodman?" was the recurring question. "No, he didn't," I was able to report. "He had an intestinal obstruction."

Did Bumbley have a compulsive behavior that wouldn't respond to Prozac or was there something else going on? At the time of this writing, I really don't have all the answers, but I did read an interesting article about compulsive eating in humans that provided food for thought. The study explored the hypothesis that bulimia might be related to a seizural behavior in some patients. The authors pointed out similarities between binge eating and seizural disturbances in certain patients, and reported brain-wave abnormalities in sixty-four percent of a large series of human patients they evaluated for problems of compulsive overeating. In addition to making these observations, they treated their patients with an antiepileptic drug, phenytoin, and found that the majority of them improved. I believe one antiepileptic medication had been tried on Bumbley prior to the antiobsessional treatment, but it may have been the wrong one or at the wrong dose. I wish I had read about the study before I saw Bumbley. If I had, perhaps things might have turned out differently.

I hasten to point out that not every dog that eats junk off the floor is compulsive or has seizures, just as not every dog that loses its appetite occasionally or pigs out has a problem with anorexia or binge eating. It is all a matter of degree. Sometimes, from the dog's point of view, there may even be a good reason for eating an object it has in its possession. One dog I saw recently always guarded items that it had stolen from family members. One day, while in possession of a tennis ball, it was approached by the lady owner. Presumably to prevent her from removing the tennis ball from its jaws, it swallowed it and sat there bug-eyed, looking at her sheepishly. Advantage dog. This naughty dog was taken down to the vet's office, where the foreign body was removed surgically. Game, set, and match to the owner.

FEAR-BASED CONDITIONS

One day, after racking my brains about a particularly difficult case involving a dog with multiple fears, I decided to consult with my colleague Dr. Richard Shader, psychiatrist and (at that time) chairman of the Department of Pharmacology and Experimental Therapeutics at Tufts University School of Veterinary Medicine. As the medical school is thirty miles from the veterinary school, I telephoned rather than visited him in person and was lucky enough to find him at his desk.

"Richard, would you be willing to help me out with one of my veterinary patients?" I began. I could almost see the twinkle in his eye as he replied, "I'll try, but I don't have many dogs on my panel, so I don't know how much help I will be."

"Working from first principles will be just fine with me," I replied.

"All right, go ahead and tell me the story," he agreed.

After giving him a fairly lengthy account of the precise nature of the problem in hand and a brief rundown of the multiple treatments I had tried, I finally posed my question. "So there are two questions I have for you. Do you agree with my assessment, and what else can I try with this dog? And what would you do if this were a human patient?"

There was a pause.

"I am intrigued by the problem, Nick, but you know, in psychiatry we don't recognize fear as an abnormal condition. Fear is regarded as a normal reaction to a fear-inducing stimulus. We just don't treat it."

I was completely taken aback. There are normally such close parallels between the study of animal behavior and human psychiatry that I had assumed Dr. Shader and I would be talking in the same language. "Fear is normal," I repeated slowly. "So what do you call it if a person is terrified of unfamiliar people?"

"A phobia," he replied. "A phobia is an extreme and apparently irrational fear."

"Yes, we talk about phobias, too," I said. "For example, noise phobia and agoraphobia, but I had always thought of fear as being one step down the ladder of intensity."

"That isn't how we see it," Dr. Shader responded, "and you will not find fear listed as a category in our bible, the *Diagnostic and Statistical Manual of Psychiatry.*"

With my terminology readjusted, we were able to resume our discussion, which drifted toward the treatment of phobias. As it turns out, treatment of phobias was no cakewalk in people, either, with cures far from guaranteed even when medications were employed. Our conversation drew to a close as Dr. Shader's secretary coaxed him away from the phone to attend to an awaiting appointment.

I hung up the phone and pondered the terminological discrepancies. To brand a dog as fearful seems to describe perfectly well the situation that arises when an insecure dog goes to pieces when faced with an intimidating class of objects or persons. I can hear my client's words now: "He's a wonderful pet with the family, Dr. Dodman, but he is extremely fearful of strangers and hides when we have company." Or, "His main problem is fear of loud noises but he also gets very frightened at the vet's office."

These are all common complaints, and terms like *fear aggression* and *inanimate fear* or *situational fear* are commonly used to describe them. At least we know what we mean by these terms, even though the conditions may be more aptly termed phobias. Perhaps the difference is that in behavioral medicine we have developed terms to describe what we observe, the fearful response, rather than how our patients feel. But by the time an animal is evidencing fear severely enough to alert our suspicions, a fearful condition has almost certainly reached the level of a phobia.

The difference between a fear and a phobia might be illustrated as follows: If a stranger approaches and threatens a normal, well-adjusted dog that cowers and backs away, this response would reasonably classify as fear. The reaction is entirely understandable and a natural one. If this same dog subsequently generalizes its fear to include all strangers that look in the remotest way like the stranger, whether they actually threaten it or not, and then reacts excessively, this would classify as a phobia. The fear has now intensified and been conditioned to occur in response to a more general stimulus.

Anxious, apprehensive dogs are more likely to develop these excessive reactions, however classified, on account of their sensitive dispositions. It is as if they expect bad things to happen to them, and fearfulness becomes a self-fulfilling prophecy. Anxiety is fear of something that is perceived as impending rather than something that is actually happening. In other words, anxiety is a type of anticipatory fear, and, because of this, can be much more sustained.

Anxiety and fear involve practically identical changes in bodily functions, including an elevation of the heart rate and blood pressure and the release of stress hormones. The body is put into a state of alertness in preparation for fight or flight, and the animal involved will demonstrate one of several possible behavioral responses to the imagined or perceived threat. These responses include freezing (in hopes that whatever it is will go away), fighting (a proactive approach when the fear-inducing stimulus is present), beating a hasty retreat (flight), or clinging to the sides of a containing area (thigmotaxic behavior). All these behaviors are accompanied by various forms of posturing, ranging from hunkering down, to become as small and nonthreatening as possible, to open-mouth threats, lunging, and biting. As an external manifestation of the inner turmoil, the pupils of the eyes dilate to form large black pools and the hair coat of the ruff and all along the spine and tail may stand erect, adding an element of intimidation to the proceedings by increasing the dog's apparent size.

What determines a dog's response in a particular situation depends on the dog's temperament and the perceived magnitude of the threat. Subordinate dogs will attempt to defuse the situation by adopting submissive postures (such as crouching and rolling over and urinating) or may run and hide. More-dominant dogs are likely to take the proactive approach and engage in an aggressive response. In the latter case, it can be difficult to determine whether fear or pure dominance is driving the behavior, but by inquiring about the dog's behavioral history, events leading up to the attack, and by observing subtle signs of submissive posturing, such as early balking or a tucked tail, you can glean vital clues as to the dog's motivation. The magnitude and duration of the fear-inducing challenge can range from mild and protracted to brief and extreme. Mild, protracted fears create an effect bordering on anxiety, whereas sudden, intense fears can produce much more extreme effects.

And how do these fears arise? What makes a dog frightened of people, thunderstorms, or of being left alone? The answer is some mix of natural and nurturing influences, the exact proportions of each depending on the case in point. Some fears seem to arise primarily as a result of genetic programming. A genetically nervous strain of pointers kept at the National Institute of Health in Bethesda, Maryland, exemplify this point. Affected dogs collapse in fear when they meet a new person or are brought out into a wide-open space, yet the environment in which they are raised is perfectly adequate. Clearly genetics is at work here. In other instances, adverse environmental events seem instrumental in the genesis of fear. The majority of seriously affected dogs that I have seen have experienced psychologically traumatic experiences, often while young.

One way I favor for classifying fear is into three separate components based on the motivation. I call this my three-cornered-hat approach or Bermuda Triangle fear approach. The latter has a nicer ring to it, and has the added advantage that it implies that the fearful state, once entered, is relatively permanent, and for the most part this is true. The three corners of the triangle represent fear of animate cues, fear of inanimate cues, and fear of certain situations. Animate cues may be animals of the same species or animals of a different species—usually humans, but sometimes other animals such as cats, or even flying insects. Fear of inanimate cues is largely represented as a fear of noises, particularly thunderstorms, but also gunshots, fireworks, power equipment, vacuum cleaners, camera flashes, et cetera. Other inanimate fears can be of various sights, sensations, and even smells. Situational fear is a composite fear epitomized by separation anxiety (see "D—Destructive Behavior"), fear of car travel, and fear of the vet's office. Frequently dogs have fear in more than one of these categories and sometimes they have a behavioral full house known as global fear, being frightened of everything and everyone.

Animate Fears

How does a dog acquire this particular type of fear? The answer is almost always as a result of adverse early exposure. Using the famous "retrospectoscope" technique, in which events of the past can be brought into sharper focus, one can sometimes identify the fear-inducing stimulus quite accurately in time and space. Even if the original offender cannot be pinpointed, a pretty good facsimile can be created. For example, you might be able to discern that the person who initially scared the dog was probably a tall man who smoked cigarettes. The technique involves taking a careful behavioral history from the owner. Fear of people usually takes the form of fear of men or children, though women sometimes generate a fear response, too. The reason men and children feature so prominently is that they tend to act most aggressively with dogs and can scare them, forming long-lasting negative impressions.

These impressions are even more indelible if they are made during the so-called sensitive period of development, which is between about three and twelve weeks of age for dogs. If a dog is frightened of men with hats or beards, I direct my line of questioning to uncover possible negative interactions the dog has had with individuals conforming to this stereotype, particularly during the early part of its life. I am always surprised at how accurate the retrospectoscope diagnostic technique is, though sometimes a full history of the dog's interactions is lacking because of what I call a behavioral black hole (a period of the dog's history during which no accounts of its behavior or interactions are available).

I recently saw a dog showing fear aggression directed toward women and children. My own daughter's behavior one day at the local park illustrates how a fear like this might develop. We were throwing sticks at a tree to knock horse chestnuts off the branches so that I might relive and teach her the thrills and spills of a childhood game I loved, called conkers. In the game of conkers you hang your horse chestnut (the conker) on a string, like a mace, and whack your opponent's conker (similarly suspended) in an attempt to destroy it (only in England, I hear you mutter). Anyway, there we were, throwing sticks at the tree, when suddenly she caught sight of a dog on the other side of a chain-link fence. "Hey Dad, let's throw a stick at that dog," my daughter blurted out. I stood there for a second, stunned and amazed. "You *do* know what I do for a living, don't you?" I asked, and saw a look of shame spread across her face. "Sorry, Dad," she muttered into her chest as the thought of throwing the stick at the dog rapidly melted away. I think it is the nature of children that they often do things spontaneously and without much thought of the consequences. Dogs sort out this kind of thing pretty quickly and take evasive action.

People may be the most frequent subjects of a dog's fearfulness, but other dogs can engender fear, too. One dog I saw recently, a fourteen-month-old sheltie, provides an example of a dog fearful of other dogs. Fable, a spayed sheltie bitch, was acquired at the age of fourteen weeks by her caring and intelligent attorney owner, Triny Gilmore. According to Ms. Gilmore, Fable had come from a good home but was the pariah dog in a litter of exceptionally dominant and willful shelties. One of her littermates, a male, had to be destroyed at the age of ten months because of "unprovoked aggression" toward family members. Whether it was because of Fable's adverse experiences at the hands (paws) of these littermates or some obscure, as yet unidentified, reason remains unclear, but she definitely did develop a dreadful fear of other dogs. Fable had other fears, too (which I will mention later), and her condition was complicated by hypothyroidism. Whatever the reason for her dislike of other dogs, her fear of them was extremely intense and pervasive.

When Ms. Gilmore first came to see me, she was not quite sure what was causing Fable to make what she called off-the-wall attacks on other dogs. The fact that Fable was aggressive to *all* other dogs, and not just potentially dominant rivals, was a good clue that fear was involved in her reaction. That dominance was the driving force behind the way she dealt with her fear was also a given. Without the insecurity she apparently felt, she would have been a different, happier dog and would have had a lot more fun. As far as other dogs were concerned she was a loose cannon, and the two other shelties she cohabitated with at Ms. Gilmore's house knew this only too well. So frequent and severe were her altercations with the other dogs that she had to spend a good deal of time separated from them. As long as the energy level in the room remained low and constant, she could stand their company for a while without conflict. By this I mean there was no commotion, no sudden movement, no barking, and no extraneous provocations of any sort. Any slight ripple in the continuum of peace and harmony would cause her to attack one or the other of her pack mates.

After correcting the hypothyroidism with synthetic thyroid hormone, Ms. Gilmore felt that Fable was about fifty percent better than she had been previously in terms of her behavior toward the other dogs—but she was still a handful. Despite dietary changes, increasing her daily exercise to aerobic levels, obedience training, agility work, and specific desensitization measures to reduce her fears, I was unable to effect much more improvement in Fable's behavior, but at least life had become somewhat livable for Ms. Gilmore.

Fable had to be confined for the first few hours of the day (until 10:00 A.M.) because that was the time she was most edgy and likely to attack the other dogs. Following this, she could be allowed to interact with them, providing that she was under someone's direct control and that attempts were made to reduce environmental provocations. The pinnacle of Fable's improvement came some months after I first saw her, occurring during outdoor agility-training sessions. Apparently she became quite familiar with several other dogs in the class, to the point that she began ignoring them and was able to focus enough to do well in the class. Unfortunately, though, the problem reemerged in the fall, when the classes were brought inside. Although initially delighted at being taken to the agility center, Fable's mood changed when she was brought indoors.

She just about coped as a new dog, a pug, was introduced to the assembled throng; began to lose it as a Brittany spaniel made its debut; and finally disintegrated when two confident Labradors entered the scene. Head held low, pupils dilated, tail tucked, she exploded into a screaming hunk of teeth and fur and had to be withdrawn from the situation immediately. The Bermuda Triangle syndrome had struck again. With patience, Ms. Gilmore was able to salvage some of the improvement that had been made, but living with Fable was like walk-ing on eggs. Fable was her own worst enemy—a product of faulty genetics—her condition reminiscent of the human condition of para-noid schizophrenia. Perhaps I should have treated her with antipsy-chotic medication.

Of course, not all fear reactions to animate cues are as extreme as Fable's. Some dogs, particularly young pups, simply run away and hide. Others avert their eyes and tremble while assuming submissive postures. The presence or absence of a trusted leader and the opportu-nity (or not) to escape will affect the response. If a dog has a great deal of faith in its handler, it will be less likely to panic or try to attack or escape. Owners can build this kind of confidence by working on a benign retraining program where the dog is required to work for all the good things in life. This so-called Nothing in Life Is Free program, normally recommended for dominant dogs, is also helpful—if applied in a milder form—for instilling confidence into fearful dogs. The more highly they regard you as their fearless leader, the less likely they are to start calling their own shots.

This program is not militaristic or bombastic, but simply one of firm, authoritative guidance coupled with warm praise for a job well done. Unlike the full-dominance program, there are times when the "schoolroom mode" does not have to be engaged and you can indulge your fearful pet. Needless to say, one of these times is not when adver-sity rears its ugly head. This is a time for the owner to assume a confident leadership position and to direct operations.

I have found head halters an invaluable asset for controlling and delivering the correct message of authority to fearful dogs. Halters deliver a biologically appropriate signal of leadership and control in a way that dogs understand and to which they conform. The result is frequently the defusing of a delicate situation before things get out of hand. A conventional flat collar or choke chain does not send the same message, and restraint of a fearful dog by such a means will likely augment its fear. The dog collared this way often receives no convincing signals of control or authority from its owner and knows that escape is not possible. This unnerving realization leads to either submission, panic, or "attack mode" as possible outcomes. A fearful dog will be less aggressive if it is free to keep its distance or if it is restrained by means of a halter.

Fearful dogs are most likely to attack an intruder who imposes on them directly when they are confined in a crate or other small space. I learned this long ago in my days in anesthesiology when I quickly found that the best way to approach a fearful dog in a cage was to open the door and stand to one side. A dog that would practically take your head off if you went in after it would then almost invariably trot out as the door was opened and, once free, would be a totally reformed character. Cornering a fearful dog is a sure way to promote aggression, because in this situation it has nowhere to go except forward.

Inanimate Fears

I have come across some pretty bizarre inanimate fears in my time, ranging from fear of microblinds, garbage bags, lawn tractors, linoleum surfaces, and Thursdays, to garbage trucks and Dumpsters. And, believe it or not, I have managed to determine a fairly precise explanation for most of these fears. Occasionally, however, I hit the behavioral-black-hole syndrome and can only guess at or presume the initial cause of the problem.

Rusty, a lovable golden retriever with award-winning ways, put me to the test. Somewhere along the road of life Rusty must have had an adverse experience with or near his owners' oven. Their description of his problem behavior was that he suffered panic attacks whenever the oven was turned on. He would leap onto people's laps, shiver and shake, and drool saliva profusely, sometimes screaming around the apartment and jumping through screened windows in attempts to flee from his nemesis.

As a matter of academic curiosity, I tried to figure out what had originally caused this fear and I laid the obvious facts on the table: Ovens are associated with food and ovens are hot. I figured that the owners had perhaps been cooking a roast some day when they had opened the oven door, leaving the roast on the door to cool while they went off to do something else. Rusty might then have approached the tasty meat and ended up by burning himself in some sensitive area, such as the tip of his nose. Now, dogs are not that great at deductive reasoning. Under these circumstances, a dog might conclude that the ticking noise the oven made as it cooled down (or warmed up), or the heat that it threw off, heralded impending pain and should be avoided at all costs. One dog that made an even more irrational association was terrified by the smell of lamb cooking. Not beef, not chicken, only lamb.

Anyway, Rusty's owners resolved his problem on their own by getting a new oven. After the change he presumably no longer associated the oven with the earlier adverse experience. In retrospect, there must have been something unique about the original oven that, when it was turned on, delivered warning signals to Rusty. Perhaps it was the glow of a light on the control panel or inside the oven door. Perhaps it was the sound of the fan. It couldn't have been the heat, because all ovens are hot, so at least we eliminated one potential trigger.

Probably the most common types of inanimate fear involve fear of sounds, and of these sound fears, thunderstorm phobia is the most prevalent. Although the primary cause of thunderstorm phobia may appear obvious at first glance, there are still doubts in my mind as to precisely what initiates it. In addition, there is no guaranteed cure for advanced cases, so there is still a lot to learn about this apparently uncomplicated condition. It is an enigma among fears and becomes so intense in some cases that even we vets use the term *phobia* to describe what occurs.

Curiously, genetics seems to play a role in determining susceptibility to this condition, as certain breeds are overrepresented in the demographics. Larger dogs, particularly Labradors, retrievers, German shepherds, and northern breeds, seem to be most at risk. The same types also appear to be more susceptible to other anxiety-related conditions, such as lick granuloma, so perhaps the mystery factor predisposing them to the condition has something to do with their temperament. One possible explanation is that herding dogs and some sporting breeds that were selectively bred to inhibit their bite are therefore more sensitive. This may have some relevance for these kinds of dogs, but the same cannot be said for northern breeds, which are as near to the wild type as any breed. Using the white-swan/black-swan argument, the theory of sensitivity is seriously flawed. In the white-swan/black-swan argument, the reasoning is that identifying any number of white swans does not prove a theory that all swans are white, but identifying one black one proves that they are not all white.

One explanation for the breed predisposition for thunderstorm phobia might have something to do with conformation, as T-storm-phobic (thunderstorm-phobia-susceptible) dogs are usually of larger and heavier-coated breeds. If confirmed, this correlation would lend support to the static-electricity theory of thunderstorm phobia. Essentially, the "static" theory is that dogs could become statically charged during a storm and receive painful electrical shocks unless they somehow "ground" themselves during the storm. Random unavoidable electric shocks would certainly produce a syndrome similar to what is seen in thunderstorm phobia. This is not to say that fear of loud noises (including thunder), darkening skies, lightning, wind noise, and rain are not also involved—just that they may be secondarily conditioned fears.

In support of the static-electricity theory, thunderstorm-phobic dogs are often found nestling in the bath, sink, shower stall, or pressed behind the toilet tank during storms. A factor in common to all locations is that they provide excellent electrical grounding because of the associated plumbing. It is conceivable that dogs discover safe places by trial-and-error learning (rats do if shocked in a cage provided with safe havens). A further piece of evidence bolstering the theory is that some clients of mine have reported receiving electrical shocks from their dogs during a storm. Add to this the possibility that a particular conformation, including a dense coat and thick footpads, might favor the buildup of static electrical charge, and you almost have a case. One other tenuous piece of evidence in support of the electrical theory is that the only three dogs with severe thunderstorm phobia that I have ever cured have been ones where I have combined pharmacotherapy with antistatic measures, such as having the owner rub the dog down with antistatic laundry strips at the onset of a storm.

I have struggled to think of ways to confirm or refute the electrical theory of thunderstorm phobia but have yet to strike the right chord. The most recent information on the subject has come from a sizable survey conducted by an interested dog owner in Australia. This owner,

Karen Damiani, designed a questionnaire to identify factors associated with the development of thunderstorm phobia, its signs, and the dog's response to conventional treatments. I enlisted the assistance of two Tufts students, and together we helped Ms. Damiani analyze the data and publish the results of the survey. An abbreviated version of the results is that we confirmed a high prevalence of thunderstorm phobia in herding breeds; many of the survey dogs sought electrically screened or grounded locations during storms; and desensitization to the sound of thunder was an ineffective treatment. Some of these findings lend additional support to the static-electricity theory but still do not confirm it.

Thunderstorm-phobic dogs are usually in a sorry state. Even before a storm arrives (changing electrical fields?) they start to look anxious and begin to pace and whimper, sometimes seeking solace from their owner. As the wind and rain pick up and the storm rumbles closer, the state that some dogs enter can only be described as one of panic or sheer terror. It is even worse for the dogs if they happen to be alone during the storm, and many tear through screens, some hurtling out of second- or third-story windows to the ground below and injuring themselves in the process. The damage they cause to the home may be the main owner complaint, and because of this the condition can be confused with separation anxiety. Careful questioning of the owner will reveal that the dog acts fearfully during thunderstorms and that the damage only occurs on stormy days. The relevant meteorological evidence can sometimes complete the picture.

Owners of dogs with thunderstorm phobia often report that their dogs were mildly anxious during storms as pups and that this state of affairs prevailed for some years before a cataclysmic worsening that can be pinpointed to a particular storm on a particular day. Those who regard thunderstorm phobia as a primary-sound phobia would argue that the storm must have been especially close overhead and noisy on that day. Proponents of the static-electrical theory would reason that the dog may have received its first serious static-electrical shock during the precipitating storm. That these dogs are frightened of sound is irrefutable. The question is only whether the sound phobia is primary or secondary. During a storm there are many things going on, any and all of which might trigger the phobic response. I have encountered thunderstorm-phobic dogs who were terrified of wind noise or rain alone, and one or two that were cued by strobelike flashing lights. No one would imagine that either wind, rain, or flashing lights could be so aversive that any one of them would act as a primary impetus for thunderstorm phobia, so their significance must have arisen by association with some other noxious event. Could thunder that is tolerated for many years suddenly become that noxious? Perhaps, if there is a sharp crack of thunder directly overhead during a particularly violent storm. Or could it be that a severe static-electrical shock is the primary aversive event, with all other cues, including the sound of thunder, being conditioned secondarily? The jury is still out on that one.

So, what can be done for thunderstorm phobia, if anything? The classic treatment is desensitization to the sound of thunder using high-quality tape or CD recordings. The thunderstorm sounds are played first at low volume and then gradually increasing volumes as the dog's reaction permits. It is extremely important during desensitization that the dog is not exposed to the full fear-inducing stimulus, which is often difficult to arrange. During the thunderstorm season it is virtually impossible. But even if the program is conducted properly during the nonstorm season, the success rate with this particular desensitization program is extremely poor, with most dogs relapsing during an actual storm.

The results of the Australian study indicated that treatment with "tapes" was only effective in a single case. This is remarkable. It is unusual for a desensitization program to be so ineffective in the treatment of a fear-based condition. One explanation for the failures could be that people are desensitizing their dogs to the wrong thing, or to only one component of a complex phobia. Another problem is that desensitization in one location does not generalize to other locations. This said, I still use sound-desensitization techniques with thunderstorm-phobic dogs because at the time of presentation, affected dogs certainly are frightened by thunder. To stack the deck in my favor, I have the owners desensitize to sounds with the dog on a "safe" mat that is moved around during the retraining process.

Desensitization is not the only treatment I employ. I also engage in various other measures designed to prevent the buildup of static electricity. These are fairly simple measures to effect, are safe, and who knows, they may even be effective. As well as the antistatic-laundry-strip trick, other strategies that I have employed include misting (with water from a spray bottle), arranging for the dog to be on a conducting surface, such as tile or a linoleum floor, spraying the dog's feet with antistatic spray, or having the owner put the dog inside his car during the storm. The latter measure seems to soothe a lot of dogs. Again, this tends to support the static-electrical theory, since automobiles, which are essentially metal boxes on wheels, act as Faraday cages, and (theoretically) should shield the dog from the buildup of static charge. Many dogs are happy as bugs in a rug when put in a car and driven around during a storm.

All of the above treatments may be combined with antianxiety or antidepressant medication to facilitate recovery and for the psychological benefit of dogs that are in great distress. I have had some success using the antianxiety drug BuSpar, but have had better results recently using the antidepressant Anafranil.

Situational Fears

Far and away the most common situational fear is separation anxiety. In this condition the fear is not of somebody or something but of the vacuum created by an owner's departure. This is fear that is engendered by adverse experience rather than underlying genetics. Affected dogs have almost all had some rift in the fabric of their early attachment experience and are, in a way, dysfunctional. Because the most common presenting sign is damage to the owners' property during their absence, separation anxiety is dealt with in more detail in the section entitled "D—Destructive Behavior." I reiterate, though, that there are other presenting signs of separation anxiety, such as house soiling, anorexia, and barking in the owners' absence, that are often not recognized by owners as components of the syndrome.

The classical program used to treat separation anxiety is another form of systematic desensitization referred to as the planned-departure technique. As part of this program owners leave their dogs for increasing periods of time, starting from just a few seconds and building up to minutes, fractions of an hour, then finally hours. Counterconditioning is usually employed simultaneously. Counterconditioning is a technique by which the dog is conditioned to engage in a behavior that is incompatible with the one that it was previously exhibiting. One form of counterconditioning is to teach the dog to sit or lie down and relax instead of pacing or barking during brief absences, and to gradually build from this base. Another counterconditioning technique is to offer a long-lasting food treat, such as a Kong chew toy with the inside smeared with peanut butter, to the dog as the owners prepare to depart. Independence training, a modification of the basic desensitization and counterconditioning program, is described in detail in the Appendix. Independence training, which is a lot less demanding than the classical program, is usually used in conjunction with antidepressant medication.

Another common situational fear is of traveling in cars. There are any number of reasons why dogs develop this fear in the first place. I feel certain that some dogs experience genuine motion sickness. Other dogs may associate car travel with going to the veterinarian's office and receiving shots or having some other memorable experiences. Whatever the cause, desensitization is the cure. Desensitizing the dog to the stationary car with the engine off, then with the engine running, the car moving slowly in the drive, and finally brief car travel on the roads, is the common progression. As is often the case, providing some pleasurable distraction, usually food treats, to condition a different effect at each stage of the proceedings helps to speed things along.

Finally, there are some more unusual situational fears, such as fear of crowded city streets. Some dogs I have treated recently were affected with the latter phobia, collapsing helpless as the owner tried to encourage them to exit the home. The reason or development of such a fear is often definable by appropriate questioning of the owner and usually amounts to some sequence of aversive incidents associated with being walked. Noisy juggernauts and attacks from other dogs feature prominently in the list of possible causative factors. In the end, the whole experience of being walked on the street becomes abhorrent to the dog and, if of faint heart, it may collapse, refusing to move and exhibiting apparent agoraphobia. Medication is a mainstay of treatment, and I have had wonderful success with the antidepressant Elavil in the cases I have treated. However, I usually attempt a graded reintroduction to the great outdoors simultaneously as the behavioral component of therapy.

Global Fear

Global fear involves all of the above fears occurring in one dog. One case of global phobia that I saw involved Lisa, a six-year-old female basset that was born in a puppy mill and remained there as a breeding bitch until four weeks before she was adopted. The owner reported that Lisa was afraid of everything, and knew very little about anything. I think that was a pretty fair assessment. When she first brought Lisa into her multidog home she regarded her as a passive, somewhat submissive dog, clearly at the bottom of the household's canine hierarchy. The owner added that in four weeks she had never seen her wag her tail, never heard her bark, and that the only emotion she ever exhibited was fear. Apparently it was awhile before Lisa allowed her new owner to approach her without running away, and the approach was only permitted as long as the owner was on her hands and knees.

Basically Lisa knew nothing of life. She had never seen stairs before and had to learn to use the ones that went up to the deck. She didn't know what a dog biscuit or rawhide treat was and wouldn't even accept a treat, possibly as a result of fear. She never played and became petrified if her owner tried to coax her into any sort of game by jockeying her along. Her owner said that Lisa was not stupid but that her problems appeared to be of an emotional or psychological nature. To be more specific, Lisa had animate fears (toward human strangers and dogs), inanimate fears (of thunderstorms and of almost any other noises), separation anxiety, and other situational fears; in essence, a behavioral full house. Although it is possible to have such extreme fear result from a genetic anomaly, hypothyroidism, or partial seizures, the weight of evidence was in favor of a dysfunctional, tortured early existence as being instrumental in this case. Lisa's owner was on the right track with her hands-and-knees desensitization approach, but medication with Elavil was a necessary part of Lisa's eventual rehabilitation.

Conclusion

The bottom line is this: A stable social base and optimal environmental experiences, particularly early in a dog's life, can go a long way toward preventing problems of a fearful nature—whether animate, inanimate, or situational. It is ideal to start out with a young puppy and guide it along the right lines each step of the way. Don't leave a thing to chance. Although genetics can tip the scales against even a good owner in some instances, optimizing rearing practices to provide insulation from adversity, socialization of pups to both people and other dogs, and benign exposure to a variety of novel stimuli will produce the best adult possible. With genetics on your side, of course, you can produce a real winner.

For dogs that have already established fears, all is not lost. But it will take equally strong doses of effort and luck to produce a significant turnaround. In such cases, reacclimation by desensitization requires a lot of patience, and sometimes medication, to rectify the situation. With firmly ensconced fears, however, there is always the possibility of a resurgence, particularly if the original fear-inducing situation is presented at full intensity. Relapses aside, understanding your dog's plight and accomodating for it is an important first step on the road to eventual rehabilitation.

GERIATRIC BEHAVIOR PROBLEMS

At least in part due to modern management practices and better health care for our pets, the population of elderly animals is increasing at quite a clip. Approximately one in six dogs is older than ten years of age. Because of this trend, gerontology increasingly has become a must-know topic for veterinary practitioners, and vets have even begun exploring home-based hospice services to further prolong the quality existence of terminally ill pets as an alternative to euthanasia. The change in demographics of the pet population mirrors what is happening in the human population and for similar reasons: more widespread preventive medicine, better management, early diagnoses of diseases, and improved health care. But living for a long time comes at a price. Despite what you hear on the news today about gene therapy or injections of pituitary extract, progressive physical and mental deterioration is inevitable. All that can be said in favor of getting old is that the alternative is even less attractive.

Owners and veterinarians alike are, for the most part, prepared for the inescapable consequences of aging in animals in their care. Vets, for example, half expect to see a graying of the lenses of the older dog's eyes, typical of nuclear sclerosis. They almost anticipate detecting a heart murmur or noisy lung sounds when they listen to an old dog's chest, and are not surprised when an elderly dog starts to drink water excessively, indicating a decline in the kidneys' concentrating ability. A gradual decline of visual and auditory acuity and some deterioration of mental processes, leading to "the old-dog syndrome," are also predictable, to some extent. Most of us already know that many of the medical conditions associated with aging can be successfully managed these days and would not hesitate to take an older pet to the vet's to get some advice on the management of what they perceive as an age-related health problem. What is not appreciated is that the cognitive deterioration associated with aging is also potentially reversible. You don't have to live with a vegetable.

Some three million dogs come to an untimely end each year in the nation's shelters and pounds. The reasons why these dogs are relinquished are myriad but, reading between the lines, behavioral problems feature prominently. From surveys, we know for sure that some twenty percent of them, approximately six hundred thousand dogs per year, are surrendered because they are "too old." However, the physical changes of old age don't cause these pets' death knell to toll prematurely so much as geriatric behavioral changes do. In a study of geriatric behavior problems tendered to the Veterinary Hospital of the University of Pennsylvania, Dr. Barbara Chapman found that separation anxiety, destructive behavior, and house soiling were high on the list of owner complaints. Since separation anxiety and destructive behavior are not mutually exclusive diagnoses, and since nonmedical causes of house soiling are often due to cognitive decline, anxiety-related behavior problems and cognitive dysfunction together appear to account for the majority of problems encountered.

Let's take a closer look at geriatric-onset separation anxiety. Why would a dog that has lived happily with its owners for some nine or ten years suddenly develop separation anxiety in its golden years? Here's how: Developing medical problems makes life miserable for them, and misery loves company. Apprehension arising from pain and discomfort seems to cause these dogs to feel insecure and to develop an increased need for company and attention. It's the same with young children when they are hurt or in pain. The first thing they do is run to their mother and cling—sometimes even Dad won't do in these situations. Time and time again I have been presented with older dogs with separation anxiety whose angst has turned out to be due to some disease process unidentified at the time. Affected dogs seem to know that something is wrong before their owners do. I have encountered old dogs that have developed severe separation anxiety secondary to brain tumors, eye tumors, bone cancer, slipped discs, arthritis, and neurological deterioration, to name but a few examples. In each case, the most noticeable change has been sudden overattachment to the owner, leading to problems when the owner is away. Destructive behavior during the owner's daytime absence is the usual presentation, though some dogs also exhibit nocturnal separation anxiety in which they can't bear to be separated from their owner, even by the physiological state of sleep. Dogs that have slept alone for years may suddenly start waking up in the early hours of the morning, barking, pacing, and demanding attention. The latter can be really distressing for working owners, who have their own and their dog's welfare on the line simultaneously.

So what can be done to improve this situation? Anything and everything is the answer to that question, depending on the underlying cause of the problem. Tumors can be removed or contained, slipped discs can be treated either surgically or medically, and arthritis can be dealt with using anti-inflammatory and analgesic drugs. Pain is a common factor in many of these conditions. Dogs can never tell you when they're in pain but their behavior is an excellent indicator of their inner well-being. The involvement of pain in a behavioral syndrome can be confirmed by noting a positive response (improved demeanor) to treatment with painkilling medications. In geriatric separation anxiety I explore this avenue of investigation early on in the proceedings for both diagnostic and humanitarian reasons. Low on the totem pole of analgesic potency is our old friend aspirin. Aspirin should be used with great caution in dogs and only under veterinary supervision because of potential adverse effects on the gut and the kidneys. An aspirin-cortisone combination (trade name Cortaba) provides even more effective relief of pain when inflammation is involved; for example, in the treatment of arthritis. Finally, there's the ultimate in pain relief, the morphinelike analgesics, the opiates ("God's own medicine"). Fortunately, modern opiate drugs are not so highly addictive and are much safer to use than their precursors. For inoperable conditions, such as some forms of cancer, treatment with analgesics may be the only option.

One case of geriatric-onset separation anxiety I saw that was medically induced had a different spin. The dog was one of the nicest, calmest, handsomest Dalmatians that I have ever seen. He had been a faithful family pet for some nine or ten years when one day he suddenly developed gait problems and seemed to be in pain. The local vet diagnosed a prolapsed cervical (neck) disc causing pressure on his spinal cord as the cause of the problem. Surgery, to which the owners agreed, was the solution.

Following surgery, and a brief period of rehabilitation at the practice, the dog was taken home and made as comfortable as possible. The main problem remaining was that the dog, suffering from residual nerve damage and postoperative pain, could no longer climb the steep stairs to the son's room on the third floor, where he usually slept. The son had left for college a year earlier but the dog, who was extremely attached to the boy, seemed to get comfort from sleeping next to his bed while his young master was away. In his incapacity, the dog took to wandering around on the second floor of the home, outside his owners' bedroom, like a tormented soul. For most of the night he would pace and whine but then, in the wee hours, would start to bark outside his sleeping owners' door. If they opened the door and let him in he would simply curl up on the floor next to the bed and go to sleep. A fairly simple solution, you might think—but the husband insisted that the dog should not be allowed in the bedroom. A rock-and-a-hard-place situation for the wife if ever I heard one.

It was the wife who finally brought the dog to me as a last-ditch measure prior to having her dog put to sleep, and she was in tears as she explained the predicament. Apparently her husband had given the dog's marching orders in the event things did not change (and quickly) and had even forbidden her to come and see me, as he "did not want to spend any more money on the dog." I promised to follow the most expedient and economic path as we began our deliberations. The upshot of the dialogue was that I decided to treat the dog with an antidepressant, Elavil, because of its mood-stabilizing and analgesic properties. I considered that this medication might circumvent the problem by helping the dog to relax and feel more comfortable at night. Behavior modification by retraining the dog was out of the question in this case.

As the woman left with her faithful companion and a prescription, I prayed for speedy and complete resolution of the problem. I was delighted when the good news finally came a few weeks later during a "recheck" appointment. Apparently my spotted friend had made a complete recovery and was now able to make it through the night peacefully sleeping on a dog bed on the second floor without disturbing his owners. I was never quite sure what component of this dog's recovery was due to my intervention and what was attributable to the passing of time, but it really didn't matter. The important thing was that the dog had been spared and was comfortable and at ease with his new sleeping arrangements. It was a great moment for me when I learned of this outcome because I was painfully aware of the alternative. As the appointment drew to a close, I asked the woman whether she would have been able to follow through with her husband's mandate if the treatment had been unsuccessful. Her answer was that forced to choose between the dog and her husband, she probably would have chosen the dog.

In contrast to the often acute anxiety-related problems associated with various disease processes are the more insidious changes of cognitive decline. But how can mental functioning be evaluated in a dog? Well, there are ways and ways but all necessitate a degree of extrapolation. We can't ask a dog whether it remembers its birthday or where it was last week but we can observe its behavior. Relevant behaviors include the dog's activity level, curiosity, social interactions, responsiveness to family members, the amount of time it spends sleeping, and how it performs routine maintenance behaviors. Typical changes of cognitive dysfunction include a decrease in spontaneous activity, decreased interactions with family members, and increased time spent dozing or sleeping. In addition, there can be deterioration of normal maintenance behaviors, such as the ability to locate food if the food bowl is moved, loss of fastidiousness regarding eating habits, and a breakdown of house training. Some affected dogs also suffer apparent loss of hearing with inability to localize sounds, whereas others wander aimlessly, sometimes stopping to stare at walls or ending up trapped in corners. Stairs present a real obstacle to these old-timers, for physical as well as cognitive reasons.

The syndrome of cognitive dysfunction that some old dogs display is strikingly similar to an equivalent condition in humans, Alzheimer's disease. Alzheimer's affects some forty-seven percent of people over eighty-five years old. People who are lucky enough to escape it are referred to as successful agers. Dogs, too, are either successful or nonsuccessful agers. According to one definition, thirteen percent of all dogs are diagnosable with cognitive dysfunction by the time they are eleven years old, and fifty percent are affected by the time they are sixteen years old. This is strikingly similar to the percentage of humans affected at equivalent ages. The time course of the disease from its onset to its most severe state (or death) is also equivalent, though the absolute progression in dogs is quicker because of their relatively compressed life span. The average survival time following the diagnosis of cognitive dysfunction in dogs is about one and one-half to two years, with the demise of some dogs being directly related to the syndrome while others die of unrelated physical causes.

In humans, physical changes in the brain, particularly the cerebral cortex and nearby areas, correlate with the onset and severity of Alzheimer's disease. The same is true for dogs, though there are some subtle differences in the actual changes that occur. Neurochemical alterations accompany the physical changes that occur in the brains of human patients with Alzheimer's, as they do in dogs with "canine cognitive dysfunction syndrome." In dogs, deficiency of a vital neurotransmitter, dopamine, seems to be inextricably linked. It stands to reason that restoring appropriate levels of dopamine by pharmacologic means should reverse some of the behavioral changes of aging in dogs, and this reversal has, in fact, been demonstrated. The drug used was L-deprenyl, which, like some of the older antidepressants, prevents the metabolic destruction of dopamine, allowing it to hang around longer. The clinical effect in dogs can be dramatic. One aging Irish setter in an early study was sleeping its life away before L-deprenyl. After four short weeks of treatment the owners told the investigator that their dog was behaving like a two-year-old. "That's terrific," said the investigator. "No, that's terrible," said the owners. "He was hyperactive when he was two and now we're suffering it all again." The dose of L-deprenyl was lowered to bring the dog's behavioral age to about six, and the owners were satisfied.

Summarized reports of clinical trials with L-deprenyl in the treatment of canine cognitive dysfunction syndrome are extremely positive. Though criticizable because of their unblinded nature, early studies demonstrate improvement in almost every trait examined. The company that developed L-deprenyl has since conducted more controlled studies with the drug, and because "Anapryl" (its trade name) is slated for FDA approval, I gather that these studies support the earlier conclusions. The behavior targeted in the more formal studies was house soiling occurring as a result of senile dementia. The reason why this particular behavior was singled out is because it is (relatively) easy to assess and because it is a common, life-threatening condition of older dogs. Owners will survive almost any other component of the cognitive dysfunction syndrome with some forbearance, but not house soiling. There is no surer condition causing owners to throw in the towel. (Incidentally, this is a common end point for people taking care of their elderly relatives, too.) But now, at last, canine cognitive dysfunction syndrome, with its house-soiling sequela, is potentially treatable. The inexorable progression of aging changes cannot be totally arrested, but the clock can be wound back to some extent.

One final point about L-deprenyl that seems too good to be absolutely true is that L-deprenyl has been shown to increase life span in laboratory rats and dogs. On the basis of presumed life-span-enhancing properties, one client of mine living in Baltimore decided to have his eleven-year-old German shepherd, King, treated with L-deprenyl for this reason alone. German shepherds usually live to be about thirteen or fourteen years old, but King made it to fifteen and a half before finally succumbing to pneumonia. I like to think the drug bought him that extra time with his devoted owner.

Some other problems that can manifest as behavioral problems in older dogs relate to sensory deterioration. Failing eyesight and hearing loss can lead to behavioral changes of uncertainty and aggression. For example, a dog with cataracts or retinal atrophy may not see a stranger approaching and could easily wind up being blindsided (literally). The dog's reaction to this can be anything from a simple startle to retaliation, depending on its temperament and the exact circumstances. Either way, the apparent increase in irritability is often viewed by owners as a purely behavioral problem. The same sort of thing can happen with a dog that is getting hard of hearing. Such dogs' first warning of your approach when they are resting with their eyes closed is physical contact. Sleeping dogs, especially deaf ones, should be allowed to lie, as rude awakenings are often greeted by a retaliatory response.

And then there's endocrine deterioration. I was once told by a senior anesthesiology professor in England that all the common signs of aging in people, from wrinkling to graying, were the result of an insidious deterioration in the function of the thyroid gland. Though this was something of an overgeneralization, thyroid function may well deteriorate with advancing years, contributing to some aging problems. Recently we have found that borderline-to-low thyroid function can be associated with significant behavioral change. The paradoxical effect of subthreshold hypothyroidism can sometimes be to increase anxiety and aggression, though when the thyroid bottoms out the converse is true and lethargy and weight gain prevail as cardinal signs. As a matter of routine practice it is advisable to have an older dog's thyroid function checked, especially if it develops behavior problems related to increased or decreased irritability or aggression. (Hypothyroidism is discussed in more detail in "V—Veterinary Causes of Behavior Problems.")

Not all behavior problems that arise in older dogs are related to physical deterioration. Some could occur at any age but happen, by chance, during the latter part of a dog's life. These problems must also be factored in when making a diagnosis of an age-related problem. A case in point was a twelve-year-old golden retriever/German shepherd crossbreed dog owned by a film screenwriter, George Page, who lived on a beachfront property in Santa Barbara, California. This lucky dog, Sam, enjoyed several beachside acres separated from the ocean only by a train track. Sam's history was one of sudden-onset aggression. It all started one day when Sam was found collapsed thirty yards from the track. When Mr. Page approached to see what was wrong, Sam growled menacingly and attempted to bite him. This was totally out of character for Sam, who was normally a pretty mellow dog. Eventually Mr. Page managed to assist Sam to his feet and Sam was able to walk off reasonably well, though with a slight hitch to his gait. In the weeks that followed, Sam was found to be terrified of train whistles and the sight of approaching trains, running and hiding in the bushes at the earliest opportunity. His fear of trains and train whistles waned over time but other physical problems appeared, with his lameness increasing to the point that it affected his ability to ascend stairs. Sam's entire personality changed in association with his infirmity. He became aggressive when Mr. Page hosed him down—a practice that Mr. Page had engaged in for years without any problem. Also, Sam now seemed generally nervous and apprehensive outside and Mr. Page had a feeling that the dog could no longer be trusted with strangers. He came to this conclusion because Sam had begun to act standoffish and hesitant in the presence of strangers, whereas formerly he had been happy and outgoing in this situation. Not sure what had caused these changes, Mr. Page began wondering whether Sam might have been injured or mistreated by a passing surfer.

It was at this point that I became involved, asked to explain what was going on as much as anything else. I told Mr. Page that I thought Sam had almost certainly been hit by a train as he tried to cross the tracks and had managed to stagger twenty or thirty yards before collapsing. "So what about his aggression to me?" quizzed Mr. Page. "And what about his developing anxiety and mistrust of strangers?"

I explained what I thought had happened as follows. The aggression Sam displayed following the trauma was almost certainly pain-related, self-protective aggression. This is a fairly typical response of dogs following injury. Similarly, hosing Sam down probably caused him to react out of pain or discomfort. The generalized outdoor-anxiety problem, I thought, was likely a remnant of the initial adverse experience, and on further questioning, it came to light that Sam was terrified when brought close to where he had been found collapsed.

Sam's case was one where there was a probable history of trauma, but his owner could not figure out how this explained the behavioral changes that unraveled in the weeks that followed. The sequence went trauma, pain, and self-protection coupled with anxiety and a form of post-traumatic stress syndrome. I was fairly certain of my reasoning. Even if there had been no train connection or possibility that an itinerant surfer had injured the dog, I would have concluded that I was dealing with a traumatically induced problem. Dogs don't normally suddenly develop behavior problems of this nature at any age unless there is an associated traumatic event, or possibly a seizural disturbance. Admittedly, the postulated traumatic event could have been one of extreme psychological trauma, though frank trauma is the usual explanation. Since Sam was found collapsed by the side of the train tracks and subsequently developed a fear of trains, I was pretty sure of my ground. He improved with rest and time but never quite forgot the events of that dreadful day, as was evidenced by his continued avoidance of the spot where he was found collapsed. The Bermuda Triangle of fear was at work again.

Sam's scenario could have occurred at any age and may have had nothing to do with geriatrics, but then again it is tempting to speculate that the reason he was hit by the train was because his senses were failing. I imagine he had crossed the tracks uneventfully many times before the fateful day, but this time he just didn't see or hear the train coming or couldn't move fast enough to get out of its way.

There are many things that can cause behavioral problems in elderly dogs, ranging from those of an acute onset to those of a more nebulous nature. Whatever the cause of the altered behavior, the problem should be properly diagnosed before being treated. The good news is that many geriatric conditions can be treated. I can hear some people saying, "But why would you want to extend the life of a decrepit old dog?" The answer to this is simple: I wouldn't if the remaining time that the dog had was not likely to be enjoyed at some level. There is no point in prolonging suffering or keeping alive a totally confused and unresponsive dog. But if I feel that I can provide that dog and owner with additional quality time together, then treatment is a go.

HYPERACTIVITY

By now almost everyone has heard of the syndrome of medical hyperactivity that is supposed to affect so many schoolchildren. These children have difficulty concentrating, are not good at following directions, fidget constantly, find it hard to sit still, and are easily bored. Another name for this nebulous constellation of signs is attention deficient hyperactivity disorder, or ADHD for short. In girls, the hyperactivity component is often lacking, giving rise to a purer attention deficit disorder, just plain ADD, whereas in boys, the hyperactivity component is more common and the syndrome is often associated with aggression. Although it used to be thought that ADHD was confined to childhood years, it has come to light recently that the disorder persists throughout life, though it often goes unrecognized and undiagnosed. Typical signs of ADHD in adults include difficulty in getting started on projects, forgetfulness, procrastination, and a constant need for stimulation that manifests as thrill-seeking behavior. The question is, could dogs possibly be affected with a similar syndrome? Some say yes, and some say no.

The term *hyperactivity* has vernacular implications as well as being a possible medical diagnosis. It is common for owners and trainers to refer to a particular dog as hyperactive, meaning that it runs around a lot and won't listen. According to this rather loose definition, almost all puppies are hyperactive; observation tells us that puppyhood and hyperactivity are virtually synonymous. But do all puppies grow up to be forgetful procrastinators? I don't think so. On the other hand, if we always interpret restlessness, limited attention span, and a high activity level in dogs as normal behavior, or a variation on a theme of normalcy, we will never diagnose hyperactivity.

Behaviorists' views on the existence of hyperactivity in dogs are equivocal, with opinions ranging from one extreme to the other. The head of the behavior clinic at the Veterinary Hospital of the University of Pennsylvania, Dr. Karen Overall, says that she has yet to diagnose a case of hyperactivity in dogs. On the other hand, Dr. Walter Burghart, a veterinary practitioner in Texas with a special interest in animal behavior, believes that hyperactivity is the driving force behind many of the behavior problems that we see in domestic dogs. The case can be argued both ways, depending on your point of view. In support of Dr. Overall's position, I, too, have had precious few, if any, dogs that I have confirmed as hyperactive according to the strict medical definition of the word. In support of Dr. Burghart's view, though, I have seen many dogs that could reasonably be described as overactive or hyperactive that present with a variety of behavior problems apparently secondary to this underlying disturbance. Some might say that the proof of this pudding lies in the response to stimulants, such as Ritalin and amphetamine.

The paradoxical response of hyperactive schoolchildren to treatment with the stimulant Ritalin is almost legend. I have even heard parents and schoolteachers say, "Oh, that kid's hyperactive. He should be put on Ritalin." Now, Ritalin would make a normal child tear around like a turkey with its head cut off, but for some reason it has a calming effect on hyperactive children, enabling them to pay attention and focus on the job at hand. In fact, in their book *Driven to Destruction,* psychiatrists David Hallowell and John Ratey liken the effect of Ritalin on a hyperactive child to that of putting a pair of spectacles on a child that is nearsighted. It has the effect of permitting him to focus.

If supposedly medically hyperactive dogs were to respond to stimulants in a similar way, you would think that this would be powerful evidence in favor of a true medical-syndrome hyperactivity. And wouldn't you know it; some hyperactive dogs do calm down when treated with stimulants. One veterinary behaviorist colleague of mine, Dr. Andrew Luescher, now head of the behavior program at Purdue Veterinary School in Indiana, employs a diagnostic test in which putatively hyperactive dogs are administered a small dose of amphetamine by mouth and their behavioral and physiologic responses are monitored for four hours thereafter. Dogs that become restless and whose heart rate and respiratory rate increases following medication are considered "normal," whereas hyperactivity is confirmed in dogs whose activity level is reduced by this treatment and whose heart rate and respiratory rate subsequently is slowed.

Dr. Burghart uses a slightly more protracted but analogous approach to diagnosing hyperactivity in some of his patients. He advises a course of the antidepressant Elavil to be given at home and for the owners to monitor and record the dog's response to this treatment. Elavil (whose very name is a pun on the word *elevate*—as in *elevate mood*) has stimulant properties and it can be argued that it produces a stimulant effect analogous to that of amphetamines. Again, the diagnosis is (supposedly) confirmed if owners report calming of the dog's behavior as a result of this test. Unfortunately, Elavil also produces a calming and mood-stabilizing effect by a different mechanism, leaving these conclusions somewhat open to debate.

All this talk of hyperactivity in dogs and its similarity with hyperactivity in children was initiated by scientist Samuel Corssen and co-workers in the 1970s. Corssen produced a behavioral change he called hyperkinesis in a cruel study on laboratory dogs by stressing them with inescapable random electric shocks. It is of little surprise that some of these dogs developed an increased heart rate, heavy breathing, salivation, and metabolic changes associated with stress. What is more surprising is that some of the dogs in the experiment did *not* show the same signs, or at least adapted quickly. He described the traumatized responders as antidiuretic dogs because their urine production fell. Finding that these antidiuretic dogs became calmer when treated with Ritalin or amphetamine, he drew parallels with the human condition of hyperactivity. More relevantly, Corssen also found that amphetamine had a beneficial calming effect on what he referred to as naturally occurring untrainable hyperkinetic dogs—untrainable dogs that had not yet been exposed to his Frankensteinian experiment. These dogs were so labeled because they did not cooperate with his handlers and were not easily commanded. Furthermore, they fought violently against the restraining harnesses and "tried to bite and chew everything within their reach." I'm not sure whether these dogs were truly hyperactive or just smart, but either way, they were calmed following treatment with stimulants. Actually, not all naturally hyperkinetic dogs responded to amphetamine in this way; only six of eight did. Interestingly, the two that were resistant to the treatment were both wirehaired fox terriers. (No surprise there—WHFTs seem refractory to all treatments.)

Although I don't condone Corssen's methods, I believe that his results, since they already exist, are worth reference. I too have found that some apparently hyperactive dogs become calmer when treated with stimulants and have had my most memorable treatment failures with wirehaired fox terriers. Although a delightful breed, wirehaired fox terriers, like my friends the bull terriers, can be extremely perseverant in a predatory sort of way. Both breeds really need a job to do if they (and their owners) are to stay sane.

I still haven't committed as to whether hyperactivity (or hyperkinesis) really does occur in dogs. The evidence we have for it occurring is that some excitable and overactive dogs show a positive response to stimulants. It's a pharmacological diagnosis. But is this positive response to stimulants really all that specific? I don't think so. Dr. Ratey uses the expression *noise* to describe the spontaneously heightened mental activity of his patients. He says that mentally noisy patients (those whose neural pathways never seem to shut down) often show a paradoxical response to stimulant drugs without necessarily having ADHD. The calming response is thus a general one that applies to all highly active individuals. The converse is also true—that more-sluggish individuals respond with increased activity. Thus the effect of stimulants appears to be one of normalizing patients, rather than some unique effect distinguishing hyperactive patients. Could it be that stimulants merely normalize dogs' behavior, too?

Another piece of evidence that detracts from the diagnostic value of the response is that *all* stimulants produce a calming effect in mentally noisy folk as well as those with ADHD. It doesn't seem to matter which drug is used—amphetamine, Ritalin, cocaine, even caffeine—the calming effect is the same for these individuals. This accounts for the fact that adults with ADHD have a tendency to become addicted to stimulant drugs like cocaine—because when under the influence of such a compound, they are able to concentrate properly, perhaps for the first time in their lives. This paradoxical response also explains why some people say they feel calm rather than jittery after drinking a gallon of black coffee. Little do they know they might have ADHD. The lack of specificity of response to stimulants seems to indicate that we're not dealing with a particular neurotransmitter imbalance in the brain with ADHD but rather a problem of a more general nature—an extreme of normal behavior, perhaps.

Whatever your thoughts on the medical condition known as hyperactivity in humans or in dogs, the fact is that some dogs' (and some humans') behavior is appropriately described by this term. Take Hyper (real name), for example, a sixteen-month-old castrated male keeshond. His frazzled owner, Wendy Smith, brought Hyper to see me one June day after a particularly harrowing week. It didn't take me long to figure out the nature of the problem as we moved from the appointment desk to the consulting room. Young Hyper was totally ballistic and, according to Wendy, this was nothing new. We lurched toward the fire door separating the waiting room from the consulting room as Hyper charged backward and forward on his leash, oscillating to and fro like a shuttlecock, racing around in circles, barking, jumping up, then freezing occasionally for a few seconds, teeth chattering in anticipation of his next eruption. We apologized to the openmouthed clients in the waiting room, as I untangled the lead from Wendy's leg, and struggled onward to the consulting room. After a few short minutes of trying to discuss the problem amid the racket, we decided that discretion was the better part of valor and returned Hyper to the car to continue our dialogue in his absence.

Needless to say, hyperactivity and barking were high on the list of Wendy's complaints. As I reviewed the behavior questionnaire I noticed that the frequency occurrence of the behavior problem was reported as "all of the time." Now I knew why she looked so frazzled.

Ancillary complaints were dominance-related aggression and extreme intrusiveness. In addition, Wendy reported that Hyper was overbearing when it came to affection. Although she qualified it by saying that he could be a wonderful and extremely affectionate dog, she also said that the extent of his affection was so great and he would lick her so much that she would almost literally have to come up for air. Moreover, Hyper would not obey any commands when in this demanding mode, which would occur whenever she dropped her guard. Wendy also reported that Hyper had trouble paying attention when given commands and that, try as she might, she could not get him to sit because he was always too wound up. He barked at shadows, planes, birds, insects, and people walking by, and would become excited by anything that was new in his environment.

Initially I treated Hyper using a dominance-control program to help Wendy get better control of him and to reduce his aggression to her. His exercise was stepped up and his food was switched from a performance ration to a low-protein, preservative-free diet. Although his aggression was controlled to some extent by these measures, his hyperactivity was not. At the suggestion of a colleague of mine, I had Wendy try a citronella antibark collar to control his barking. Initially the antibark collar was a big success, but unfortunately it was triggered by other dogs barking and he kept getting citronella sprayed in his face for no reason at all. This, coupled with the fact that the citronella made him throw up, led to a messy conclusion to this phase of his retraining.

It was at this time that I thought a trial with Ritalin would be in order. Wendy ran the trial at home one weekend. Hyper was given one Ritalin tablet on a Saturday night, but instead of calming him down, the medication made him tear around barking and he became even more hyperactive (how was this possible?). Wendy elected not to experiment with a second dose of Ritalin on Sunday, and with that the diagnosis of hyperactivity and the possibility of treatment with Ritalin or amphetamine went by the board. All was not lost, though, as Hyper did respond to treatment with Elavil, which seemed to bring him back to earth to some extent. It's hard to know whether this result was a paradoxical one or attributable to the more traditional calming effect of the antidepressant, because, as I mentioned, Elavil's effects can be interpreted either way. I may never know what was troubling Hyper. I wish I did because there are a lot of dogs like him, some of which show a response to stimulants and some of which do not. Without question, more studies need to be conducted to further investigate this perplexing syndrome. One thing is for sure: If a dog tears around in circles, won't listen, won't respond to commands, is impulsive, intrusive, and won't wait, it isn't necessarily hyperactive in the true medical sense of the word. To go out on a limb, I would say that such dogs do not have a psychiatric disorder homologous with ADHD in children, even though there are some intriguing parallels.

To further muddy the waters, there are a number of other problems that can lead to similar extreme behavior. I have already mentioned the possible confusion with normal puppy behavior, but there is also the all-too-common problem of mismanagement. Some dogs have no expectations made of them, have little exercise, and spend many hours alone or confined. Such dogs are bound to let rip when they finally are given some freedom. Confused owners stand there and yell at the dog, "No," "Sit," "Leave it," and all the other things they have learned at training classes, hoping that their untrained dog will suddenly see the light. Fat chance. Well-behaved dogs, like well-behaved children, require good schooling, attention when attention is due, and constant reinforcement of good behaviors. They also require a healthy lifestyle including plenty of exercise, entertainment, companionship, and clear lines of communication with the owner. All can be achieved if the owner invests time in training the dog, particularly in puppyhood. Consistent training is an essential part of the behavioral shaping process but such training should, in my opinion, be a positive experience for both the owner and the dog and it should be nonconfrontational in nature (see "O—Obedience Training").

Though not universally accepted, dietary measures may also be an important part of the management of some hyperactive dogs. It is generally believed by dog trainers and some behaviorists that certain foods exacerbate hyperactivity in dogs, as they may do in hyperactive children. The dietary culprits have yet to be identified with any precision, but high levels of dietary protein, sources of protein to which the dog is allergic, and artificial preservatives (particularly ethoxyquin) are widely touted as being involved.

One other cause of hyperactivity is metabolic dysfunction. Both hypo- and hyperthyroidism can lead to hyperactivity. Hyperthyroidism is extremely rare in dogs but can result from thyroid tumors. Hypothyroidism, on the other hand, is extremely common, and recent evidence suggests that borderline-to-low thyroid function may cause a paradoxical syndrome of increased anxiety, fearfulness, and hyperactivity. The fact that thyroid hormone receptors are affected in some cases of medical hyperactivity (ADHD) provides a fascinating link between these conditions that is worthy of further investigation. Details of the paradoxical hypothyroid syndrome are dealt with in a later section ("V—Veterinary Causes of Behavior Problems").

Before we leave the subject of hyperactivity, a word or two about the "extremes of normal" theory is warranted. You may be saying, "How can an extremely hyperactive dog be described as normal?" By way of explanation, the first question to ask is, "What is normal?" Normal is (according to the Chambers etiological dictionary) "ordinary, well-adjusted, and functioning regularly." Statistically, the normal distribution of a biological population of, say, behavior types is described by a bell-shaped curve. Most of the behavioral types fall in and around the bulge in the center of this curve, but others will lie out toward the tapering ends of the bell curve as it approaches the baseline. A small percentage of any population will lie in the nether regions of this curve, a considerable distance from the mean (average) finding. In terms of activity level this means that you would expect certain members of a population of dogs to be considerably slower and more sedentary than their "normal" peers. You also would expect a similar number of dogs to be much more active and restless than their peers. The argument about where normal finishes and where abnormal starts is a common one in behavioral circles. With some conditions (perhaps including hyperactivity), it is possible to identify individuals that conclusively fit the criteria describing an abnormal state of affairs. Dogs could be defined as hyperactive if they are more than two standard deviations from the "norm" of activity level. Note that this definition does not necessitate believing in a medical syndrome of hyperactivity, just a variation on a theme. This explanation could even encompass the Ritalin responders if you buy the "noisy" mind theory and the more general effect of stimulant drugs.

The final word about canine hyperactivity has yet to be spoken. Until that time, the behavioral camps remain divided. We are not alone in our indecision. The same debate goes on about ADHD. There are those who believe that medical hyperactivity is a contrivance, an "emperor's new clothes" phenomenon, and others who would swear by it. It has been argued that ADHDers were most likely to seek the challenge of the dangerous transatlantic crossing in the old days, and once in North America were more likely to head west in search of new frontiers. Theoretically, then, the greatest percentage of schoolchildren receiving Ritalin should be found on the West Coast. But even if this was substantiated, naysayers would argue cultural factors rather than come to a medical conclusion. You just can't win, in people or in dogs. Perhaps one day there will be some resolution to this dilemma. When that day arrives we will know for sure whether those individuals presently described as hyperactive actually do have something organically different from the rest of us or whether they're just behaving badly and looking for an excuse.

I
IMPRINTING PROBLEMS

From soup to nuts, from birth to death, nature is marvelous. It is a constant source of amazement to me that chicks know how and when to peck their way out of the egg, that foals know how to stand within an hour of birth, and that newborn pups know how to suckle when presented with mother's milk bar. It's wonderful the way that mothers and offspring always are guided about what to do and when to do it. First-time mothers give birth and nurture their young without the aid of Lamaze classes or advice from Dr. Spock. Drinking, eating, grooming, and elimination behaviors, to name a few, unfold in the offspring under Mother's watchful eye like the petals of flowers unfold. The entire developmental process is organized to precision through the interaction of both internal and external forces. Older animals, too, have an intrinsic drive to do the right thing at the right time. As it says in the Bible, "there is a time for every purpose under heaven."

But how does all of this choreographing take place? How does a dog automatically know what to do and when to do it in the best interests of its survival and that of the species? The classic answer to this question is that all behavior is determined by both nature and nurture—the precise contribution of each depending on the stage in the dog's life and the opportunity that has occurred for modification of the behavior by learning. At the beginning of life, behaviors such as locating and suckling on a nipple are so automatic that it is hard to imagine them being driven by anything other than natural forces. The fact that some rehearsal of components of these behaviors can take place in utero does not alter the argument that they are innate. That behaviors arise spontaneously when there has been no opportunity for learning to occur is evidence that they are preprogrammed. Exactly how this happens is a bit of a mystery, but the answer lies somewhere in the genes.

Purely natural behaviors are rather rudimentary and must be honed by experience. The fact that a young pup comes to associate the feel, odor, and warmth of its mother's underbelly with the flow of milk, comfort, and safety is a reward of the best kind that assures continued attraction. The mechanism that facilitates this attraction is innate, but the establishment of a true infant-mother bond requires experience and learning. The bitch finds her pups irresistibly appealing, too, and smell plays a key role in the equation of her attraction to them, though she uses every sense available to her in this respect. But there's more, as they say in the Ginsu-knife advertisement.

The attraction that a mom feels for her pups is both mental and physical, with the hormone oxytocin playing an important role in the maternal bonding process. Oxytocin released during the birthing process and during suckling facilitates uterine contractions and milk letdown, but also appears to serve as cement for the maternal bond. So powerful is the oxytocin-induced maternal bond that the behavior it elicits is considered by some to be a natural form of obsessive-compulsive behavior. In obsessive-compulsive behaviors, a constantly recurring thought—in this case, the pups' welfare—is linked with a repetitive behavioral consequence that the bitch is driven to perform; specifically, fussing over them. All this fits in with the definition of obsessive-compulsive behavior, yet does not cause us to raise our eyebrows because we are familiar with it as a normal behavior and because the consequences are functional. This intriguing parallel between a maternal behavior and obsessive-compulsive behavior, followed to its logical conclusion, provides a biological explanation for one of the most powerful emotions of all, a mother's love.

After pups' eyes have opened at about one and a half weeks of age there is a week-long transitional period, following which the socialization period begins. At this point, and for the first time in the pup's life, it becomes aware of the teeming world around it and the fun begins in earnest. Tussles with littermates, rolling around, righting, chasing, nipping, squealing, and fleeing are all products of an instinctive drive to interact socially. From those giddy playful days of early sibship develops a more outwardly exploratory mode, tempered by caution, in which pups push the envelope of their world, expanding their horizons. The curiosity that fuels their drive for exploration is innate and provides a platform for learning about the environment. Hunting, courting, breeding, birthing, care of young, and other instinctive behaviors unravel, are honed over time, and become integrated into day-to-day pack life.

The process by which certain specific, vital information is absorbed and processed early in life is referred to as imprinting. The term *imprinting* is so descriptive that even by popular usage it is widely understood to mean the acquisition of a permanent mental image pertaining to something. The first time I heard the expression it imprinted on me! But the word does have bona fide scientific implications, even though the definition is becoming a little woolly around the edges today. Imprinting was originally considered to be an esoteric, biologically relevant form of learning occurring early in life and designed to ensure the cleaving of a newborn to its parents. It was distinguished from other forms of learning by several features, including the rapid acquisition of a learned image (the imprint) and its relative resistance to extinction. Nobel laureate Konrad Lorenz studied imprinting in geese and other species of birds and noted that hatchlings would follow the first large moving object they encountered, particularly if it was making appropriate quacking sounds. Lorenz tricked hatchling geese into following large red balls and other moving objects, and even had geese imprint on him.

Unlike other types of learning, with imprinting there was no obvious reward for the behavior and it appeared it was actually enhanced by increasing the degree of difficulty the birds encountered in following the moving object.

During his imprinting experiments, Lorenz made the interesting observation that Barbary doves imprinted on him subsequently showed sexual orientation toward his hands when they reached sexual maturity. The definition of imprinting was expanded to include this phenomenon. The term *filial imprinting* was reserved to describe the bonding process between offspring and a parent, whereas *sexual imprinting* denoted the type of learning oriented toward recognizing the physical characteristics of future partners and potential mates. Both filial and sexual imprinting shared certain characteristics, including rapid acquisition, relative indelibility, and being triggered by relatively crude cues. Apparently nature anticipated little competition for these rudimentary recognition processes, which would, under normal circumstances, be fine-tuned by subsequent learning.

The time periods during which imprint learning took place were regarded as relatively inflexible and were described as critical periods. Clearly, the times for the filial and sexual imprinting had to be quite distinct to avoid biologically disastrous confusion. Since the early days, there has been greater recognition of the flexibility and scope of imprint learning, including the fact that it shares many characteristics in common with other forms of learning and is similar to conditioning. The term itself has now been replaced by the slightly less rigid and more amorphous term *sensitive period*. This period includes filial and sexual imprinting but also encompasses other pivotal learning that occurs rapidly in the early part of an animal's life.

So what does all of this have to do with unusual or problematic behaviors that develop in puppies or adult dogs? Quite a lot, as it turns out. When things go wrong during sensitive periods of development there are often long-term, possibly lifetime, changes in a dog's behavior. Take the very early postnatal period in a puppy's life, for example. It is normal for puppies to gravitate toward their mothers and to nurse or sleep in cyclic oblivion as the filial relationship solidifies. But if no mother is present, as occurs when pups are orphaned, the youngsters will still seek another warm and nutritious haven, such as that provided by a caring human foster parent. With time, pups get used to this situation and come to recognize the source of nurturing as "Mother." Unfortunately, human surrogates often don't know how to proceed from the nursing stage to foster the pups' independence. The result is that such pups can become overattached and may wind up displaying various neurotic behaviors, such as overprotectiveness, or may become overly demanding.

In addition, pups weaned from their natural mothers too early are predisposed to behavior problems associated with premature dislocation of their drive to nurse. In the absence of Mom, nursing may be directed onto some other substitute, such as a blanket, thin air, or perhaps some easy-to-reach part of the dog's own body. Although redirected nursing in the form of wool sucking is well known in early-weaned cats, the same syndrome is not recognized in dogs, though Dobermans and dachshunds are well known for blanket sucking, and bull terriers and Dobermans both sometimes engage in flank sucking. Genetics is probably involved in the tendency to develop these aberrant nursing behaviors. Perhaps pups of these breeds naturally nurse for longer than the statutory six to seven weeks usually allowed, so that a shift to solid food at six weeks of age constitutes early weaning. Alternatively, some bitches may produce less milk and be less willing to allow their pups to nurse, or the pups themselves may have a higher drive to nurse than the dam can or will accommodate. Clearly, more investigations are needed in this area to determine the true cause of behavior problems of this nature.

Although nursing and infant-mother bonding conform to imprint learning, for dogs, the term *sensitive period* is usually taken to mean the period of socialization when pups learn about each other and other creatures in the world around them. The time period denoted for this rapid socialization learning is usually taken to be from three to twelve weeks old, though there are different phases of learning that take place even within this period. From three to six weeks of age, puppies interact with each other, learning the p's and q's of canine etiquette and social interaction. For example, during a particularly rough bout of play, one pup may inadvertently nip another one too hard. The pup on the receiving end of this uninhibited bite squeals and runs away. The biter learns that this is not the correct way to proceed if the fun is to continue and will temper its bites to a lesser intensity in the future.

This type of learning approaches the kind with which we are more familiar, but it is naturally driven and the images gleaned are relatively permanent. In addition, there is biological significance to this learning, as it facilitates both social organization within the pack and appropriate interactions with unfamiliar dogs. Dogs that are deprived of such experiences as pups grow up to be dysfunctional in that they do not display appropriate behavioral exchanges with other dogs. It is common wisdom that hand-raised pups are almost untrainable if they show aggressive behavior toward other dogs, presumably because they have missed an important window of development. It is as if they fail to read the signs of submission properly and, when attacked, do not know how to signal their defeat. The result is that fights continue to the bitter end, until one dog is seriously injured, or worse.

Up until six weeks of age and probably for two or three weeks after that, puppies are fairly accepting of unfamiliar things in the environment around them, investigating and learning about everything with which they come in contact. But toward the end of the socialization period, arguably somewhere between the eighth and twelfth week of life, natural apprehension and fearfulness develop to close the window of socialization learning. The pup now starts to develop a healthy respect for the sometimes not-so-friendly world around it. From this time on, charity begins and ends at home. The transition into this less trusting state may be a nuisance for dog owners, but it has survival value in the wild. Once a pup has made the appropriate family ties and explored its immediate environment, it is time for it to look further afield. This is the stage when youngsters start to wander progressively farther from home with an increased chance of meeting some hostile adversary: It is the beginning of a critical period for imprinting fears. I have encountered several cases in which dogs have developed permanent fear and suspicion of objects or people if they have suffered unfortunate exposure to them during this sensitive phase of development. A typical scenario was the one that I quoted in *The Dog Who Loved Too Much* about a pup that had a negative exposure to a man with a white beard when it was ten and a half weeks of age. This dog subsequently went on to develop a lifelong fear of all men with white beards, a fear that escalated to phobic proportions when the dog was confronted with the original perpetrator of the "crime."

Chronologically speaking, the sexual-imprinting phase is the next important learning stage. The correct experience at this stage, or the lack of it, can shape a dog's opinion of what constitutes a proper mate.

In sheep, males that are separated from the flock while young and raised in same-sex groups develop a high incidence of homosexuality that affects some fifty percent of the flock. Raising sheep in mixed groups reduces the incidence of this productivity-lowering behavior into the low single-digit range. An orphan kitten I saw had only a pair of socks for company during a critical period of its development and, though neutered, this kitten subsequently adopted the balled-up socks as a mating partner. To its owner's horror and embarrassment, the kitten would then hump the socks in front of astonished guests, no doubt fulfilling some primordial need in the process. Dogs sometimes develop a penchant for humping people's legs, or cushions. Certain males, and even females, will almost compulsively exhibit same-sex mounting behavior or may hump cushions. It is quite possible that the reason dogs engage in these vacuum activities is that they were not exposed to appropriate members of their own species during a critical period of development—say around five months of age—and thus had no more fitting object for the behavior available to them.

If sexual behavior can imprint, why not predatory behavior, too? Some aspects of predatory behavior, particularly the appetitive or pursuit phase, are largely inherited. Other aspects are learned, honed, and fine-tuned as a result of experience. Predatory learning probably takes place at a certain stage of development to complete a sequence that, in nature, is responsible for sustaining a dog's life. In the domestic setting, where already-prepared foods are the order of the day, prey-seeking and -killing behaviors are redundant, but the natural drives and learning mechanisms are still in place. It seems likely that if appropriate prey subjects are not available during this period, dogs would be compelled to displace their predatory focus onto prey facsimiles such as tennis balls, joggers, skateboarders, automobiles, or even their own tails. Factoring in genetics and environmental factors, it would seem most likely for this displacement to occur in breeds with high prey drive, such as terriers and herding dogs, especially if they are kept isolated from "real prey" when young. Tennis balls and shadows or lights may present the best opportunities these dogs have for imprinting and will subsequently become the vehicles through which their innate prey drive is released. In the extreme situation of being raised in a crate, the only thing onto which the predatory dog can displace its frustrations is its own tail. Compulsive tail chasing and other forms of compulsive chasing behavior present something of a problem in some breeds (see "P—Predatory Behavior"), but as you will now appreciate, if these dogs had been properly imprinted while young they would never have developed their unusual fetish in the first place.

This process, by which important facts about life are acquired as a result of innate drives and natural curiosities, is essential to normal behavioral development. One famous behaviorist, Dr. Patrick Bateson, likened the process of early learning to a train ride through life in which the windows are opened into certain cars intermittently during the journey. When a given window is open the occupants of that car are able to learn about the surrounding terrain. The window is then closed and the train speeds on. The train analogy is a good one, as it indicates the full complexity of learning during development. Trains travel at different speeds, the countryside is constantly changing, the passengers are different, individuals may or may not be looking out when the window is open, and so on. By the end of even very similar rides, different trainloads of people may have quite different impressions of the journey they have just experienced.

The importance of early learning is indicated by certain experiments that have involved isolation of animals during critical periods of their development. The most famous experiments of this nature were conducted with monkeys by Harry Harlow and colleagues. Neonate monkeys were separated from their mothers at birth and were then raised in complete isolation. Infants isolated in this way immediately gravitated toward a sometimes felt-clad, wire-framed maternal facsimile, but on receiving no reciprocating behavior from the mummy dummy they proceeded to sit in corners and rock back and forth. Monkeys raised in this manner were never normal. All showed permanent psychological scarring. Monkey infants raised by their moms but isolated during the socialization period of development also became dysfunctional. Some would develop the floating-limb syndrome, in which monkeys cause one hind leg to rise up slowly from behind a shoulder and, on seeing it, act surprised and attack the foot. In the fierce battles that ensue, sometimes the monkey wins and sometimes the foot wins. Clearly there is never any resolution to this pseudo-dominance struggle and no biologically satisfying learning comes of it. Other aspects of social and sexual behavior are also disturbed in these poor creatures, which frequently mutilate themselves (as do humans who have been seriously abused while young) or engage in other mindless stereotypies.

Dogs, too, have been the subject of isolation experiments, and although the effects are not as dramatic as with the monkeys, they are nevertheless undesirable from an owner's point of view. In general, lack of appropriate geographic and social experiences during puppyhood leads to excessive timidity and submissiveness. This syndrome has been referred to as kennelitis (or kennelosis) and is associated with hyperactivity, decreased social behavior, and reduced mental ability. This kind of behavior plagues dogs that have been improperly raised. The importance of proper exposure during the sensitive period of development cannot be overstated. Socialization is critical for pups if they are to exhibit normal, well-adjusted behavior as adults. Until recently the significance of the sensitive period has been underrated by most breeders. Too often I hear of pups raised in basements, garages, or outside runs, that have developed problems related to shyness. To raise a dog in a kennel situation with littermates will permit normal maternal and sibling interactions but will leave the dog open to socialization deficiencies, setting it up for fear-based and territorially related problems. Since half the dogs in the United States don't make it to their second birthday, with behavior problems as the leading cause of death, it's about time we changed the way we do things.

The ideal situation for a pup is to be raised with its mother and siblings for the first seven or eight weeks of life and then to be seamlessly transplanted to a loving, caring, nurturing environment. For the first three or four months the new owners should actively arrange appropriate exposure of the pup to whatever it will be required to tolerate when fully grown, including visitors, children, and mailmen. It is important to arrange benign social experiences and contact with the outside world in as many different shapes and forms as possible. I fully support the preventative work of Dr. Ian Dunbar in this respect. Ian has always preached the gospel of socialization, making it something of a signature theme of his life's work with dogs. I believe that socializing dogs is one of the most fundamental ways in which they can be prepared for their future.

The most wide-scale example of inappropriate imprinting experiences is provided by reference to the puppy-mill situation. These dogs are batch-raised, early-weaned, and transported miles across the country to be deposited in pet stores to peer at the world through the bars of their solitary confinement. No wonder we feel sorry for them. No wonder we buy them. No wonder many come with built-in problems. But finger-pointing is not helpful in resolving this problem and that is not why I tender my opinion. Understanding is the key. I want people to understand what is wrong so that they can figure out what to do about it. The fact is that there is a large national demand for puppies that cannot be met by private breeders alone. Puppy mills are here to stay. The way forward is to educate puppy-mill owners to raise their pups differently to ensure appropriate early social experiences and to find other ways of distributing them to their new owners. The middlemen in the current practice are the pet-store owners who, like cigarette manufacturers, secretly appreciate the problems that they purvey. Try calling your local pet store to see if they will allow you to bring in a video camera to film the pups in the cages. The answer will be no. Sensitivities exist, and for good reason. I'm sure there is a way on from here, though, and I, for one, would be happy to work with whoever comes forward to optimize the currently indecorous practice of churning out pups.

Although we have talked largely about positive and negative imprinting experiences of puppies under four months of age, as an addendum, it is worth noting that imprinting experiences may also occur later in life. Extreme stress or trauma usually triggers this day-late-and-a-dollar-short imprint learning. Sudden release of high levels of stress hormones (catecholamines) causing plastic changes in central nervous structures is instrumental in this respect. The ability to imprint under these circumstances makes good sense, biologically speaking, because for an animal to imprint an indelible image of a potentially dangerous situation or experience might benefit it in the future and help it survive by avoidance. Although rapid and permanent learning can take place by this mechanism, the majority of rapid learning takes place earlier in life.

Imprinting of whatever type is a form of conditioning for which the dog is biologically prepared, and the consequences of which are relevant in terms of survival. One of the areas of preparedness for the young is possessing an (albeit biased) memory like a steel trap. For older dogs, the trap can be pried open by extreme stress or under hormonal influences. It is important to recognize all aspects of imprint learning and conditioning when raising and living with dogs so that appropriate experiences can be fostered while negative imprinting experiences are avoided. All things considered, it should take a lot of hard work to raise puppies properly, but the results of this labor are always well worth it.

JEALOUSY AND GUILT

Elizabeth Marshall Thomas, in her book *The Hidden Life of Dogs,* starts off by warning readers about her anthropomorphic approach to canine behavior. She rationalizes that science has gone overboard in its attempts to depersonalize animals and makes no excuse for her interpretations of what dogs are actually thinking.

Proving what is going on in dogs' minds, however, is still beyond our reach at present and the field of cognitive ethology remains equivocal and contentious. If you don't believe that dogs have emotions similar to those felt by humans, you can deny their existence without fear of contradiction. On the other hand, if you *do* believe dogs have feelings, you can interpret their behavior in this light and no one can prove you wrong.

Personally, I believe that Elizabeth Marshall Thomas is on the right track, but some scientists practically spit blood when they hear such "heresy" because, as they say, there is no evidence to support the existence of feelings or emotions in dogs. Some of my colleagues say that to encourage people to believe that their dogs experience anger, guilt, jealousy, and remorse is to do them a disservice. These individuals believe that owners already overinterpret their dogs' behavior, wrongly ascribing human-type feelings to their pets, and that these misguided convictions lead to miscommunication and mismanagement. There is some truth to this, but I still can't accept that animals are completely devoid of thought or emotions. Although "doubting Thomas" behaviorists tend to underinterpret the thought processes underlying canine behavior and some owners clearly overinterpret their pets' actions, the correct interpretation probably lies somewhere in the middle of this spectrum of persuasions—though, in my opinion, nearer the "cognitive" end.

Take jealousy, for example. Do you think a dog can be jealous of another dog or person? There's not much doubt in my mind that it can. The dictionary definition of jealousy is as follows: "Intolerance of rivalry or unfaithfulness; disposed to suspect rivalry; apprehension regarding the loss of another's exclusive devotion; distrustful watchfulness; vigilance in guarding a possession." "Intolerance of rivalry" is exactly the way some dominant dogs behave toward subordinates that are receiving attention, food treats, or praise from a favorite family member. As discussed later (see "Q—Quarreling"), the term *sibling rivalry* is widely used to describe this state of affairs and I think it is an appropriate one to use. But what is going through the dominant dog's mind when he growls at or attacks a fellow pack member who is receiving attention from a human caregiver?

Scientists would say "nothing" and dryly explain the behavior as an innate, almost reflexive response engaged in by dominant dogs when unwitting owners contravene unwritten (pack) rules. They regard it as a sort of behavioral knee-jerk reaction, initiated by activation of hard-wired neural circuits governing law-of-the-pack behavior and reinforced by conditioning. This interpretation depersonalizes the behavior, explaining events in robotlike terms, apparently to avoid more complicated cognitive implications. A scientist called Morgan encouraged this type of approach earlier in this century with his famous canon that, paraphrased, said that no behavior should be interpreted as due to a higher nervous-system function if it can be attributed to a lower function. Or basically, animals are assumed to be guilty of mindless action/activity until we can prove otherwise.

I prefer to reason the other way—that higher animals, like dogs, appear to think along the same lines as we do, and since they can't speak to communicate their feelings precisely, we should give them the benefit of the doubt and assume that the most obvious interpretation of their behavior is the correct one. It is clear to me (and most owners) that jealousy underlies sibling rivalry—jealousy of attention that the other dog is receiving. To interpret the aggressive behavior that results any other way is to go around the houses to arrive at the same place. The selfish behavior of sibling rivalry is the antithesis of generosity and altruism and, in accord with the dictionary definition of jealousy, involves apprehension about the loss of another's exclusive devotion. That pretty much sums it up for some of these characters.

Most dogs with sibling rivalry coexist peacefully in their owners' absence, but the more dominant of the two will attack its housemate when the owner returns home. The purpose of the attack is to reestablish ground rules relating to pack order to head off any potential expropriation between the subordinate dog and the owner. Because most owners don't understand the way their dogs think, they often inadvertently tip the scales of canine social justice on their return by, for example, greeting the subordinate dog first. This is guaranteed to put the dominant dog's hackles up and sensitize it to incidents of a similar ilk. The dictionary definition of jealousy includes the phrase *disposed to suspect rivalry,* and that is exactly how the more dominant dog of a pair acts.

Some dogs that have no problem with respect to the other dogs in the house are jealous of interactions between their human owners or between their owners and their friends. A typical scenario is that a dog throws itself between two embracing humans with the express intention of preventing their interaction and regaining the limelight. This is what some young children do when their parents' attention is diverted by someone else. With both dogs and children, this interruptive behavior can escalate to the point of aggression and may be quite disruptive. Children may shout at their parents, pull at clothing, and kick or punch, whereas dogs bark, jump up, and nip or bite their owners. Again, behaviorists go out of their way to come up with dry and dusty scientific explanations for this behavior in dogs—"possessive aggression," "protective behavior," or "guarding"—but owners see it for what it really is. "He seems to be jealous of my husband/boyfriend/wife," they say. Right on. What other reasonable explanation could there be? Why should we get inventive searching for other explanations for the behavior when the obvious one is right there in front of us? If something looks like a duck, waddles like a duck, and quacks like a duck, I reckon it probably is a duck.

The last part of the dictionary definition of jealousy—"vigilance in guarding a possession"—also lends itself to interpretation in the light of canine behavior. Typically, dominant dogs will growl, or worse, if approached or challenged when in possession of a bone. What has that got to do with jealousy, you might ask? It's just plain old protection of a valued asset, isn't it? Maybe so, but it could also be viewed in the context of jealousy.

If an approacher was to take a bone away from a dominant dog, it would likely seethe in frustration and anger. But what, exactly, would the dog be thinking at this point? It is not unreasonable to assume that the deprived dog might be "envious." It might even "covet" the missing object. We can extrapolate that it might have feelings of *jealousy*—the kind of feeling that "have-nots" experience when forced to acknowledge the "haves." The growling exhibited by the dog in possession of a bone or other valued asset can be viewed as a proactive approach designed to prevent this situation from occurring. And there is one good cure for jealousy—never let go of what you are likely to be jealous about. Every jealous boyfriend knows all about this. This doesn't mean we have to stop calling possessiveness in dogs for what it is, just that we should realize that there may be more to it than meets the eye.

Sometimes more than one component may be necessary to activate a dog's possessiveness. I once saw a neutered male Yorkshire terrier with a compound problem of this nature. If the man of the house tarried while turning out the lights last thing at night, the Yorkie would immediately jump into bed next to the man's wife. Any attempts to remove the dog caused a huge furor and resulted in the dog biting the man to protect what it apparently regarded as prime real estate. The man described himself shaking his hand up and down with the dog still attached to one of his fingers. At the time of the consultation, the man was sleeping in the spare room to avoid such scenes. Interestingly, the dog did not guard the bed unless the woman was in it, and did not show aggression around the woman unless she was in bed. Both of these factors were required simultaneously to catalyze the dog's reaction. Perhaps the height of the bed off the ground added to his confidence, or perhaps the whole situation was just too overwhelming for this possessive little dog.

This problem was resolved by means of a dominance-control program and initially by avoidance of the circumstances leading to the event (the dog was not allowed upstairs at night). The man's wife was an integral part of the problem. It's likely that the dog's "overprotectiveness" stemmed from its fascination with her, and that its aggression was designed to monopolize her in this situation. I'll leave you to decide whether the dog's behavior signaled jealousy or whether a law-of-the-pack explanation suits better. Both interpretations work. When male dogs show protectiveness over a female human companion it is tempting to speculate that the dog somehow regards its human companion as a mate of sorts. Under this premise, jealousy is even easier to imagine because the term is often used in the context of jealous lovers, jealous boyfriends, and so on. Whether dogs have such aspirations is not clear, but jealousy is still quite possible without such divinations.

So far I have only discussed jealousy, but there are other canine emotions that have been relegated to fairy-tale status under the influence of the so-called scientific approach to animal behavior. Guilt, for example, is another term dog owners commonly use that causes behaviorists to have their mouths washed out with soap if they utter it in any scientific communication. The fact that dogs appear "guilty" when they have had an accident on the floor or have destroyed something while you were away does not (apparently) sanction the use of the word. It's not guilt, the pundits say knowledgeably. The dog simply associates your presence, its presence, and the presence of the damage as a tripartite cue for punishment. Maybe so, but what the dictionary says about guilt is that it occurs "after an individual has committed a breach of conduct, especially violating a law and involving a penalty: the state of one who has committed an offense, especially a conspicuous one leading to feelings of culpability."

A feeling of culpability for an offense. I can't think of a more appropriate description of the way I believe dogs feel when their owners return to find the house trashed. Sure they're thinking penalty, and no, they didn't feel guilty while they were doing it. Why should they? There was no one around at the time to worry about. Guilt is often experienced after the fact. Doing whatever makes you feel guilty afterward can even be fun, under some circumstances. It's later that the realization sets in and the worries start.

So why on earth do scientists constantly and conscientiously avoid attributing human-type feelings to dogs (and other higher animals)? Do they believe that humans are the only ones graced with feelings? What are they afraid of? Do they come up with contrivances to explain animal behavior because they want to preserve an impression of human uniqueness? Theories of evolution would tend to support the gradual development of thought processes, including emotions, in animals other than ourselves. And anyway, it just makes sense to interpret behaviors in terms of what is almost painfully clear.

I once had a group of M.D.s quizzing me about the use of the term *anxiety* in a communication about dog behavior. "How can a dog be anxious?" they said. "Anxiety is a uniquely human emotion, isn't it?" It looked for a moment as if I were going to have to find some other way of saying what I wanted to say, but in the end they allowed me to leave the term in as long as I justified it. I used a modified "duck" analogy to make my point. "If dogs *look* anxious in situations where anxiety would be anticipated," I said, "show physiological changes associated with anxiety, and respond to treatment with human antianxiety drugs, then I think you should accept that they probably are anxious." They all agreed.

Animals have been regarded by some as automatons since the time of Descartes, and a mechanistic view of their motivations prevailed for the first half of this century as a result of what was termed behaviorism. Even the European ethologists carefully avoided cognitive issues and stuck to reporting measurable phenomena, such as honeybees' waggle dances, promenading ducks, and song learning in birds. Luckily, Dr. Don Griffin, the father of cognitive ethology, put us back on the right track, stepping outside the stifling constraints of conventional science to champion a cognitive explanation for animal behavior. In essence, he supported the contention that animals can and do make decisions about their actions and are not as ritualistic and reflexive as some would have us believe. The ability of animals, dogs included, to respond in this way is most likely related to a need they have had for decision making in the course of their evolutionary development. To make decisions, an animal has to rely on past experience, weigh the situation, and act accordingly. Any action embarked upon will cause internal feelings: of accomplishment when the desired result is successfully achieved; and of failure when the goals are not met. For group-living animals, the behavior of others must be taken into account when making decisions. The group dwellers must be programmed to be cognizant of the responses of those around them and to react accordingly. All this points to something more complicated than a knee-jerk reaction. Because of this and for the other reasons mentioned, I feel that dogs can and do experience feelings of jealousy and guilt, though they may not possess a full house of human emotion.

One difference in the thinking capacity of dogs likely stems from their relative lack of ability to dwell on and project from the immediate situation. Most animals I have encountered seem more immediate and superficial in their responses than human adults, at least. Dominant dogs, for example, can go from anger to indifference in seconds, once their demands are met. There may be a physical, developmental reason for this shallow level of concern. Ruminations and deliberations in humans are supposed to arise in a region of the brain called the prefrontal cortex. If this structure is present in dogs, it is not a patch on the human equivalent. The prefrontal area is concerned with projection, planning, worry, and doubt. It is involved in decision making and the weighing of consequences. I doubt if dogs are capable of much along these lines, but they certainly do retain memories associated with events, anticipate events, and show anxious behaviors when expected outcomes do not materialize.

In many ways, dogs are like children. They act and react as things happen and they do what they do for pretty straightforward reasons. Children, however, go on to develop into more cognitively complex adults, whereas dogs do the Peter Pan thing, remaining immediate and relatively superficial for the rest of their lives. They do, in a way, wear their hearts on their sleeves, so that only a scientist could misunderstand their true feelings. As a recent book title suggests, dogs don't lie about love, and, as it happens, cannot conceal feelings of jealousy and guilt, either.

KISSING

The almost universal response to having a dog approach and lick your face is to say, "Oh, look—he's kissing me." My usual (though mostly unspoken) reaction to this is, "In your dreams," because in nature, as well as in the domestic situation, dogs just don't kiss. It's not one of the things that they do, along with hugging and shaking hands (which, incidentally, is subtly different from being trained to "give a paw"). Although face licking can reasonably be interpreted as a compliment (of sorts), it is not exactly kissing in the true sense of the word. In her wonderful book *The Hidden Life of Dogs,* Elizabeth Marshall Thomas describes dogs kissing as a romantic gesture. Although I have tremendous respect for Ms. Thomas's insights into canine behavior, I find it difficult to accept this particular point of view, not for the usual stick-in-the-mud scientific reasons but because there are, I believe, other more plausible explanations for what she observed.

To understand "kissing" it helps to analyze its form, function, and significance and then to go from there in terms of any conclusions that might be drawn. First, let's consider the form of the behavior. When dogs "kiss" they do not apply their lips to each other, flutter their eyes, and almost certainly do not think romantic thoughts as humans sometimes do. Let's face it, they lick. Hands, feet, faces, whatever they can get their tongues on, they lick. Licking first appears in the mother-infant situation when the bitch grooms her pups immediately after birthing to clean them up and perhaps, unbeknownst to her, to stimulate respiration. Later, she continues to groom them as a function of hygiene, and grooming directed to the pups' anogenital area serves the vital purpose of stimulating urination and defecation. That the bitch loves her pups is not in question, though that still doesn't make grooming the equivalent of kissing. Human mothers bathe their infants and change diapers because they care, but no one would confuse the act of bathing or changing diapers with kissing, either in its form or function. Because dogs can manipulate things better with their mouths than their paws, it makes sense for them to employ their tongues rather than their toes in their hygienic pursuits.

In time, pups begin to lick and clean themselves and to engage in a certain amount of so-called allogrooming. Allogrooming is a caregiving behavior that serves the social function of enhancing bonding between individuals, but I see this apparently altruistic activity as more closely akin to a back rub or the proverbial nitpicking than to kissing per se. It must be quite satisfying for dogs to have a buddy help out with those hard-to-reach places, and reciprocation, which increases the likelihood of future gratifying interactions of this nature, is a logical sequel. If friends groom friends as a goodwill gesture, grooming obviously does serve as some kind of communicative function. But what exactly is the dog communicating? The most reasonable answer to this is appeasement—a sort of "I'm being nice to you/don't hurt me" type of signal. I would classify licking of one littermate by another, along with rolling over and submissive urination, as a gesture of goodwill and surrender. Humans and other primates also groom and massage each other by way of pleasurable exchange. The behavioral significance of this is similar to that of canine allogrooming in that it denotes friendly intentions and serves as a mechanism for reducing stress.

Pups lick their mother's face around the time they are making the transition from milk to solid food. This face licking is part of a greeting ritual in the wild when a bitch returns from hunting with a belly full of food. The purpose of face licking in this context is to cause Mom to regurgitate partially digested stomach contents for the pups' dining pleasure. This type of face licking still occurs in domestic dogs and sometimes with the same result, yet it is not kissing. Face licking of this variety is a care-soliciting (etepimeletic) behavior, not to my mind what kissing in humans is all about.

Another form of licking that pups display is licking their own lips. Initially this behavior may have evolved for the purpose of cleaning the lips after feeding, but when it occurs out of context it indicates emotional reactivity and serves as an indicator of stress. It is, in a sense, analogous to lip biting in humans. Lip licking decreases as pups gain in confidence and feel more comfortable with their surroundings but it doesn't disappear entirely, even in adult dogs. I often see dogs nervously licking their lips in my consulting room as they ponder their fate with me. These same dogs often approach their owners and lick their faces too, kowtowing and hoping for clemency. If you ask animal scientists about the relevance of face licking by dogs, most would characterize it as submissive behavior. This is because face licking, like lip licking, is exhibited by dogs in situations of stress or conflict. Face licking is particularly likely to occur when a subordinate dog has summoned up enough courage to approach a more dominant one.

This brings up a possible parallel between face licking by dogs and kissing in nonhuman primates, if not humans. Apparently, kissing is a common greeting behavior expressed when a subordinate chimpanzee greets a more dominant one. The dominant chimp may in return also kiss the subordinate during such meetings, though kissing by the more dominant chimp is only about half as likely. Could it be that when your dog greets you at the door with wagging tail and licks your face as you kneel to say hi that he is actually acknowledging you, chimp-style, as his dominant leader by this gesture of deference? This sounds plausible to me, and might explain some dogs' face licking, but how does this relate to kissing between people? Do you think that a wife who kisses her husband when he returns home from work is signaling submission? I don't think I would take the analogy that far. And what if the husband kisses her back? Is he signaling dominance or is this a case of mutual submission?

In one of her scientific communications, primatologist Jane Goodall reported, "Occasionally a mature male (chimpanzee) pressed his lips to the face of a female when she approached . . . after he himself had been kissed submissively. When the dominant individual responded to a submissive kiss with a similar gesture, this sometimes resulted in mouth-to-mouth kissing." Goodall also mentions that she feels there may be a sexual element in such greeting behaviors, at least between individuals of opposite sexes, and believes that kissing may have evolved from the infantile response of suckling. I can accept some parallels between face licking by dogs and kissing in primates. They can both be greeting behaviors; they both involve tête-à-tête contact; and they both seem to provide some reassurance for the donor and the recipient. However, there are notable differences between these behaviors in form. Dogs that face-lick do not actually apply their lips to another individual's lips. They lick. Face licking by dogs is a unidirectional phenomenon from one individual to another and is not particularly intimate or mutual. Though face licking by dogs does appear to serve a communicative function, it is one of respect and deference and not necessarily a gesture of love.

Under some circumstances, face licking by dogs can represent a tacit assertion of dominance and control. When this occurs in the context of unsolicited (literally and metaphorically), in-your-face licking, it qualifies as a challenge. I sometimes find myself the subject of unsolicited face licking by known dominant, aggressive dogs in my clinic. Are these dogs surrendering to me? I doubt it. Or are they attempting to signal their mastery over me? I think the latter is more likely. Even in human terms, when a kiss is forced and unwanted it becomes an assault and is not a sign of affection. In would-be dominant dogs I believe that licking behavior can be provocative, too. "No lick" is definitely a useful command to master for use under these circumstances and should be incorporated into the retraining of all dominant dogs that lick their owners excessively. I have heard of at least one dominance program failing because this issue was overlooked. The dominant dog, which was not responding to treatment, was being allowed to lick its owner's legs when she got out of the shower. This deferential gesture by her was enough to allow her dog to remain in charge and refuse to submit to her requests at other times.

Face licking can mean many things but the one thing I can't accept about it is that it is romantic. I don't believe that dogs kiss each other or humans in this way, not unless you stretch the definition of the word *romantic*. It might be nice to think of two dogs nose-to-nose in the moonlight thinking endearing thoughts of each other, but that isn't the way it happens. That's the stuff only dreams are made of.

LEAVING HOME

Several years ago, shortly after I first opened the doors of the behavior clinic at Tufts, I received a call from our development office to say that Ms. Edith Davenport, a generous benefactor from nearby Paxton, was having serious trouble with her dogs. The problem was that the dogs, Jason and Jenna, a pair of two-year-old sibling golden retrievers, would not stay in her backyard and kept charging out onto a busy main road, endangering themselves and passing motorists. It was time for the cavalry to arrive for the rescue so, along with reinforcements, I agreed to pay her a visit.

At the time, trainer Brian Kilcommons was visiting from New York so we teamed up and made the house call together; after all, two heads are better than one and I wanted to do everything possible for this special friend of Tufts. I had never been to the Davenport residence before but had heard that it was quite special—and the rumors were not unfounded. After a pleasant run up Route 140 north in Brian's car, we crackled up Ms. Davenport's stone-covered, sweeping semicircular driveway and came to a halt right outside her impressive front entrance. Set on what can only be described as a country estate, the slate-clad, stuccoed house was large but cottagelike, with leaded-light windows and an old-world charm all its own. Sam, Ms. Davenport's caretaker, gardener and right-hand man, greeted us at the front door. He wore the wry smile of a skeptic but cordially invited us in and called down the hall for Ms. Davenport.

Finally the grande dame emerged from a Persian-rugged living room, obviously delighted to see us, and launched into a detailed description of the difficulties she was experiencing with her dogs. We walked as we talked, down to the kennel where Jason and Jenna stayed. Their home was fit for a king and queen. It was a well-appointed outbuilding, designed after the style of the main house in every detail, right down to the retriever weather vane, and had a half-acre run out back. There was only one luxury the dogs were not allowed. They were not permitted to go into the main house. They were just too rambunctious to be allowed to romp in Ms. Davenport's finely appointed home, and this meant that they spent many long hours without human companionship. Whether a cause or an effect of their incarceration I'm not sure, but when people arrived they went ballistic. Brian and I were subjected to a barrage of jumping up, face licking, and nudging from the pair as Ms. Davenport finished her tale about the runaway dogs and posed her question. "So you see, I have no way of preventing them from running across that busy road and if something isn't done I feel sure there will be a horrible accident. . . . Can you help me?"

"What happens when you call them back?" Brian quizzed.

"Nothing," Ms. Davenport admitted. "They just don't listen. They heed Sam sometimes but won't do much for me."

"I can't stop them when they decide they're gonna take off," Sam added. "They just make a beeline for the road over there," he said, beckoning toward a remote corner of the sprawling front lawn, "and pretty soon they're just specks on the horizon."

I spent a little while talking with Ms. Davenport about socializing the dogs more, perhaps allowing them into the home, and stressed the importance of exercise and a healthy diet (which, as it turned out, they were already receiving). We also discussed motives for their wander-lust, trying to discover some pertinent fact that would defuse the situa-tion. However, I was able to conclude little more than that these two youngsters had found something attractive out there—whether it was canine company, an interesting refuse heap, or a duck pond, I will never know.

"You know, Ms. Davenport, you'll never get them to come back when you call unless you have perfect control of them in less emotive situations," Brian chipped in. "From what you are telling me, this pair doesn't pay much attention to you even when they have nothing much to do."

"That's true," Ms. Davenport conceded, "but I don't really need them to be that obedient. I just want them to stay in the yard and come when they're called."

I looked at Brian and he looked at me. It was time to educate Ms. Davenport.

After he had explained that training, like charity, begins (but shouldn't end) at home, Brian managed to persuade Ms. Davenport that it was *she* and not Sam who should work with Jason and Jenna. He showed her step-by-step basic obedience training for the dogs, demon-strating first, and then coaching Ms. Davenport to do the same. He showed her how to secure the leash (with thumb inside the loop); how to walk and praise them; how to get them to sit and wait; and how to make them come when called. In essence, he taught her that the dogs had to learn to walk before they could be stopped from running away. Within a couple of hours I saw the dogs improve from paying no atten-tion to Ms. Davenport, to listening to some of her commands and work-ing for her. The transformation was most rewarding for all concerned. Ms. Davenport thoroughly enjoyed the session, which ended on a memorable note—as she called Jason, from a short distance, he recog-nized her call and actually came to her side. Brian and I headed back to Grafton, a job well done, and eventually went our own ways—until the next time.

I called Ms. Davenport a few weeks later to see how things were going. Sam answered the phone. I knew he would prefer, for Ms. Dav-enport's sake, that the problem was resolved, though I detected a note of vindication in his voice as he relayed the bad news that Jason and

Jenna had succeeded in several more hair-raising escapes since our visit.

"Something has to be done about this, Doc," he said in a friendly but definite tone. "Ms. Davenport just can't go on like this. The town is already on the case and she would hate to lose the dogs. You know what I mean?"

I certainly did.

I called Brian to see what he had to offer. "I'd try an invisible fence, Nick," he said. "That'll keep them in, I bet."

I didn't like this idea, having never advised an invisible fence before, and was naturally skeptical about this punitive method of control.

"Doesn't it hurt them?" I asked.

"Not much," Brian said. "It just delivers a mild electric shock when they cross the buried wire, and anyway, the dogs can avoid the shock if they want by staying within the designated area."

"But they have to get shocked to find that out," I wrangled.

"Only the first couple of times," he replied. "Besides, what's the alternative? We've done the best we can without going that route and the dogs are going to get in serious trouble if something isn't done soon."

Reluctantly I agreed, but for reasons of conscience I called the Humane Society *and* the invisible-fence company to hear some divergent points of view. The people at the Humane Society were really down on the fence at that time and told me why. First, they thought it was unfair to confine a dog electronically without means of escape, where it could be persecuted by any itinerant Cujo of a dog cruising the neighborhood. Secondly, they were concerned that if a dog broke out of its confine it could become trapped outside the electric field, unable to return without receiving a shock. They also pointed out that some dogs wearing shock collars might receive random shocks triggered by television sets and that this might result in various neurotic behaviors. On another negative note, they maintained that electric fences were prone to damage by lightning strike, and for this and other reasons were not a reliable way of containing dogs. Even when the fence works properly, they added, many dogs will accept the shock to escape if the motivation is sufficiently strong. Their formal position on electric fences (of whatever variety) was that they were a relatively inexpensive way out for people wishing to save the cost of the gold standard of restraint, a real fence.

The invisible-fence company put my mind at ease on some of these issues. The Cujo story, they thought, was a bit far-fetched and more of a visceral reaction than a considered response. The fence, they assured me, had been modified in more recent designs to circumvent the possibility of random shocks—and the control box had been protected to prevent it from being deactivated by lightning strike. A delay circuit had been added so that dogs, once out, could reenter the zone without getting zapped. In addition, the magnitude of the shock administered was modifiable to accommodate even the most sensitive (or resistant) individuals, and very few dogs were not completely contained by the setup. Only one and one-half percent of dogs restrained by invisible fences blasted through the electric field, accepting the jolt to chase a jogger or catch a squirrel. The company termed these few renegades the hounds from hell.

I still didn't like the concept of the electric fence, but the lack of a suitable alternative, the company's guarantee of efficacy, and the serious consequences of having Ms. Davenport's dogs running loose on the main road all came together to persuade me to recommend that she have one installed. Ms. Davenport seized upon this option and the invisible fence company was called without delay. A few days after the company had completed the installation, Brian and I visited Ms. Davenport again for a follow-up appointment. This time there were little white flags along the sides of the drive to inform the dogs where the hazard lay. About seven acres were marked out in this way. The dogs had been brought close to the flags once or twice, a buzzer on their collars had sounded, and they were then walked on to receive a shock. One or two shocks was all it took. After those experiences the buzzer and flags signified bad news and flagged areas were conscientiously avoided by both dogs. These were not hounds from hell. They responded exactly as planned and did not forget the boundaries even when the flags were eventually removed—the buzzer made sure of that. The experiment had worked well and Ms. Davenport was delighted with the result. The dogs were free to run in the seven acres but were safe from the perils of the road; because of the fence they were much more likely to be around to see their next few birthdays; and to crown it all, the roads around Ms. Davenport's estate were now a lot safer for motorists.

Although the conclusion of the Davenport case was satisfactory, I remain somewhat skeptical of the electric-fence concept. I know that dogs, once trained, can avoid the shock but to have them shocked in the first place, and then to have them spend their outside lives avoiding the experience for a second time, doesn't ride well with me. In an attempt to overcome my reservations, I decided at one veterinary meeting to take the manufacturer up on an offer of trying out the collar on myself. I wandered into their commercial booth and, at the invitation of a salesperson, applied the two electrodes to my own forearm.

"Should I try low or medium?" I questioned.

"Try it on low first," the salesperson responded confidently.

I pressed the button and a searing charge, like death by a thousand knives, ran through my body. I leaped back in pain and amazement.

"What the . . ." I muttered, nursing my tingling arm in disbelief.

The salesperson's smile transformed into a frown.

"Painful?" he quizzed.

I don't know what the problem was—whether it was my low pain threshold, an exceedingly good contact, or that the collar was adjusted wrongly—but I got zapped. I'm just glad I didn't put the collar around my neck. I would probably have curly hair now if I had.

Another problem with electric collars that came to my attention recently is that some dogs' necks become ulcerated by the electrodes if the collars are put on too tight, or if they're left on all the time, without careful attention. I have a slide of such in my collection to remind me of this and to inform others of what can happen if you don't take care.

For those opposed to invisible fences, and for those who can't afford them, the question remains, what to do about dogs that roam? Beyond training, leashing, and a real fence, I am at a loss as to what to advise. In the section "S—Sexual Behavior," I discuss the effects of castration in preventing roaming by male dogs, but many females and neutered males roam, too. An idea I had recently, that may not completely resolve the problem, would, if correctly deployed, at least help contain dogs while the owner is around by improving re-call. The idea occurred to me one day while I was reading the *Boston Globe,* when I noticed a headline "The Invisible Lead." Thinking dogs, I read on but found myself reading about an epidemic of electronic paging devices in Asia, including voice pagers and cell phones. The popular term the Chinese had adopted to describe these remote-communication devices was invisible leads. What if, I thought, I set my pager to beep or vibrate, attached it to a dog's collar, and then called it up? Obviously the pager would be activated and the dog would sense the signal. If I had previously paired the sound or vibration with some irresistible reward, perhaps a food treat or favorite toy, I could see the dog returning enthusiastically to collect the reward when summoned. It made sense to me.

I called a friend of mine who designs complicated electronic circuitry and he confirmed the feasibility of the idea. We even got into details of infrared versus radio-frequency activation. He thought it would be a cinch to build a transmitter no bigger than a key-ring pendant and a receiver for the dog's collar that would be practically flush. I was so enamored of the idea that I had our patent office run a search to see if we could get some legal protection before we approached a manufacturer. As it turned out, a patent was not possible because of some "prior art" technology, so the idea died shortly after its inception. But there's always the option of the pager, cell phone, and the redial button for those still interested in checking this out.

I imagine some people are thinking, why not just let the dogs come and go? What's the big deal? They'll always find their way back, won't they?

Well, dogs do have a great homing system and, like cats, have been known to traverse great distances to find their way home. But that's not the point. I have already alluded to the dangers of traffic and the potential for road accidents, and that's a major concern, but there are other problems associated with allowing dogs to run free. Some dogs chase people and scare them when they are out. I have heard of dogs running wild down the main streets of towns, terrorizing whole neighborhoods until apprehended. One pit bull I was consulted about recently attacked an old man who was cradling his pup for safety and the man ended up in the hospital with serious injuries. Also, in the section "Z—Zoonosis," you will read about packing behavior and the risk of injury to children. Then there's the problem of dog fights, which are bad news whether your dog is on the giving or receiving end of the fray. And you know what happens when unneutered dogs are allowed to run together. The list goes on.

The bottom line is that it is not cool or safe to allow dogs to run free in any urban or suburban environment. They should always be under their owner's control or suitably restrained. It's not fair to the dogs or to people to have it any other way. How an individual owner achieves this is less important than the fact that he does.

MATERNAL BEHAVIOR

(Mind over Mother)

Behavior makes a fascinating study. It is the outward expression of inner thought processes and gives clues as to what animals (and people) are actually thinking. Actions, as we say, speak louder than words. The odd thing is that, like us (although we hate to admit it), what animals think, and therefore how they act, depends on their prevailing brain chemistry. For example, in people and animals, high (but not too high) brain concentrations of the neurotransmitter serotonin create a mood of assurance and behavioral stability. Low serotonin, on the other hand, is associated with underconfidence, depression, and aggressiveness. People who mass-murder strangers in a fit of rage and depression invariably have low brain serotonin, as do people who commit the ultimate self-directed aggressive act, suicide. Aggressive dogs have low brain serotonin, too, and increasing serotonin by whatever means seems to stabilize their moods and reduce aggression. Changes in other neurotransmitters, such as dopamine (the subject of Dr. Oliver Sacks's epic book, *Awakenings*), acetylcholine, and norepinephrine, can also produce dramatic alterations in the behavior and mood of man and animals.

Hormones play a role in organizing aspects of the neurochemical extravaganza, facilitating certain behaviors and inhibiting others. Testosterone alters the drive for aggression and fuels several other male-oriented behaviors, but female hormones also shape the perceptions and actions of the so endowed. The essence of good politics (it is said) is to think globally and act locally. This describes how reproductive hormones operate, being disseminated globally (into the bloodstream and throughout the tissues) but acting locally on specific brain centers in and around a structure called the hypothalamus. What with brain centers and neurochemicals, plus or minus input from hormones, it makes you wonder what we animals actually do conjure up versus what is biologically driven. The answer to this question can be a bit disturbing to those who believe only in pure, primordial thought, because nothing cerebral or behavioral can occur without the prerequisite neural circuitry and relevant biochemical milieu. Altered brain chemistry can be a real mind bender.

Maternal behavior mechanisms can be fooled by biochemical influences, highlighting the mechanistic side of this behavior. And it can happen right in the middle of an otherwise ordinary life and when least expected. Take Maggie, for example, a six-year-old German shorthaired pointer who normally knew her own mind. Maggie's owners had not had her spayed, even though they never intended to breed her, and had tolerated the inconvenience of her six-monthly heat periods for all her life. The problem was that Maggie started to have false pregnancies sixty days or so after each heat. During these times she would put on weight, show enlargement of her mammary glands (some bitches actually produce milk), start running around with a stuffed toy in her mouth (a puppy facsimile), and begin to make a nest to accommodate the new arrival. Sometimes she would curl up next to the stuffed toy in nursing posture and would actually defend the surrogate against intrusions from the outside world. Although Maggie was never given the opportunity to become pregnant, this omission did not stop her body from going through phantom pregnancies and engaging in prosthetic puppy-rearing at appropriate times. Her mind and body told her she had given birth, though definitive evidence was lacking. Not to be deterred, she simply adopted a pup facsimile and went about her duty.

The cause of this curious nonevent was post-estrus hormone fluctuations, including falling levels of progesterone, "the hormone of pregnancy." When we saw Maggie for the first time she was having her nineteenth nervous breakdown of this kind and treatment was definitely indicated. The duration of the false pregnancies had increased progressively over the years, and when she was finally brought to Tufts, this time she had not responded to her vet's usual treatment, oral progesterone therapy. We prescribed a synthetic male hormone, milbolerone, instead and were rewarded with a fairly rapid resolution of the immediate problem—but the treatment was not a long-term solution. Sure enough, the next time she came into heat she had pseudopregnancy again, this time on an even grander scale. It was at this point that her owners elected to have her spayed to prevent further problems—just as well, really, because the combination of recurrent pseudopregnancy and the vet's progesterone treatments may eventually have led to a potentially dangerous uterine infection, pyometra.

As an aside, sometimes milbolerone will not hold a pseudopregnancy in check. In such difficult-to-treat cases, vets occasionally resort to another drug called bromocriptine. Bromocriptine facilitates the action of the neurotransmitter dopamine, which, in turn, blocks the release of prolactin from the pituitary gland. Prolactin is a lactational hormone, though it has other effects, too.

Nine months ago I was consulted about a two-year-old castrated male golden retriever called Bill, who had begun discharging milk from his nipples, building a nest, and had become aggressive. I immediately realized that these changes could result from a pituitary tumor, increasing prolactin secretion from his pituitary gland. To confirm my supposition I had his blood-prolactin level checked and it was three times the normal amount. I was convinced I was on the right track and treatment with a dopamine enhancing drug produced the desired effects both biochemically and behaviorally. Treatment success aside for a moment, just think about what had been going on: maternal behavior and lactation in a male. Talk about soup from a stone.

Although the maternal behavior shown by both of these "phantom pregnancy" dogs, Maggie and Bill, was duped into action by altered brain chemistry, there are learned components that modify maternal behavior, too. It would be a shame if a bitch functioned simply as an automaton with no appreciation or memory of what she was doing. Fortunately, that's not the case. Experienced mothers are more efficient and better mothers than rookies, who act purely out of instinct. Moms do learn from practice, and no doubt appreciate the mothering experience, however driven they feel. As usual, the combination of nature and nurture working together produces the most satisfactory results.

There are several aspects of maternal behavior that deserve attention. The first is nesting. There was a question in an examination I took that quizzed, "Which of the following species build nests?" The choices were dogs, cats, birds, pigs, and monkeys. I was thinking of nests as being things built in trees and made of grass or twigs, or at least the ground-level equivalent, such as a swan's nest. I didn't have a problem coming up with birds' nests, of course. I also happened to know that chimps build nests in the trees, and I had learned, to my great surprise, that lady pigs (sows) gather twigs and sticks together at parturition time and build a fairly respectable nest (making the old saying "If pigs could fly" somewhat less poignant). I was down to the choice of whether to include dogs and cats. Although I knew that dogs use a whelping box and may grab some strips of material or paper to lie on, and that cats curl up under a deck or in a cupboard, I didn't feel that these efforts could be classed as true nest building—after all, there were no sticks or twigs involved. But I was wrong. When I checked the textbooks after the examination I found *nest* everywhere in descriptions of the whelping and kittening. Now I describe what Maggie and Bill were doing as nest building, even though it is still strange to think of a dog or cat sitting on a nest.

Nest building precedes whelping, another behavior that is programmed—no learning required. It is relatively easy to grasp the automatic nature of the birthing process but far more of a stretch to fathom the behavioral aftermath. How is it that a first-time mother feels compelled to lick herself, clean any soiled bedding, and lick her pups dry? How does she know that she should sever the umbilical cord, extract her own placenta, and consume the placenta once it is delivered? And what stimulates her to lie down and allow her pups to nurse or herd them back to her with a few well-directed swipes of her tongue? No one really has all the answers to these questions, but behaviors certainly are passed on from generation to generation, so the answer lies somewhere in the genes. We do know that genes control the timely manufacture and disposition of proteins, creating the structures and neurochemicals that facilitate behavior, and that environmental cues and learning help kick-start and propagate biologically relevant behaviors. But, whatever the technical underpinnings, the consequences of this genetic-behavioral link still represent something of an ongoing miracle.

A bitch's licking of her pups, which is directed primarily toward each pup's head, navel, and rear (perineum), serves several distinct but vital functions. Licking of a pup's perineal area helps stimulate the elimination of urine and feces; attention to the navel aids proper healing of this structure; and licking of the head (and perhaps other areas) facilitates the pup's neural development and its ability to deal with stress. The beneficial effects of early handling of pups by humans are probably due to increased licking of handled pups by moms when they are returned to the litter. (In rats' pups, the rate of maternal licking has been shown to double immediately following handling, and the benefits that this confers parallel those found in lucky pups whose moms are naturally ardent groomers.) And incidentally, well-licked pups may be less susceptible to some of the deleterious neurodegenerative consequences of aging (described in the "G—Geriatric" section).

Another tale of misdirected mothering illustrates the powerful biological drive of bitches to adopt, nurture, and groom small, furry neonates or, in this case, a neonate facsimile. Sarah, a six-year-old female McNab shepherd, found herself accompanied by the neighbors' pet rat, which was boarding over the weekend while the neighbors were away. Instead of displaying a predatory reaction to this rodent, Sarah became obsessed with it in a maternal sort of way. During the rat's stay she wouldn't leave it alone. She didn't want to go outside, which was very unusual for her, and if encouraged to go for a walk she would only make it about two blocks from the house before turning around and bolting back to the house to check on the visitor. On returning she would grab a bite of food from her bowl and then head straight for the rat's cage, where she would gaze at the rat fixedly. Periodically, she would run off and grab another bite of food before checking on the rat again. I believe that if the rat had licked her face she would have regurgitated for it.

In an attempt to divine her true motivation, Sarah's owners took the rat out of the cage and showed it to her, taking suitable precautions lest she should scoff it. She didn't. She examined it lovingly and then began to groom the little sucker. As a touching finale to this heart-warming story, Sarah became terribly depressed when the rat was taken home. She would go outside and stand peering at the neighbors' house for hours on end and was off her food. She got over it eventually but probably still dreams of the day that she had her very own living doll. Incidentally, for people who like long words, the phenomenon by which nonpregnant moms accept foreign offspring following a period of exposure to the youngster is called *concaveation*. This phenomenon, well documented in sheep, is not widely touted in other species, though cuckoos depend on it and Sarah was on the receiving end of a lot of it.

Next on the list of a bitch's maternal responsibilities is nursing. Bitches naturally know when it is time to initiate bouts of nursing and when it is time to repel borders in the interests of their pups' independence. You can't set your watch by it, but bitches initiate their pups' nursing for the first three weeks of lactation. After that their patience wears a little thin and they get progressively more fussy about what they will tolerate and what they will not, sometimes driving their pups away with a growl or a weak bite. Nature has determined the time line that works well to get pups experimenting with solid food—by four to six weeks of age. Nursing does not occur by trial and error. There are strong drives operating in both the pup and the bitch that guarantee success. Pups gravitate toward Mom's nipples like there's no tomorrow (and there wouldn't be if they didn't), and the bitch relishes the power-fully reinforcing, positively euphoric, suckling-driven hormonal milieu that results. Anyway, all good things must end, and with the recession of the hormonal tide, nursing peters out, usually by about sixty days following parturition.

During the first three weeks of lactation, pups are totally dependent and the bitch has to keep an eye on them in more ways than one.

Not only does she have to facilitate their feeding and elimination behavior, but also it is her bounden duty to retrieve them should they wander too far afield. Licking the pups is one way of orienting them back to safety from short-range excursions. The bitch licks the pup's head as she backs away from it and it follows her to the sanctuary of the nest. Bitches also collar the little tykes and physically carry them back when greater distances are involved. One would imagine that some breeds would be better at this form of return than others because some have been selectively bred to enhance their retrieving properties—golden retrievers, for example. In the only study on this subject that I could find, John Scott and John Fuller did indeed note some breed differences in retrieval but were surprised to discover that cocker spaniels were not as good at this as most of the other breeds they tested. Since cockers were bred to retrieve game, they concluded that retrieving young and retrieving game were two different ("not closely related") behaviors. But I have known several misguided retriever-type dogs who brought back shoes or socks like clockwork during periods of anxiety and stress. These dogs then took the spoils to a nestlike location, in one case under a bed, and curled up around them in a typical nursing posture. This doesn't sound too predatory to me. It sounds more like puppy-retrieval behavior. The question is, how do you explain Scott and Fuller's observations on their cockers? Well, there are a few possible explanations. One is that the strain that they tested was not particularly good at retrieving pups and may not have been much good at retrieving game, either. Then again, the results of their experiment were not really that convincing. They found that three out of thirteen cocker mothers and six out of eight basenji mothers retrieved at least some of their pups. Because of the nature of the study and the low number of dogs, these results are a little wobbly. Finally, I understand that cocker spaniels were actually bred for flushing woodcock rather than simply retrieving game (hence the name "(wood)cocker of Spanish origin"), so they might not have been the optimum breed from which to extrapolate such conclusions. Now, if Scott and Fuller had studied twenty or thirty golden retrievers and found that only three were good at retrieving pups, I would be more convinced by their conclusions.

One final responsibility of motherhood is to defend the young.

Bitches notoriously display what is referred to as maternal aggression if they feel that their pups are being threatened in any way. Maternal aggression comes and goes under the influence of, what else, hormones and neurotransmitters. Graphs charting maternal aggression in rats show aggressive behavior exactly paralleling the rise and fall of the hormone prolactin. It is possible that there is no cause-and-effect relationship, but a top-drawer neuroendocrinologist I know believes there is. The fact that progesterone is plummeting after birthing, too, will hardly improve mood either, in rat moms or bitches, so perhaps maternal aggression is more complicated than the prolactin data would suggest. I am not implying that a bitch's defense of her young is performed without true feeling. Quite the reverse; I believe that the hormonal changes inspire nursing bitches to greater heights.

Occasionally the well-oiled machine of motherhood goes awry. And when it does, the result can be disastrous—as it was with a bull terrier bitch I treated called Lila. Maternal rejection is what occurred in Lila's case—rejection manifesting as escalating aggression to both her pups and to her owner. Lila started to have her pups one May day in her New Hampshire home. Halfway through the delivery, her joyous owner, Kathy, showed Lila the three pups she had delivered to that point and tried to encourage them to nurse. Perhaps it was too much too soon. Perhaps Lila was in pain, or perhaps she was just one of nature's psycho mothers. We may never know the answer to that question, but on seeing the pups Lila sat up and let out a bloodcurdling snarl, and that just isn't right.

I love bull terriers. They are one of my favorite breeds, with their characterful faces, curious but endearing ways, and their apparent sense of fun, but as any bull terrier breeder will tell you, you can't afford to fool around with a really aggressive one. They are just too powerful and too tenacious. Kathy, somewhat intimidated herself, immediately took the pups away to safety until the rest of the litter was delivered. As the remaining three pups were born, Lila payed no attention to them at all. Not even a lick, just a grim and slightly distant look. An hour and a half later Kathy muzzled her and retried the introduction. This time Lila became violent, growling and lunging at the pups so that she had to be restrained to prevent her from hurting them. Kathy's joy turned to tears. Nevertheless, for forty-eight hours she continued to present the pups to Lila for nursing, with limited success, though she did manage to get some colostrum into each of them. By the forty-eight-hour mark Lila had disintegrated into an unmanageable land shark every time she saw her pups, and Kathy had to abandon her valiant attempts to make a mother out of Lila. It was hand-rearing all the way for these pups.

Then the really bad stuff happened. Lila started to become aggressive to Kathy and her nineteen-year-old daughter. This occurred first when Kathy reached into Lila's crate to retrieve an empty food bowl. Lila, who had never shown any aggression to family members before, suddenly lunged at Kathy, just missing her arm. Kathy shut the door to the crate quickly but Lila continued to snarl and throw herself against the door in an attempt to break out and attack Kathy. God forbid. The growling and lunging continued when Kathy or her daughter went anywhere near the crate, so they had to cover it with a cloth and immediately arrange to come and see me.

I had maternal-behavior expert Dr. Bob Bridges in the consulting room with me when Kathy arrived. Kathy left Lila in her crate in the car at first so that we could discuss the diagnosis and game plan. The conversation drifted from hormone this to hormone that until we had exhausted all possibilities. It was possible that the hormonal changes of late pregnancy had triggered latent behavioral seizures, not unheard of in the breed, but Lila's sudden change of heart could also have represented normal behavior gone awry. We weren't really sure what was going on, but we knew what to do to get things back to the way they were before Lila lost her cool, and to prevent further problems. We did examine Lila (from three-feet range) and confirmed what Kathy had reported as Lila obviously regarded us as threatening and emitted a low growl. I found myself behaving like Niles Crane (of *Frasier* fame) with his whippet. "Stop that immediately, Lila," I ventured tentatively. Lila continued to growl, lower and louder. "H'okay, let's go back to the consulting room, folks." (I know when I am beaten.) The discharge orders were for Kathy and her daughter to keep themselves safe, to have Lila spayed, and, post spaying, to treat her with synthetic progesterone. The plan worked like a dream. Within days Lila was her old playful, hand-licking, body-wiggling self and there were no further problems in that household. I did wonder, however, about the genetic legacy Lila had left for us in the form of her pups.

It continues to amaze me that dogs' (and perhaps humans') behaviors are so fickle, being dependent on these inner goings-on. They occur, it seems, at the whim and fancy of the hormones and neurotransmitters that are secreted. It almost doesn't leave much room for a personal agenda or unbiased thought. From progesterone to prolactin, from LSD to angel dust, what we secrete (and what we eat) is what we are. I am exaggerating a little, of course, but it's an exaggeration to make a point. We are all subject to the whims and fancy of our internal environment from cradle to grave. It's just lucky that most of the time the whole process runs like clockwork, especially the birthing and rearing processes, or none of us would be here.

NUISANCE BEHAVIORS

Attention Seeking

"Hold yer *whiesht*," my ex-mother-in-law, Jesse, would say to her unique piano-playing, Gaelic-comprehending collie cross, Djelias (phonetically: je-lus, meaning "faithful"). The cue for this command, literally translated as "hold your tongue," would be Djelias's whining and yipping, as she stared into Jesse's eyes with laserlike intensity, backing up in front of her as she walked and practically tripping her up. The express purpose of this complex behavior was to obtain Jesse's attention and then some favor. For Djelias, her intrusive attention-seeking behavior could elicit any one of three possible outcomes. The first—and least desirable, from her point of view—would be nothing at all. The second option would be that she might be spoken to in affirmation or chastisement—either way, she would have Jesse's attention. On the affirmative side, Jesse might say, "What's the matter, Djelias? Are you talking to me?" Or, when not in the mood for Djelias's shenanigans, she might say, *"Soay shiez"* (translated as "sit down") or *"Nach ist* you" (meaning "be quiet"), at which point the obedient Djelias would sit down and be quiet as instructed, though she would continue to gaze at Jesse with her head tipped to one side and with a look that would melt ice, waiting for a response. The third possible outcome would be not mere acknowledgment but some more positive consequence as well, such as petting, praise, food, or being let out. For example, once Djelias had Jesse's attention she might then back toward the door and Jesse would say, "D'you want out?" At this point Djelias would bark once or twice in affirmation and wag her tail in joy, knowing she had been understood. The door would be opened.

Children use this ploy, too. Does this sound familiar?

"Mommy, Mommy. *Mommy*."

Child tugs at Mom's coat.

"Mommy. Mommy, I want to go to the bathroom."

Mom suddenly tunes in.

"Okay, dear. I'm sorry. I didn't realize. Come on, let's go."

Notice the order. Attention first . . . bathroom trip second. Now I ask you, what child will not learn that the magic words *I want to go to the bathroom* will rapidly attract otherwise absent attention? Not many. Of course, most kids are smart enough to learn that this trick can't be overdone or it will wear thin, but during an attention-withdrawal crisis it's any port in a storm. I know. I have been on the giving and receiving end of that ploy, depending on the stage of my life. I wish I had a quarter for all the times I've been dragged off to the bathroom by one of my kids, only to find that the fruit of their labor was about as impressive as the rainfall in Baghdad. The lesson here is that attention-seeking behavior can be employed either as a means to an end or as a way of getting attention for attention's sake. It is the latter situation that accounts for the nuisance variety of attention seeking.

Dogs will not seek human attention if they already have a surfeit of it, though dogs' needs for attention vary. People who pamper their dogs virtually all of the time may experience quite the opposite of attention seeking; they may find that the dog sometimes attempts to rid itself of their attention. Some dogs move away from their owners or even growl at them when overindulged, simply to get themselves some space. Dominant dogs tend to be independent and frequently growl to ward off unwelcome advances. Attention for dogs, like candy or hard-to-get toys for children, only becomes a treasure when rationed and/or in short supply. This is one of the tenets of the "Nothing in Life Is Free" program used to treat dominance aggression. At the other end of the spectrum are needy, dependent dogs that crave attention because of an insecure past or because their owners are absorbed in their own whirlwind lifestyles. These latter dogs resort to all kinds of antics to get the attention they desire and may become quite overbearing.

Practically any behavior can be reinforced as an attention-getting behavior. Whether we realize it or not, attention is one of the key rewards that we provide to dogs in training as well as during the course of everyday life. When we tell a dog to "Sit" and praise it and pet it for a job well done, we are actually engaging several reinforcers of the desired response. We are looking at the dog, talking to the dog (in high praising tones), and also delivering a powerful tactile reward. All this amounts to attention. Appropriately directed and rationed, such attention can reinforce the behaviors we desire from our dogs and maintain a healthy human-to-dog relationship. However, if a regular supply of well-timed rewards and attention is lacking, dogs can learn to pester for attention and can be very insistent. Jumping up on owners and guests is one of those attention-seeking behaviors that occurs all too frequently in greeting. Fair enough; if your dog is petite and you and your guests don't object to its jumping up, you don't have a problem, but it is important to realize that jumping up occurs because it is rewarded. The reward is your attention. Even if you push your dog away and yell "No," the dog is not discouraged and may even start having fun as you become more animated. It is hardly surprising that the dog comes back for more. To yell and push a dog like this does nothing to resolve the problem and often makes things worse.

What does work to curb jumping up is masterly inactivity from all those imposed upon, the zero-sum game. I advise people to become silent, "turn to stone," or walk away when their dog jumps up on them. Though this treatment initially may exacerbate the jumping up as the dog tries to reactivate a reward system that once worked, the behavior will eventually extinguish because the rewards, attention and touch, are no longer supplied. Okay, I hear practical folk snort, but what if I have a large dog pummeling me like a ninety-pound sack of potatoes on a pogo stick? Do I have to allow myself to be knocked to the ground while I wait for the treatment to work? The answer is no, you don't have to get beaten up by your dog. There is a simple way in which jumping up can be rapidly and humanely curtailed for the gravitationally challenged and those with fine clothes or a delicate skin. I refer to the use of negative reinforcement by means of a head halter. The idea is that the dog will increase the frequency of four-on-the-floor behavior (all feet on the ground) in order to avoid the mildly disconcerting effect of having its head drawn to one side by the halter when it jumps up on someone. This is negative reinforcement. Because of the way head halters are designed, they send a clear message of control from the owner to the dog and require very little physical strength to operate. The noseband tightens around the dog's muzzle, delivering a message of rebuke, just like Mama used to do, and the high-riding neck band delivers pressure to the nape of the neck akin to scruffing. Many trainers refer to these halters as power steering, but many don't often recommend them. I never did understand why halters are not more widely employed. If a halter is used, however, it is important also to address the reason for a dog's overexuberant tendencies and attention seeking. This entails providing ample exercise, a more entertaining environment, and plenty of attention at the right times.

Some owners of jumping dogs are told to knee their dogs in the chest or to stand on their back paws to discourage or punish the behavior. As jumping is probably something of a compliment, this treatment is rude, inappropriate, and unnecessary. Aside from this, punishment of this nature does not teach the dog anything that will stick and on its own does nothing to address the cause of the behavior. To knee a dog to the ground and then smile and praise it for staying down is not my idea of a "positive" training method, as is sometimes claimed (because reward is involved).

Aside from jumping up, there are several other behaviors that are reinforced as attention-getting behaviors that patient owners merely tolerate or suffer when performed to excess. There's whining, nudging to be petted, face licking, hand nibbling, barking at people, and that old chestnut of a game, "keep away." Remember, though, as I run through a few examples of these behaviors, that I'm not expecting dogs to be saints (Saint Bernards excluded). Just as the child who never cries is an anomaly, so dogs that never engage in any of these behaviors are unusual and in some respects pitiful.

With attention-seeking behaviors, more often than not, we are talking about the degree of the invasiveness rather than the behavior itself. Dogs that nudge their owners in situations where they really *do* need something from them are not being a nuisance. They are merely communicating this need. Dogs that constantly nudge their owners for no good reason, however, can be real pests. I call these dogs nudgers. They are not the kind of dogs you want to have around when you have genteel company visiting and are trying to make polite conversation while holding a cup of tea in one hand and a plate of cucumber sandwiches in the other. The chances are that everything will go flying, however many times you say "Off," "No," "Leave it," or whatever else.

Nudgers just don't take no for an answer. They don't appear to be able to take a hint. The reason for this is that they are actually oblivious to your plight because they are so enrapt in their own. Bigger dogs are best at attracting attention in this way and are often impossible to ignore. Large, dominant dogs can be particularly pushy when they are demanding attention. Little dogs can also be problematic, but most are not able to reach up far enough to be really good nudgers. Some develop other winning ways, however, such as bouncing around and yipping. That usually gets them picked up. From their new thronely position they are then able to engage in phase two of the assault, face licking and line-of-vision blocking. These hand-held dogs seem to revel in the fact that their owners have to crane or arch away from them to avoid their quicksilver tongues or to maintain visual contact with their friends during a conversation. This very avoidance reaction communicates to the dog that its message is finally getting through and that its lack-of-attention problem is finally . . . er . . . well . . . licked.

Then there's barking. Barking can be used in exactly the same way to attract attention. My neighbor's dog, Fletch, barks, and barks, and barks to get the attention of a would-be stick or ball thrower. Fletch has learned that some people have limited noise tolerance and will interrupt what they are doing to attend to what she wants (as if they didn't know). Is it a problem in this case? Not really. Fletch's attention seeking only occurs periodically when she wants to have some fun with people and when they are ignoring her. It's really quite understandable and amounts to nothing more than overenthusiastic vocal communication from a dog that loves people and sticks to otherwise stick-in-the-mud, boring human adults. Other dogs overuse this particular attention-getting ploy. Such dogs can be said to be behaving badly but, in most instances, it's the dog's owners who should shoulder most of the blame.

One relatively common, and to some extent understandable, attention-seeking behavior manifests itself as the game "keep away." The rules of this game (for a dog) are first to find something that really seems to animate people, like stealing a pair of socks, grab the object, and run like the wind. This game produces hours of seemingly endless fun and causes human adults to race around yelling wildly and waving their arms about. To the dog, the owners probably appear to be enjoying the game too. Now, from the human point of view, it is important to realize that dogs that entertain themselves this way are probably in need of the right kind of attention for doing something worthwhile, and providing attention at the right time is part of the ultimate solution. Also, as dogs are very fast and hard to catch, you have to ask yourself, "Is the chase really worth it?" Let the dog have the tissue or the towel if you can possibly bear to part with it and if the dog is not actually ingesting great gobs of the material. By not chasing the dog you remove your attention from the equation and reduce the thrill of the game to practically zilch.

If you could do this every time, you would be home and dry but, of course, there are some stolen objects that you just can't ignore, such as cooked bones (the dog may crunch them up, swallow the pieces, and develop intestinal problems) or your credit cards (without them you would never be able to pay the veterinary bills to have the remnants recovered). Under these circumstances some kind of intervention is necessary to resolve the problem, but the correct solution does not entail chasing the dog. It is far better to change the whole tenor of the situation by coming up with some other, more interesting, activity to replace the unwanted behavior. You could call your dog to you and reward it handsomely for obeying. You could stand by the food cupboard or back door to make your command more tantalizing. You could get your dog's lead and get ready to leave. You could even open the door and ring the doorbell. Whatever you do, you shouldn't chase an attention-seeking dog. Chasing a dog when it has stolen something will simply ensure more of the same behavior in the future.

So far I have discussed some reasonably normal and some excessive, nuisance-level attention-seeking behaviors, but there are other complex, almost pathological, behaviors that arise in dogs from a desire to be noticed. These problems, which are really too severe to be labeled nuisance behaviors, are often the ones that behaviorists think of when the phrase *attention-seeking behavior* comes to mind. One of the difficulties in diagnosing these maladies is that sometimes they appear similar to behavioral seizures and canine compulsive disorders (there may even be some overlap between the various conditions). Take fly snapping, for example. In this bizarre behavior, affected dogs appear to focus on imaginary flies hovering above their heads and snap at these illusions, initially to the amusement of their puzzled owners. At some point, however, owners realize that there is a genuine problem as the behavior occurs with greater frequency and intensity than seems healthy for the dog. The dog may start out snapping at real flies, only to discover that the performance has attracted its owner's attention. Thus the behavior is reinforced. I know a couple of owners who are convinced that their dogs started snapping at imaginary flies because of this.

In support of this contention, I have successfully treated one fly-snapping dog by advising the owners to withdraw their attention while it was so engaged. The dog responded dramatically and has not relapsed since. I told the owners to make a neutral sound (using a tuning fork or by striking a note on their piano) and then leave the room whenever the dog began to engage in the behavior. The neutral sound, a "bridging stimulus," was used to make an explicit connection between the dog's behavior and the owners' departure. It worked. This dog's owners had been told by their own vet that the behavior had neurological roots, was progressive, and that the dog would probably succumb to some nervous disorder in due course. Needless to say, the owners were delighted with the results of the attention-withdrawal treatment and wondered how their vet could have been so wrong. But the vet wasn't too far off base. There are about five publications in the veterinary literature in which fly snapping has been linked to seizure activity and has been shown to respond to treatment with antiseizure medication. I myself have witnessed apparently seizure-related, barbiturate-responsive fly-snapping behavior in a bull terrier with a demonstrably abnormal (epileptiform) electroencephalogram (EEG).

Finally, some pundits (including myself) believe that some cases of fly-snapping behavior represent a form of canine compulsive disorder related to predation and often recommend antiobsessional medication as part of the treatment plan (see "C—Compulsive Behavior"). In favor of the compulsive-predatory theory, one coydog (coyote-beagle crossbreed) I know that is an occasional fly snapper has the behavior exacerbated each time it is fitted with a flea collar. The flea collar contains a poison that increases the concentration of the neurotransmitter acetylcholine in the brain and acetylcholine is responsible, amongst other things, for enhancing a predator's prey drive.

Treatmentwise it's whatever works in a particular situation, starting with simple measures and escalating to more-involved approaches. I usually start by having owners withdraw their attention when the dog is engaging in the behavior and then go from there. Whether antiobsessional medication or antiseizure medication is selected as the next step, it is imperative to optimize the dog's management and the dog's environment to minimize stress.

Light chasing or shadow chasing is another behavior that has been similarly classified as everything under the sun. Affected dogs chase lights or shadows mercilessly, sometimes to exhaustion. I have had two dogs with this condition that have responded dramatically, though not completely, to attention withdrawal. In another I had an EEG performed because of the possibility that light chasing results from seizure activity in the visual cortex, but nothing suspicious of seizure activity was found on the trace. I have had my best success treating light and shadow chasing with a combination of environmental enrichment and antiobsessional drugs. The latter finding supports a compulsive-behavior basis for this problem, but clearly there's room for more studies on this confusing behavior.

Sometimes attention-seeking behavior can be novel, complex, and really quite confusing. A neutered male cairn terrier called Andy developed a behavior that his owner, Diane Fronzac, described as fishtailing (serially jerking his back legs forward from a sitting or semi-lying position). Andy engaged in this bizarre behavior (that I never actually witnessed) several times a day, causing Diane great concern. She took him to her vet's office and the vet diagnosed partial seizures and treated Andy with the anticonvulsant phenobarbital—but he didn't improve much. Next came a trip to a veterinary neurologist for a second opinion. The neurologist confirmed seizures as the likely cause and supplemented the phenobarbital with potassium bromide (for added effect). There was still no joy in the Fronzac household.

Finally, Diane and her mother came to see me. I could understand the other vets' diagnoses and was leaning that way myself, but in the end I tried attention withdrawal as the first measure, using a duck call as a bridging stimulus before escalating to more-invasive therapies. The response was better than I dared hope for. Andy was fifty-percent better after two weeks; seventy-five-percent better after four weeks; and cured after six weeks. I weaned him of his antiepilepsy drugs and after six weeks he was not only cured but also drug free. He certainly presented an unusual manifestation of attention-getting behavior. If he could learn a complicated maneuver like "fishtailing" as an attention-seeking behavior, I don't know where the limit is. It's no wonder the Japanese retitled my last book on dog behavior *So Your Dog Is Strange*.

Food Stealing

Of course, attention seeking is not the only form of behavior that can be deemed nuisance behavior. Sometimes dogs get themselves into trouble behind their owners' backs. One such problem behavior is raiding countertops, otherwise known as food stealing. Now, you don't need a Ph.D. in criminology to know why dogs steal food, or one in psychology to know why people inadvertently leave food out. Voilà: a problem.

I have heard some outrageous food-stealing stories in my time, involving the disappearance of whole cooked birds and roasts of beef that were only just out of the owners' eyesight. It was therefore with great interest that I noticed my sister Angela's dog, a German shepherd, walking around nonchalantly beside a countertop laden with the kind of food about which most dogs only dream. Not once did this dog raise its head even close to this veritable feast, and yet no one was in attendance. So I asked Angela, "How come Fawn doesn't swipe a piece of meat? What have you done to make her so well-behaved?"

Angela told me the story. "When Fawn was young, around six months of age, we caught her trying to steal something from the table one day, so Peter [Angela's husband] and I decided to rig up a booby trap for her. What we did was to build a towering pyramid of pots and pans and attach a piece of meat to the center pan by means of a piece of fine black thread. We placed the piece of meat right on the edge of the counter and went to bed. We hadn't been in bed for more than five minutes when we heard a tremendous crash as the pots toppled over and bounced around all over on the tiled floor. Somewhere amidst the ruckus we heard Fawn howl in terror and we ran downstairs to see what was going on. She was sitting pressed into a corner of the kitchen, shivering in fright and whimpering. We comforted her and cleaned up the mess and from that day on she never raided a countertop again."

The reason why this punishment was such an effective strategy was that no one's presence was required to make it work. It was "remote" punishment. If Angela had trained Fawn to "Leave it" when there was food on the counter, Fawn would have just taken her operation underground; that is, she would have only stolen while their backs were turned. Things in my sister's favor were the breed and age of her dog. A dominant five-year-old Rottweiler would have been much less impressionable and might have attacked the pans to teach them a good lesson.

Attacking Mail

Talking about attacking inanimate objects, some dogs attack the mail and shred it. This can be quite exasperating. Perhaps the reason dogs shred mail is that mail is foreign and viewed as invasive by the dog, though I believe that dogs that do this are usually territorially aggressive and, given the opportunity, would like to shred the mailman's coattails and pant legs, too. In this case the arriving mail could be the substrate for displaced aggression usually intended for the unreachable, unassailable mail carrier. The best treatment for mail bashing by your dog is avoidance; pick up your mail from the post office or arrange an alternative drop-off site at your home. Because many mailmacerating dogs are anxious characters, desensitization is the crux of behavior therapy, though the program is fairly demanding and is time-consuming. The goal of therapy is to inure the dog to the mailman to negate the "foreign" concept the dog has developed of him and the mail he carries. Counterconditioning by means of food treats can be invaluable in this war of perceptions. The program goes much better if the door facilitates an unobstructed view of the mailman. It is also more likely to be successful if the mailman did not previously use Mace on the dog.

Digging

Another nuisance behavior that troubles some owners is the digging of holes in the yard. Some dogs are champions at this "destructive" behavior, particularly those that dig holes in the wild to survive, such as northern breeds. Some hole digging is to be expected in an outdoor dog confined in the yard. Dogs dig to escape from heat and cold, to excavate or bury bones, and sometimes just for fun. But there is no denying that the behavior can reach compulsive proportions in some dogs. I have seen yards that look like they have been the targets of mortar fire or like London bomb sites after the Blitz.

In terms of understanding this behavior I agree with trainer/behaviorist Bill Campbell. In one of his books he tells a story about the treatment of a dog that was digging holes in the yard. During his interview with the owner he asked the $64,000 question: Where did the first hole appear? The answer was that it was right outside the back door. And why was the dog outside the back door, he asked? Because it jumped up on people and couldn't be controlled, came the reply. Campbell interpreted this dog's digging to indicate frustration about being shut outside. The dog wanted to be inside with its owners and ended up digging holes as a displacement behavior. The hole digging eventually reached epidemic proportions and there were holes all over the yard. The treatment: to teach the dog to behave well indoors so that he could remain inside when visitors arrived. Once this was achieved, the hole digging ceased.

Maybe not all hole digging is caused by dogs not being trained to greet visitors properly, but the message about frustration and boredom is definitely one to take home. Whenever problems of this nature are encountered, it is best to review the whole situation and lifestyle of the dog involved and to make changes for the better. Trying to stop the behavior by putting wire under the holes or by using remote electric shock makes no sense at all.

Balking

One last nuisance behavior that I will discuss before concluding this topic involves balking on walks. Balking may not seem like such a big problem to someone who has not experienced it with his dog, but I can tell you that in the course of my travels I have come across several very unhappy campers who have practically pleaded with me to help them out of their abyss. One such case involved an eight-and-a-half-month-old neutered male Jack Russell called Duncan. Duncan's New York City-based owner, Mary Maguire, a first-time dog owner, acquired him from her sister, a Jack Russell breeder, at the age of four months. All was well for a couple of weeks, but then Duncan began to balk when taken outside for walks. He would simply plonk his derriere on the ground and refuse to move. This would occur up to ten to fifteen times per walk, anywhere from right outside her apartment door, to the lobby, and anywhere outside the building. This was very frustrating for his new owner, who had no notion of how to handle the situation. She simply waited him out, which took about five minutes each time. In desperation, she would sometimes pick him up and carry him. Walks were no fun for her anymore. It was time to seek professional help.

Help came sequentially in the form of five trainers and finally a local behavior specialist. The advice Mary received included bribing Duncan to move with food treats, coaxing him in dulcet tones, issuing stern commands, applying leash corrections, plain old dragging him along, and the use of a dog halter. But little Duncan, though better at the threshold and in the lobby, still balked on the street, and often enough to constitute a traffic problem. That was when I became involved. Mary sent me a full report of his behavior and called me up to make sure I understood. I read the notes with interest: "balks consistently at certain places"; "balks when I go in a different direction from usual"; "balks when we leave parks"; "aggression to strangers"; "doesn't like children, drunks, or loud men"; "barks and lunges at strange dogs"; "doesn't like fireworks"; "follows me around the house."

Duncan was a fearful dog that, among other things, had not taken kindly to the streets of Manhattan. Not surprising, really, for one of his disposition. Who could blame him for being skittish, with all the hustle and bustle, the noise of traffic, and the strange encounters he no doubt had on the street? Duncan's reaction: a classical fear response—he simply hunkered down and became immobile.

The treatment I planned for Duncan was to build his confidence both inside and outside his home and to desensitize him to his fear of strangers and situational fear of the street. Considering Duncan's age, I believed he would learn quickly and gain enough confidence to walk properly along the sidewalks while on leash. I was concerned, however, that he might have some lingering memories of prior aversive events that could escalate as fear aggression as he matured.

Although Ms. Maguire had to cancel her initial appointment at the last minute, I finally did get to see Duncan when he was one year of age. As I had surmised, his balking eventually melted away as his confidence grew; he could at last circumnavigate the busy streets of Manhattan without sitting down on the job. Unfortunately, however, my second prediction also came to pass. In fact, the only reason his owner finally committed to make the long haul to my office from the Big Apple was that Duncan had started lunging at and attempting to bite children and strangers when approached or petted. Fear aggression was now the primary concern. I advised Ms. Maguire on how to deal with this Jekyll and Hyde-style metamorphosis (see "A—Aggression" and Appendix) but warned her that he would probably always be a bit shy (as well as "sharp") and would have to be managed carefully in the company of strangers. Sometimes I hate being right.

One story of balking with a totally different cause and treatment involved a sensitive toy breed that balked on walks after a dental "prophy" procedure. Following the experience the poor wee bairn was delivered home a shaken, nervous wreck, refusing to stand, walk, or eat on its own. The dog's owner was struck with guilt and grief and pampered her pet to an impressive and almost complete recovery. Complete, that is, except that the dog would not walk on lead, plumping itself down and refusing to move. The concerned owner went to her vet, who said something about possible physical injury and pain and suggested an X ray. The owner then went to the breeder for a second opinion. "What do you think is wrong with my dog?" the owner asked. "I think there's nothing wrong with him," the breeder said. "He's at it. Don't cater to this behavior. I want you to take him down to the park, attach your lead, and start walking." The owner was surprised at this apparently hard-line approach, but she did what she was told. She took her dog for a drag, striding along with the creature skidding behind her in the dirt. After thirty yards or so it was obvious that the scheme had worked. The dog suddenly started to run along next to her and for the rest of the walk and ever since has been right as rain.

The breeder was right. It wasn't a pain that was causing the problem. The only pain in this case was the dog itself, sitting down on the job to attract its owner's sympathy and attention. When the strategy didn't work anymore the dog realized he'd been rumbled and quit.

Conclusion

I could expand further on nuisance behaviors, but you probably have the drift by now. Many of them stem from attention seeking, but others are just dogs being dogs, sometimes fueled by particular wants or needs. In all cases it is important to review the facts carefully to determine the precise nature of the problem. Sometimes I have to explore quite broadly to elucidate contributing causes, which may range from factors relating to the dog's exercise level and daily routine to the adverse impact of environmental and developmental experiences. And remember, whether a behavior is considered a nuisance behavior or not depends on the observer's perception. One person's meat is another one's poison. Some folks like their dogs to keep nudging them and paying them attention, and others couldn't care less if the yard gets dug up. "Problem? What problem?" their response might be to some of the behaviors I've discussed. I agree that many of the behaviors mentioned above can present at non-nuisance levels and others could be construed as positively endearing. Take Djelias's behavior, for example. Old nudger and singer that she was, her humans wouldn't have wanted to change her for the world and I know for a fact that she's sorely missed.

OBEDIENCE TRAINING

Most people who get a new puppy try to do everything they can to get it a good start in life. The initial advice on what to do usually comes from breeders or pet-store staff.

"Don't forget to take him to your vet for deworming and his shots . . ." the staffer might call out to the new owners as they leave, ". . . and remember to take him for puppy training after he is vaccinated."

Balancing advice on what to feed, the importance of keeping the pup inside at first, crate training, house training, and various other bits of first-aid advice, they stumble out of the establishment on circuit overload and head for home. The weeks pass and eventually the veterinary side of things is under control. Their pup is now roadworthy, fully protected against most of the serious infections that can afflict a neophyte. Around this time, or shortly after, the pup's owners often begin to notice that their new charge is starting to develop some mildly annoying behaviors such as nipping, chewing, jumping up, running away on walks, excessive yappiness, and so on. They hardly need a postcard to remind them of the breeder's parting words on puppy training, and if any one of their many friends hasn't enthusiastically endorsed a particular training operation, this is when they turn to the pet section of the yellow pages and let their fingers do the walking.

If you stand outside the doors of a puppy-training operation and watch the novice owners arrive, it's like watching the two-by-two approach to Noah's ark. Cars pull into the lot and expectant owners of all varieties exit their vehicles, spend a few moments apprehending their dogs, and then weave across the parking lot while their little bundles of joy zig and zag between their legs, almost tripping them up. These untrained dogs act virtually independently of their owners, stopping to investigate this and that on the way and periodically veering off in different directions until they come to a jerking halt at the end of their tethers. Some valiant owners discreetly submit to the uneven struggle and carry their dogs the final few yards to the training center.

Excitement is high in the arena as the dogs investigate each other in the melee that ensues. Then the games begin. Half the fun for the owners is meeting people in the same or a worse predicament than themselves. It's like group therapy for new owners—puppy owners anonymous. "Hi. My name's Mike and I have a basenji." Instructors lecture groups of ten to fifteen people at a time, periodically stopping to assist an exasperated owner who is having exceptional difficulties, break up a tussle between pups, or direct a cleanup operation.

The initial gist of training is to direct the desired response with food (food—magnet; dog—iron), or to physically assist the pup into position by means of so-called placement techniques. Either way, owners are taught to reward a job well done with warm praise, properly directed petting (under the chin or stroking the side of the dog's face in the same direction the hair grows), and/or morsels of food. In this way pups are taught to sit, wait, walk to heel, lie down, and come. These are fairly noble goals when you consider that highly trained police dogs are only required to exhibit refined versions of the same skills in public demonstrations and by so doing usually draw the oohs and aahs of the crowd. The long remote "down-stay" of Schutzhund training is often a stumbling block even for these highly trained dogs.

As simple as the principles of training appear on paper, they are not that easy for the inexperienced owner to grasp. Body language, voice intonation, and coordination are all critical to success. Many people do not properly master the requisite skills immediately, and some never will. It takes practice, practice, and practice and requires a certain natural flair. Trainers themselves invariably have this flair, which is why they do what they do. To me, trainers always appear very confident (sometimes for good reason and sometimes not), have naturally assertive ways, and have body language to match. Owners and dogs take one look at these individuals and know that there is not much point in resistance—they must toe the line. To demonstrate their prowess, trainers often bring their own highly coached dogs to class and put them through their paces to the openmouthed amazement of the amateurs before them. Such bravado always reminds me of a guitar tutor I once had who periodically astonished me by playing elaborate riffs. I suppose such solos confirmed his competence and should have provided me with a goal, but instead I found myself intimidated by the huge gulf between our skill levels. I recently heard of a trainer who had four large dogs (Dobermans, I believe) stationed at the four corners of his training room like sentinels. None of these dogs moved a muscle unless the trainer commanded them to. Very impressive, if not a bit unnerving for the clients.

One hour per week and eight weeks later into training, owners have often mastered some basic skills under the direction of the trainer, and pups graduate with a certificate of accomplishment that can be proudly displayed on their kennels. Some pups do very well in training class, apparently enjoying the whole experience and performing like little soldiers. Others are more unruly and learn less—though they still receive certificates. (It's a bit like grade school, where everyone is a winner.) At the end of the classes the owners contentedly weave their way back to their cars with their pups darting between their legs, almost tripping them up. Déjà vu all over again.

I am not implying that puppy training is a fruitless affair, even for these characters. Far from it. The experiences encountered and the learning that results are necessary forerunners of what should be a continuing process of lifelong learning for both dog and owner. Dogs that learn to sit and come at these boot camps retain at least ghostly images of the commands for many years later, but unless owners follow through at home their dogs will become rusty, only obeying occasionally and never, it seems, when a prompt response is needed. What *is* required by way of continuing education is to reinforce and build on learning that has occurred in class by means of brief daily training sessions and the routine use of one-word commands followed by immediate praise. To omit this all-important follow-up is like not practicing a guitar after the first ten introductory lessons—you may know where the notes are and how to play a couple of chords but you still can't play anything worth listening to (I know). Likewise, "been to puppy training" as a qualification is no more a guarantee of good behavior than the famous "BTA" degree (meaning been to America) signals business prowess for a European returning home.

With reference to training adult dogs, some owners say, "But I don't want a highly trained dog," or "I just don't need that degree of control." I can understand this view. And to some extent, these owners have a point. There are several things owners are asked to master in most training classes that are not really necessary—such as having their dogs walk "to heel" when all that is required is for the dog to walk on lead without pulling. Heeling is show stuff and is quite unnecessary for garden-variety dog owners. Even having your dog sit squarely on command or make sharp right or left turns on lead is not really necessary.

Some training, however, is essential if you wish to control your dog in difficult situations and avoid awkward or dangerous moments. Only three dependable responses are needed to ensure the requisite control. The dog should be trained to come when called; to stop doing something that it shouldn't be doing on command; and to lie down, wait, or stay when instructed. To have a dog obedient in these three commands creates a well-behaved and safe dog—and a happy owner. If your dog comes when you call, you can keep him out of trouble; if he stops fooling around or otherwise getting into trouble when instructed, he will be a better canine citizen; and if he stays in one place when directed, he will be a safer, more respectful, and more enjoyable pet.

In training there are two factors to consider: owner factors and dog factors. Most trainers acknowledge that they are not training dogs so much as they are training owners. With an owner who is quick on the uptake and a dog that is receptive to training, everyone is a winner. It's a marriage made in heaven. The combination of a good owner and a difficult dog, or an average dog and a less-than-adroit owner, can produce good results, too. Problems occur when both parties are out of "sync," and in this situation trainers have their work cut out for them.

Unfortunately, some trainers use increasing levels of coercion in an attempt to fit these square-peg dogs into round holes. The time-honored escalation is from flat collar to choke collar, from choke collar to prong collar. To check aggression, some even resort to stringing dogs up (the so-called hanging method), whirling them around on the end of the lead ("the helicopter"), or using electric shocks. One trainer I know treats dogs with "food aggression" by positioning the dog and a bowl of food under a tree branch and having the owner approach the food bowl as if to take it away. The dog is controlled by a long rope attached to its collar and passed over the branch, to be held by two strong men in nearby bushes. When the dog begins to growl or shows any signs of aggression, it is hoisted up a few feet into the air and allowed to hang there pirouetting for several long seconds before being lowered back down to the ground. This procedure is repeated as often as necessary until the dog no longer growls. Even one of our former students, a large-breed aficionado, told me that when one of his dogs growled at him he strung it over a door and let it hang there until it "almost saw its maker." Apparently this produced the desired effect because the dog did not growl at him again. I want to be clear about this, I am totally against such methods and don't believe that the end justifies the means.

Harsh training techniques used to be applied to children, but fortunately such methods are now considered abusive and are outlawed. I grew up in an era when "Spare the rod and spoil the child" was the axiom of the day. In my school we had our knuckles rapped with a wooden ruler for being out of line; we were "slippered" (beaten with a size-thirteen gym shoe) for talking out of turn; and were "caned" (beaten with a bamboo cane) for more serious offenses. The threat of corporal punishment did keep many of us honest for most of the time, I'll grant you, but looking back I can see that there are more appropriate methods by which we could have been discouraged from our crimes.

So it is with dog training. Hard-line methods can produce the goods, as they did with us schoolchildren, but at the price of mutual

understanding and real respect. I believe that in our school our coop-
eration would have been better ensured by means of positive reinforcement of desired behaviors and appropriate punishments selected to fit
the crimes; time out for social misdemeanors; loss of privileges for
breaking rules; early bed for talking after lights out; and so on. Benevolent solutions to problems of recalcitrant dogs can be engineered
along similar lines. Desired behaviors should be rewarded immediately, with failed responses and unwanted behaviors punished by
omission of some valued or sought-after resource. For heinous crimes,
time out can be an effective punishment, though a cold shoulder works
well, too.

Once a pup has been taught to sit it should be required to sit to
obtain praise, petting, or food treats. Employing an intermittent schedule of reward will reinforce the response, increasing the likeliness of
its occurrence. The reward that is selected is important, too. If food is
used it should be a favorite food: not just kibble, the ten-dollar reward;
not just chicken, the fifty-dollar reward; but freeze-dried liver or
cheese, the one-hundred-dollar reward. Some dogs couldn't care less
about food, however, but would almost die for a tennis ball, attention,
or petting. Whatever is a particular dog's primary motivator should be
used as the reward in training by positive reinforcement. I have seen
police dogs complete a circuit without obtaining any reward except
petting and a kind word following successful completion of the course.
To make the dog this grateful for such a meager reward it is important
to ration it carefully. You can't pet a dog whenever it wants to be
petted and then expect it to jump through hoops for a scratch on the
chest.

With respect to the two different approaches to training, forced
versus reward training, there's nothing new under the sun. A training
book from the turn of the century describes gentlemen's training and
ladies' training as two alternative methods, the former based on coercion and the latter on direction and encouragement. During the Second
World War the armed services appointed servicemen to look after and
train military dogs. Like the recruits themselves, these dogs were
trained using fairly uncompromising techniques. After all, there was
no room for error. Following the war some of these dogs could not be
successfully rehabilitated because they had become aggressive. This

doesn't speak well for the training methods used or the dogs' psychological welfare. Perhaps desperate needs warrant desperate measures—and (supposedly) all is fair in love and war—but domestic dog owners do not have such pressing requirements.

Postwar, some military trainers continued to practice in "civvy street," establishing training operations in several major cities. Successful practitioners were joined by apprentices, and so the same skills were transmitted to another generation of trainers who knew nothing of tanks and planes—only how to get a dog to obey . . . on the double. Alpha rolls (rolling and holding the dog down on its back), scruffing, and grabbing the dog by the jowls were commonly used strategies and became the three R's of this type of training. The message was, dominate or be dominated. One athletic trainer I know thinks nothing of leaping on a growling Doberman and wrestling it into a subordinate (supine) position amid the clacking of its jaws. I know it can be argued that dogs deal with each other in similar ways, but we are not dogs, and I don't believe we should stoop to physical, combative methods when more subtle and more humane techniques work as well, if not better. It is always better to command respect than to demand it.

In the 1970s a revolution spread through the training world in the form of the late Barbara Woodhouse and her "Woodhouse way" of training. Woodhouse, a physician's wife, had a lot of time to spend with dogs and, adopting a more benign version of military training, delighted a nation or two with her apparently novel techniques and quaint phrases (such as "walkies" and "hurry up"), not to mention her trademark (a heavy-gauge choke collar) and philosophy: "There's no such thing as a bad dog, just a bad owner." Though a choke-chain exponent, she always argued that it was not the collar being jerked that made the dog respond but the sound of the chain as the links slid through each other. I am not so sure about this. I *do* know that a noiseless thin-linked collar, especially placed high up on the dog's neck, produces the most dramatic results, suggesting that mechanics rather than acoustics are primarily involved.

I don't mean to detract from Barbara Woodhouse's contribution. She was a philosopher and an innovator in her own right who performed wonders in the training idiom of her time. Her influence has continued to flourish since her death. Woodhouse techniques used today vary only slightly from those originally described by the great lady and are similar to what was referred to as gentlemen's training at the turn of the century. The difference between training by the Woodhouse way and gentlemen's training (or military training) is really one of presentation and degree. I remember, back in England, seeing Barbara Woodhouse on TV, striding along in front of a rose-covered cottage, warbling the unforgettable and inimitable expression "walkies" to the dog at her side. The novice dog trotted next to her as if the two were joined at the hip. On taking the lead for the first time, Woodhouse trainers always march off with the dog on their left, chattering benignly. "Let's go. Good boy, Pogo. All right. What a good dog. I'm so proud of you." What the dog doesn't know, but will shortly discover, is that the trainer will not stop until ready to do so and will make sharp right turns every twenty yards or so. If the dog does not trot nicely at his side, it will feel a fairly strong tug of the choker around its neck, and if it fails to anticipate the sudden right turns it will receive a nasty jolt. Usually one run up and down is enough to convince most dogs that these trainers mean business.

Dogs respond to body language, not reasoning, and the language they are perceiving here indicates that they had better pay attention—or else. Following the initial surprise, most dogs toe the line quite nicely, much to the delight of their exuberant owners, who are often overwhelmed by the trainer's immediate influence on their formerly unruly pet. Now it's just a matter of explaining to the owner how it's done, though it is the trainer's mind-set that helps achieve the end result—not just some protocol to be followed by rote. The process of transmitting this "my-way-or-the-highway" message to the dog may appear quite innocuous from the sidelines. If the trainer says "sit" and the dog doesn't respond, a mild jerk of the choke chain reminds the dog who is in charge. If there is still no response, a second, sharper signal is then delivered with lightning speed and quick release. If things get really bad, the trainer might push the collar up higher on the neck and bounce up and down a few times with tension applied to the lead (not so good for the old vertebrae). Realizing the trainer is not fooling around, the dog sits. Unfortunately, many owners just don't have what it takes and once outside the sphere of the trainer's influence find that their dogs revert to their original unruly ways. You only have to stand by our reception desk for five minutes to see what I mean, as owners of previously trained dogs command "Sit . . . sit . . . sit . . ." to their unheeding hounds while they struggle to keep them in check and pay the bill simultaneously.

British Prime Minister William Gladstone once said of opposition party leader Benjamin Disraeli, "The man has a smile like the silver plate on a coffin." I have thought of this expression when I have seen "extreme" trainers at work. This hard-line training is sometimes performed under the guise of positive training because reward is involved. The word *punishment* is hardly mentioned. Instead the euphemism *correction* is used to describe the method of castigation. More accurate terminology would probably send most owners packing.

I must admit I don't much like physical methods of dog training. I am not alone, either. Dr. Dennis Fetko, alias Dr. Dog, a Ph.D. canine behaviorist in California, says that the word *jerk,* as it is used in dog training, is not a verb—it is a noun (presumably to describe those who rely on this method). This said, there are many good trainers who use a combination of approaches when training dogs, and their approaches might happen to include the carefully rationed use of leash corrections. Such trainers employ these corrections only in dealing with certain (dominant) types of adult dogs and carefully ration the punishment to suit the occasion. To know how and when to use one training method over another is a skill in itself, and to do this successfully, the trainer must be highly skilled at interpreting canine body language. This is the only scenario in which I find punishment-based techniques even semiacceptable.

Let's suppose for a moment that you have a timid or even a run-of-the-mill mutt and are a responsible pet owner who simply wants to have some control over his (or her) pet. Let's also suppose that you have an objection to the use of force in training, as you have read some pretty worrying things about choke chains and prong collars. What alternatives are available for you? The first that bears some discussion is the head halter, a device that has evolved over the years from prototypes, the Come Along and the Alpha M, to modern-day equivalents such as the Halti and the Gentle Leader. Such head halters deliver a biologically appropriate signal to the dog that ensures the utmost control. An adjustable nose loop tightens when gentle tension is applied to the lead, sending a message of authority in just the way Mama used to do—via the muzzle. Simultaneously, gentle pressure is applied to the scruff region by a high-riding neck band—again, a biologically appropriate signal of authority.

The beauty of head halters is that they never have to be jerked and are virtually impossible to abuse. Also, the signal they deliver to the dog has an effect like power steering, enabling even frail owners to obtain good control of their dogs. Finally, the successful application of a halter does not require the hours of training most people need if they are to learn how to deliver a well-timed "pop" with a choker. Unfortunately, some dogs do not have the physiognomy to keep halters on (Pekinese and pugs spring to mind) and others hate them with such a passion that they never tire of trying to get them off. As far as the really short-snouted dogs are concerned, they should probably be fitted with flat collars or harnesses instead. I don't see any other way around the anatomic dilemma. Application of halters earlier in life, however, would go a long way toward addressing problems of head-halter resistance. This would require a cultural shift away from the practice of graduating pups from food-reward training directly to slip collars, to a new paradigm involving head-halter acclimation. Pups take to new things much more quickly than adults and could easily be accustomed to accept halters as part of life. Introducing an eighty-pound raging bull of a dog to a head halter at the age of three is not an optimal scenario, although even this task can be accomplished without bloodshed.

In Britain, the cultural movement toward accepting halters is already underway. Some sixty percent of dogs in Britain now wear halters for the reasons outlined above, so comments like "Is that a muzzle your dog is wearing?" are much less common than they would be in the U.S. Of course, halter systems are not muzzles and do not physically prevent dogs from opening their mouths to bite, pant, eat, drink, or anything else (except perhaps to hold a tennis ball). Halters are simply control systems that allow you to gently direct your dog's behavior, pull up to enforce a "Sit," pull down to enforce a "Down," pull to the side to discourage unwanted behavior. And there you have it. Naturally, warm praise, petting, food treats, and other rewards following the desired response, whether enforced or not, will facilitate the dog's rapid response in the future when a command is given.

"On-lead" training, discussed above, is helpful to deliver a potent signal of your leadership and control to an incompletely trained dog, and dogs must learn to tolerate a lead in public for logistical reasons. Leads are also necessary in situations where there is no room for error or when rules dictate. The ultimate goal of trainers and owners, however, is to have dogs obedient off lead. "I only want him to come when I call" is one of the most common owner cries. To have a dog come to you in the park when you call, to place *your* needs over all the other exciting things that are happening, represents a very high level of training and it takes time and patience to achieve this control. The way most dog trainers handle the transition from on-lead to off-lead control is by having the owner drop the lead after a series of on-lead commands have been faultlessly obeyed. Following close-up exercises, the distance between the owner and dog is slowly increased as success permits until distant control is possible. It is a slow process. The technique undoubtedly works, but there is another, more fun, way of achieving the same level of off-lead training that owners can explore in their homes. I refer to clicker training, otherwise known as click-and-treat training. This type of training is easy to perform, produces spectacular results, and can start from the get-go without the need for preparatory work.

Clicker training was first used by the Brelands, a couple of psychologists turned professional animal trainers, in the 1950s. They used clickers as reinforcers for learning so that learning could be accurately and easily shaped. The idea was that if a reward was first paired with a click, the click would assume significance to the animal as a reward in its own right. It would signal a very specific point in time that the animal had done something right and could thus help refine training.

Cetacean trainers employed this method in training dolphins, and it has been adapted for use in a variety of species, including an assortment of zoo animals, dogs, cats, and horses. A whistle, rather than a clicker, was employed to signal reward for the dolphins when they accomplished a desired task because the sound of a whistle travels better underwater. The only training requirements aside from the whistle were a full bucket of fish and a hungry dolphin. To train dolphins literally to jump through hoops (management buffs take note), they are first rewarded for swimming through the hoop underwater, which they do almost inadvertently. On discovering that accomplishing this maneuver results in the whistle being sounded and food appearing, they try it again to see if it has the same effect. Of course, it does. Being intelligent creatures, they also try other methods of obtaining the reward, like swimming close to the hoop, but quickly find that these other excursions don't generate the same result. Hoop swimming becomes the order of the day for a hungry dolphin or, ultimately, one that just wants to get attention and have some fun. Once the hoop swimming is reliably trained, the hoop can be raised until the dolphins will break the surface of the water, and then jump progressively farther out of the water, to get through the hoop to receive the reward. Eventually the jump alone, with or without somersaults, can be rewarded. But it isn't just hoop jumping that cetaceans can be trained to do. One killer whale was trained to launch itself out of the pool, roll on its side, and urinate into a small plastic cup (for medical reasons) . . . *on command*. Note that no choke chain was necessary here, fortunately for the trainer. If you can condition a killer whale to perform complicated feats like this using only a bucket of fish and a whistle, there are few limits to what can be achieved using this method of training.

And yes, it does work in dogs. I have seen dogs trained to walk to a door and ring a bell attached to the handle to signal that they want to go out. It took about five minutes. In one clicker-training video a dog was taught to shut an open cupboard door on command in little longer than this. What I really like about this method is that it doesn't involve punishment, only reward. It is a common fallacy that you need punishment alternating with reward in order to train a dog. The proper use of basic principles of training—shaping the desired response, the correct timing and sequencing of rewards, and the introduction of various cues and signals—can achieve anything your heart desires. You don't even have to run around clicking all the time, either, as the clicker itself can be discarded once the response has been learned. Give me a clicker and kind tones any day over a choke chain and admonishments.

After all is said and done, owners have to make their own choices on how to raise their dogs, just as they have to decide how to raise their children. In an analogous way, new parents discover fairly rapidly the various options in child rearing. With children the question is, should we employ the time-honored techniques based on the philosophy "Spare the rod and spoil the child," or do we adopt the more humane approach of Drs. Spock and Brazelton? The decisions to be made in dog training are similar: Should we use traditional forced-training methods or make reward-based techniques the cornerstone of shaping the dog's behavior? Although some trainers pooh-pooh the latter approach, considering leash "corrections" indispensable, the same trainers already employ motivational techniques in puppy training, only graduating to leash corrections as pups mature. It wouldn't be a far cry for these trainers to continue the soft-shoe approach into maturity, aided by the early deployment of halters to facilitate physical control and abetted by motivational-training homework for owners between sessions.

I can hear the critics already: "Doesn't he realize that no two dogs are the same?" "Surely he knows that some dogs have to be disciplined or they will not obey and will not come to regard you as the leader." Or, "You can teach a dog using food treats but you need corrections to enforce the behavior *once* it has been learned." I understand these points of view but I think they can be addressed. It must be appreciated that some adult dogs have learned bad habits and will not respond as rapidly to motivational training as youngsters do, but they *will* learn in time. I believe that owners should be involved in training their dogs for the long haul, and not just looking for a quick and temporary fix. However, it is better to start out the way you plan to continue and begin motivational training at the earliest possible age, certainly before vaccination is complete, though public places are off limits at this time. Socialization exercises should also be encouraged during this early phase, say between six and fourteen weeks of age, to head off problems that otherwise might push owners to consider correctional approaches as a deterrent. Dominance can also be established nonconfrontationally if owners know what to do from the start— before they get themselves into trouble. It doesn't make sense to wait until a dog is growling at its owners and then start popping it with a choke or prong collar to win its respect and curtail its waywardness.

Finally, the criticism of food-training methods as only working when food is available just isn't true. If food treats and other rewards are kept in relatively scant supply and given on a variable schedule of reinforcement, their effect can be riveting. The analogy with the intermittent rewards issued by the one-armed bandits in Atlantic City or Vegas is inescapable. No amount of punishment keeps people from the gaming machines, but intermittent reward assures that they never give up. Dog training can be more entertaining and much less of a gamble if similar principles are employed.

PREDATION

We're so civilized now that it's easy to forget that as a species we once relied on hunting for our sustenance. Our forward-looking vision, athletic design, and ability for stealth and explosive bursts of speed are redundant for us now in the well-supplied supermarket aisles. Under normal circumstances all we have to do to get food is saunter idly down the lanes, selecting the required food items to deposit in our shopping carts. Where's the skill in that?

So where did our predatory instincts go? Did they simply melt away, or are they still lurking? The truth is they're more than lurking, they're alive and well in the form of blood sports and are constantly rehearsed by sports fans. Since men were the primary hunters of our species, it is not surprising they are overrepresented in the demographics of hunting, shooting, fishing, football, basketball, and baseball, making interest in these activities almost sexually dimorphic.

And what of dogs, supreme hunters that they are? Evolution has also equipped them both mentally and physically to engage in the naturally fulfilling behavior of predation; the chasing, killing, and consuming of prey. It's one of the things they do best. How do they cope when their hunting instincts are made redundant as daily rations are spooned out from a can and arrive like manna from heaven? Most know nothing of the joys of the hunt and are driven to other outlets for their pent-up urges, some acceptable to us and others not. Only a few lucky dogs who enjoy the benefits of a large, open yard do get to run and chase small, furry varmints, or get to cavort with outdoorsman owners. Chasing squirrels in the backyard or rabbits in a hedgerow provides biological fulfillment even if the dog is rarely successful in its quest. Other less fortunate dogs discharge their predatory energies onto modern-day prey facsimiles, such as joggers and cyclists, and in this way reap the rich reward that nature originally sowed in the interest of the survival of the species.

There are individual and breed differences determining which dogs have the greatest prey drive. Dogs from breeds selected for high prey drive are the most likely to show aberrations of this behavioral system, especially if their biological needs are not met. And the kind of trouble they get into depends on the precise components of the predatory sequence for which they were bred.

The predatory sequence is divided into two distinct phases: the *appetitive phase* of investigation and searching, leading to stalking, packing, herding, pursuing, and finally, killing; and the postkill *consummatory phase* of ingestive behavior. Different breeds have been selected for enhancement or attenuation of one or more components of this sequence to facilitate the various functions they were selected to perform.

Closest to the wild type are the northern breeds, which have received little selection of this type. As a result, they display a full range of predatory behaviors. Scent hounds, like the bloodhound, have been bred as supersleuths, relying on their almost incredible olfactory ability in search-and-find missions. Herding dogs, like Border collies and German shepherds, which were selected more for the searching and stalking components of predatory behavior, are less committed to the actual killing process than, say, dogs bred for ratting. With sporting breeds, like retrievers, the situation is similar to that in herding dogs, with a tendency for inhibition of final components of the predatory sequence. A "soft mouth" was always considered a desirable attribute for such dogs. Terriers, on the other hand, including bull terriers and fox terriers, were bred for *enhanced* prey drive and perseverance in the killing of rats and mice, baiting of bears and badgers, running foxes to ground, and so on. Predatory behavior surfaces as problem behavior most commonly in terriers and in herding breeds, especially if their passions are not met. The precise manifestation depends on the breed in question.

One day a couple of years ago in New Hampshire, a Staffordshire bull terrier bitch and her one-year-old "pup" escaped from their home and roamed the neighborhood, galloping through many neighbors' backyards. Now, you've heard the expression "Let the dog see the rabbit"—well, they did. It was in a hutch in someone's garden. Not to be foiled, they broke into the hutch and killed the rabbit . . . and it happened right in front of the irate owner's eyes. He launched himself from his back-door vantage point, baseball bat in hand, and descended on the dogs, yelling abuse and brandishing the bat. They may have growled at him as he threatened them but soon ran off and disappeared into the woods. But the man was livid about the atrocity that he had just witnessed and called the police, who, in turn, called the dog officer.

The police issued the dog officer a .38-caliber handgun and asked him to set off in pursuit of these now-branded killers. Luckily for the dogs, as they weaved through the trees amid a hail of bullets, the dog officer, in hot pursuit, tripped and fell down a hole in the ground, breaking his leg. The dogs got away but the rest of the story wasn't as much fun, as the authorities insisted these "vicious" dogs should be put to sleep—and the dog officer sued the dogs' owner for causing his injuries (only in America). Nobody seemed to understand that the dogs were behaving naturally. They were no more vicious than cats that kill mice or a little old lady at a fast-food restaurant demanding "Where's the beef?" Our food starts out alive, although it's often easy to forget this fact. One vegetarian plug I once read exclaimed, "I never eat anything that had parents."

This whole killer-dog syndrome was revisited recently in another of the northern New England states, Vermont. This time the dog ended up on death row for killing someone's pet goat, and a debate blew up, culminating in petitions to the governor and a media frenzy. The dog was clearly innocent of any real crime, though it, too, was labeled vicious, a killer, and psychotic. Sure, it must have been a real trauma for the pet owner to lose his little buddy in this manner, but there isn't much anyone can do to reverse nature.

Some dogs defuse their pent-up predatory energies along acceptable lines. Many retrieve tennis balls and sticks whenever the opportunity presents and some, like my neighbor's dog, will engage in this activity to the point of near obsession. There are also those "home-alone" dogs with working owners, who are not so fortunate as to have ball throwers constantly available. If these dogs are left outside in the yard for hours on end, and there happens to be a road nearby, they will frequently discover the joy of chasing cars, joggers, skateboarders, and bicyclists. For some dogs this takes the form of fence running and barking, though fenceless yards permit stealth attacks directed toward hapless passersby. I was the subject (and nearly the victim) of one of these attacks a few years ago when I was out jogging. I saw the dog slink behind me as I ran down the street. At a critical moment I spun around just in time to prevent the dog from nipping me in the thigh. I knew what was happening but was almost too late. Movement is the trigger for the hunt, so turning around and facing such a dog will often defuse the situation.

Even dogs that are wonderful with family and friends may engage in predatory chasing behavior if left alone outside. German shepherds and other herding breeds are notorious for this. I believe that shepherd dogs that chase kids on bicycles almost cannot help themselves. They probably feel something like Toad of Toad Hall when he saw his first car, though definitely not so dreamy. I have heard trainers claim that they can break this cycle. This might be possible if the owner is actually present, but in the owner's absence, nature is bound to take over and the behavior will resurface. No dog has that much self-control. The only real solution is to put a physical barrier between the dog and any potential "prey"—preferably a solid barrier so that the dog is not constantly teased by fleeting yet unattainable images. This done, it is the owner's responsibility to supply other outlets for the dog's pent-up predatory drive. Whatever activity is selected to fulfill a dog's prey drive must involve chase and retrieval of a moving object. Fly ball and Frisbee fill the bill nicely. There may be some thrill in the chase alone, especially in dogs bred for an abbreviated predatory sequence, though even in these dogs the instinct to deliver the coup de grâce may not be completely absent.

My sister told me a story about her young German shepherd, who thrilled in chasing squirrels in her backyard. Fawn never actually caught the squirrels but would chase them up trees and off the property and then bark in lengthy exclamation. Both dog and owner were satisfied with this arrangement until one day a fleeing squirrel became entwined in the tennis net. With the dog advancing from the south and the tennis net blocking the northern escape route, the squirrel was spinning its wheels in desperation. As Fawn loomed closer, the squirrel suddenly flopped down motionless, playing possum, so to speak. Fawn had never seen anything like this before and cocked her head in disbelief, creating an image of the RCA-parlaphone signature dog. My sister, an animal lover, saw the squirrel's plight and called Fawn off in a stern tone. "Leave it, Fawn. Leave it alone!" A confused but well-trained Fawn obeyed by taking a pace back and in so doing taking her eyes off the squirrel for a split second. The squirrel, making its second error of the day, then leaped at Fawn, attaching itself firmly to her lip. Fawn howled in pain and ran around in circles attempting to detach the half-crazed rodent. She was eventually successful in this quest and, having shaken it loose, now knew exactly what to do. In one fell swoop she snapped its neck with her powerful jaws. Game, set, and match to the dog. That squirrel will not be passing on its genes to the next generation. Survival of the fittest at work in 1998.

In discussing how to encourage dogs to discharge their predatory tendencies, I haven't really talked about what happens if all chances to engage in predatory behavior are thwarted by lack of opportunity. The answer is unprompted displacement behaviors that sometimes escalate to compulsive proportions. To engineer such a behavior (not that you would want to), you would take a dog with high prey drive and confine it in a crate or kennel or tie it on a short line during the early part of its life. This results in some of the saddest behavior cases we encounter. Tail chasing, light and shadow chasing, air licking, and fly catching are some of the aberrations that can result (see "C—Compulsive Behavior").

When there is no opportunity for appropriately directed predatory behavior, the tendency surfaces as either chasing behavior directed toward will-o'-the-wisp, nonexistent prey facsimiles or as self-directed predatory behavior. Any component of the predatory sequence may be evidenced in this way. I have seen video of compulsive-searching behavior in a dog that was tethered in a junkyard on a few feet of chain-link lead. While on the lead this dog would spend almost all the time searching for something (nothing, as it turned out) around the empty oil barrels that framed its outdoor prison. Other dogs chase and may mutilate their tails while yet others chase shadows or pace mindlessly. I know genetics has a bearing on the expression of these aberrant behaviors but I believe welfare issues are implicated, too, at least at one stage of these dogs' lives.

Another time when predatory instincts can go awry is when they are misdirected toward other dogs. The formula to make this happen includes a suitably motivated large breed of dog and a small dog in rapid motion within its field of vision. The hunter in predatorially deprived dogs is reflexly energized by this scene, with the result that the full force of the pursuant's frustrated prey drive is suddenly liberated. Behaviorist Dr. Valerie O'Farrell of the United Kingdom reported such a case in a manual she prepared for the British Small Animal Veterinary Association. It involved a large dog that constantly attacked smaller dogs with apparent vengeance. Dr. O'Farrell's ethological explanation of the dog's behavior afforded the owner some relief, since the owner had previously regarded her dog's actions as deviant canicidal behavior and was on the point of having her "killer" dog put to sleep. Armed with the truth, she was able to persevere, investing time and energy in containing and averting the problem with a more positive frame of mind.

Although lone dogs are driven in the solitary pursuit of prey, the effect is compounded when a pack of two or more dogs lock onto the same target. Cooperative hunting ventures are natural for dogs. Packing, first seen in the socialization period when dogs are only a few weeks old, is an allelomimetic, or copycat, behavior. "Monkey see, monkey do" just about sums it up. This behavior had important survival value to the species at one time but in the domestic situation is unnecessary and can cause some serious problems. A typical bad-news situation is what happens when a group of predatorially motivated dogs happen across a small dog or unsupervised child careening across their path. With so many canine minds at work it is much more likely that one will be inspired by the thrill of the chase and others will then be drawn into the fray by irresistible, almost magnetic natural forces. In humans, the "lynch-mob" or "gang" mentality describes analogous behavior driven by the effects of peer pressure. In some cases the power of such forces becomes overwhelming and reason is superseded. Although they are rare, there are a number of extremely unfortunate incidents each year in the United States in which groups of "wild dogs" attack and maim or kill children. The culprits are usually me-dium- to large-sized dogs with innately high prey drive that are cruis-ing neighborhoods in groups of two to six "pack" members. I was consulted about such a case recently by attorneys representing the victim of the attack.

The case involved two neighborhood Rottweilers who set on a boy on a bicycle, causing serious injuries. Luckily the incident was broken up by nearby adults or the result could have been even worse. Points of note were that the dogs were not wild dogs but belonged to someone in the same street who irresponsibly allowed them to roam off lead together. No doubt he figured that because they were nice dogs at home they wouldn't be capable of such an attack. Wrong!

Public safety concerns aside, dog owners should not allow their dogs to roam unsupervised for the dog's sake. It is an unsafe practice and the accidents that sometimes result are costly in terms of suffering that results as well as the owner's pocketbook. And there are legal implications, too. In a different case, two dogs running free on their owner's front lawn leaped the fence to attack a passing mother and her daughter. The final settlement awarded against the dogs' owner came to eight hundred thousand dollars to compensate the victims for the physical and mental suffering that resulted from the attack. That sum should be enough to make others pay attention, but it's sad that this is what it takes to make the point.

There is no doubt that predatory behavior, especially in the form of packing, can have disastrous consequences and must be contained if there is any likelihood of its occurrence. To find that your dog has a practically insatiable appetite for chasing squirrels or moving objects is a pretty good clue that the potential for problems exists, though the possible repercussions are much less severe if the dog is small and tends to inhibit its bite. The scary thing is that several breeds of dogs have the genetic potential for such predatory attacks should the planets line up correctly. And the bottom line is that if there is any reason for concern in this department, take no chances. Dog owners have no option but to understand and control their dogs' predatory behavior. There is no such thing as a dog with no prey drive, although sheep-guarding dogs, like the maremma, which have had their prey drive attenuated by selective breeding, come fairly close. Just as every dog has its day, so every dog has certain predatory requirements, however modest they may be, that must be met. It is safest and best to take a proactive approach to dealing with this potential problem area by providing outlets for your dog's predatory instincts under direct supervision. This will ensure that frustrations do not build up and spill over into unwanted, inappropriate, or even dangerous behaviors. As always, you have to know your dog and cater specifically to its needs. After all, a dog with a job will be happier and much less likely to cause problems for itself or others. That's the end of the sermon. Let us prey.

QUARRELING

One annoying, sometimes destructive, dog-eat-dog problem that occurs between dogs living in the same household is referred to as sibling rivalry. This problem, which involves chronic and apparently pointless quarreling and infighting between family dogs, centers around dominance struggles occurring as a result of an unstable pack structure within the home. In its most advanced form, sibling rivalry leads to prolonged and vicious battles between dogs and makes life thoroughly miserable and potentially dangerous for both owners and dogs. Feuding dogs can seriously injure each other during fights, to the point of necessitating veterinary attention, and owners, too, may be injured if they attempt to break up the scraps. Queen Elizabeth II fell afoul of such misfortune and was bitten when she tried to intervene in a fight between a couple of her corgis. After the incident, an animal behaviorist who had previously advised her not to intervene in such frays went public, saying that what she should have done was to interrupt the fight by dropping one of her solid-silver trays onto the floor. The advice was good but my outspoken colleague's "clanger" landed him in a right royal jam. He should have followed my grandmother's advice, "If you can't say anything nice, don't say anything at all."

Unfortunately, owners' instincts mislead them in terms of how to interpret and handle sibling rivalry. In the classic form of this condition, well-intentioned owners unwittingly feed into their dogs' aggression problem by supporting the underdog—because they feel sorry for it. Although this approach may seem equitable to us, it ensures that fighting will continue because it prevents the establishment of a stable pack structure within the home. An owner's support of the more subordinate dog seems to lend the underdog more authority, empowering it to flout the alpha dog's dominance and break certain unwritten rules. One way of viewing this phenomenon is that the subordinate dog forms a cryptic alliance with the owner, artifactually altering dominance dynamics within the family pack. This alliance temporarily elevates the usually more deferent dog's dominance status, thus facilitating the problem. Some behaviorists believe that the subordinate dog initiates fighting in the owner's presence. My experience is a little different. I find that the more dominant dog of the pair, incensed by some liberty that the subordinate dog has taken, will often attack first. When in any doubt as to which dog is more dominant, it is advisable to support the older dog, though there are other considerations, such as size, genetics, and health status, that should also be factored in.

In mild cases of sibling rivalry, quarreling dogs may coexist quite peacefully when the owner is absent but resume the fray immediately when the owner returns home. In more advanced cases, the feuding parties cannot be left together at any time or they will seriously injure each other.

One moderately severe but otherwise typical case I saw recently involved a couple of two-year-old mixed-breed spayed female siblings called Shelby and Christy. Their owners, Janice and Jeff Bateman of Connecticut, had adopted the pair from a local animal-welfare society. All was well for three months, but then the fights began. The first incident occurred one day when the dogs came in from the yard after being outside together. The "bone of contention" in this instance was the narrow deck stair that they had to traverse en route. Access along corridors and across thresholds is so important to would-be leaders that these zones are typical testing grounds for dominance. The fact that Jeff was standing at the head of the stairs probably provided fuel for the conflagration that subsequently ensued. The dogs almost literally flew at each other, much to Jeff's horror and surprise, and though he pulled them apart fairly quickly, they managed to inflict serious physical injuries on each other. Following the cataclysm it was off to the vet's for the two of them, both drenched in blood, for anesthesia and stitches all around.

The next episode occurred a couple of weeks later while Janice and Jeff were engaging in some obedience training with them. Once again the incident occurred too quickly for either owner to see who lunged at whom. This time veterinary care was not necessary, thanks to Jeff's lightning reactions. A couple of months later, rawhide chews provided the impetus for the attack. Janice was the sole witness this time and was the one who had to ferry them to the vet's office for attention. A month later, while on lead with Jeff, one dog "accidentally" bumped into the other. Another fight ensued. The vet was getting quite used to seeing the pair being hauled out of the car and delivered to the clinic for yet more suturing and antibiotics. Things got very tedious and stressful for the Batemans, who finally separated the dogs from each other as the only viable solution. This was the stage at which Jeff contacted me for help after learning about the Tufts Behavior Clinic from his brother, a vet in New Hampshire.

Jeff gave me a detailed rundown of the problem between Shelby and Christy and asked me what could be done. I led off by explaining that most cases of sibling rivalry represent a dominance struggle between dogs of near-equal dominance status, catalyzed by the owner's input. As with many owners, it was a moment of revelation for Jeff when it dawned on him that the dogs never fought while they were alone together and that each fight had been terminated by the dogs being hauled apart. Although masterly inactivity—allowing the dogs to fight it out—is a solution in milder cases of sibling rivalry, this was not an option for Jeff. The fighting between Shelby and Christy had reached such proportions that physical injury to one or both dogs was inevitable if someone didn't intervene, yet allowing them to work out their own issues was the only way to resolve the dilemma—a catch-22 if ever I heard of one. But there was a solution; muzzles to be applied at strategic times. The idea was to permit the dogs to interact freely for a few hours each day in Jeff and Janice's presence without the possibility of serious injury. If fighting occurred, the dogs were to be left alone to sort out their hierarchical differences, which, I explained, they could still do by wrestling while muzzled, yet without injuring each other.

This made sense to Jeff, but he wondered what would happen if his dogs did not fight while muzzled. Would they still resolve their status struggle without making physical contact? Maybe not, I informed him, but that was where he and Janice came in. They were to steadfastly support the more dominant dog in all daily activities so that there was no doubt in either dog's mind about which one was the leader. First, we had to decide which was the more dominant dog of the pair. We settled on Shelby because she was most often the instigator of the fights. From now on it was first come, first served for Shelby—first through doors, first to get treats, first to be petted, and so on. Christy, on the other hand, was to receive the "also-ran" treatment, including being banished from Jeff and Janice's bed at night, where one of the more recent contretemps had occurred. As a finishing touch, I advised Jeff and Janice to assert greater control over both dogs by having them engage in a nonconfrontational dominance program.

I spoke to Jeff a couple of times over the next few weeks to fine-tune the program, but then lost touch with him until early 1998, six months after our initial contact. I was delighted to learn of the progress he and Janice had made with the dogs. Apparently the muzzles had extinguished all battles from the get-go. There wasn't even any bodychecking. After several weeks of supporting Shelby's position, the Batemans tried removing the muzzles and prayed. A delicate peace prevailed. There had been only one flare-up in the entire six-month period and the Batemans handled this well by diverting both dogs before there could be a serious consequence. The record was not perfect, but the half year following our consultation was still the most trouble-free period the Batemans had experienced for many a moon and they felt that they were heading in the right direction. As an incidental finding they quipped that Christy initially had been none too happy with her ousting from the master bed but that she had eventually accepted her new lot with dignity. It mustn't have been too much fun for her to discover her number-two status—but that's what had to be.

Dogs don't have to be siblings to engage in "sibling rivalry," and the owner's presence is not an absolute requirement for in-home dominance struggles to occur. A long-standing and refractory case of owner-independent sibling rivalry in which I became embroiled involved a couple of dogs belonging to a veterinarian in New Jersey. This long-suffering vet had devoted years attempting to resolve intractable in-fighting between his two Finnish spitzes. He had read every book available on the subject and, as far as I was concerned, had done everything he knew to resolve the problem, but to no avail. He had tried supporting what he regarded as the alpha or dominant dog and ignoring the underdog—theoretically the correct strategy. It didn't work. But because the dogs were so evenly matched, he thought he might have gauged the would-be leader incorrectly so he switched his support to the other dog. The result was the same—no change. He tried muzzling both dogs and allowing them to fight it out, with and without sedation, but the fights never came to a resolution. He tried desensitizing the pair by introducing them to each other at a thousand paces across a huge field, but the moment the dogs caught sight of each other, even at this distance, they went berserk and started lunging toward each other. Eventually the vet gave up all attempts at desensitization because he couldn't even get the program started. Finally, in an attempt to facilitate the dogs' peaceful reintroduction, he tried several different antiaggressive medications on them. Nothing worked. Then he called me.

There was nothing behavioral left for me to do. The vet had already tried all the behavior-modification techniques I knew. All that remained for me to do was to explore some pharmacologic strategies that he had not yet tried. I started by recommending that he should try treating both dogs with Prozac, on the basis that any medication that increases serotonin in the brain should decrease aggression. At the time I had just completed a study demonstrating the efficacy of Prozac in owner-directed dominance aggression in dogs and felt reasonably optimistic that we would obtain some favorable results. Bearing in mind these dogs' track record, I should have guessed that even Prozac would not temper their aggression to each other, and this proved to be the case. We tried top doses of Prozac, various pharmacologic-augmentation strategies—for example, adding Inderal to the regimen—and tried beefing up behavior modification during this treatment; nothing worked.

In desperation, I had the vet try some novel antiaggression drugs—the human antipsychotic drug Clozaril, the endorphin blocker ReVia . . . same result. Finally I called aggression expert Dr. Klaus Miczek of the psychology department at Tufts for some new ideas. Klaus thought it might be worth anesthetizing the dogs and allowing them to wake up next to each other. This plan does work in aggressive laboratory animals (mice and rats) that are somehow bonded by the shared experience. The dogs were duly anesthetized and brought together for their recovery. However, as they emerged from the anesthetic they recognized each other immediately and went at it again, stumbling and lurching toward each other with malicious intent even in their semiconscious stupor.

This extreme case of sibling rivalry just didn't respond to anything we threw at it and I'm afraid the final solution was to keep the dogs separate at all times. It was quite humbling to realize that with all we now know about the psychology and pharmacology of aggression, we still couldn't come up with a solution. I sometimes wonder why the responses to behavioral treatments are as variable as they appear to be. It is not uncommon to find that a behavior problem can be remedied in one dog by an approach that leaves another cold. The answer to this dilemma must be that the brain is a much more complicated structure than we realize. The fashionable reductionist approach to understanding behavior problems is undoubtedly an oversimplification of what's really going on. After all, modification of an animal's behavior, by whatever means, is not like taking a stroll in the park. Sometimes it seems like we're trying to fix a mainframe computer armed only with a screwdriver and a roll of duct tape.

On a positive note, I had a call a couple of weeks ago from a friend and behaviorist colleague of mine, Dr. R. K. Anderson. He was asking me about dose adjustments for Prozac in a couple of dogs with sibling rivalry that were successfully controlled by this therapy. He was absolutely delighted at the way things had turned out for these two dogs. I was happy to supply him with the information he needed, but the success he reported set me musing again about the variability of dogs' responses to treatment. One day the answer to this quandary may emerge, but in the meantime we do what we can and pray for success. As with all battles, some you win . . . some you lose. Perhaps that's the way it has to be for now.

REACTIVITY

We've all known dogs that demand affection, are highly excitable, and tear around the house at the slightest excuse, barking excessively. There may even be one living next door to you. This syndrome is so familiar that each of us can conjure up a mental image of such a dog without much difficulty. For me, Bumbley, a wirehaired fox terrier that I have mentioned earlier (see "E—Eating Disorders"), springs to my mind as the epitome of excess reactivity. Bumbley, however, may have been a tad worse than the average dog whose motor is running too fast. He may have even been one of those enigmatic cases of medical hyperactivity, because he wasn't just plain old "hyper"—he was in perpetual motion. So how do we label a dog that responds excessively to every tiny perturbation in the environment? Some would say *excitable*, others *irritable*, and yet others *reactive*. In the discussion that follows I will stick to the term *reactive* because it has precedence in the literature and is, I believe, reasonably apt.

One such reactive dog was brought to see me a couple of weeks ago. His name was Tucker and he was a young neutered male bluetick coonhound. Tucker's owner, Kassie, a final-year veterinary student, was a model student and had previously had great success training dogs—until Tucker came along. In listening to Kassie's problems with Tucker, the diagnosis of "reactive" was unavoidable. He was super-excitable, too excitable even to train, and any attention put him over the top. He was demanding, jumping up on people, leaping at them, twisting and turning, barking and squirming. Tucker wasn't aggressive at all. He just had a bad case of Saint Vitus's dance. In the evenings, when Kassie's other dogs were resting peacefully, Tucker was waiting and listening—listening for anything that would provide a good excuse for another exaggerated display of . . . well, Tucker. The sound of the doorbell and the arrival of visitors caused major problems. He could barely be controlled because of his high level of excitement, and more often than not, his rambunctiousness was unwelcome. Visitors began to take heed and only came around when absolutely necessary. In Tucker's case, though, it wasn't just the doorbell and visitors that caused problems. It was anything . . . a leaf falling, an icicle dripping, a sudden gust of wind—any excuse was a good one. He had a hair trigger. Life was getting difficult for Kassie so, after months of trying to correct this problem, she sought my input.

First, I tried to explain what might have caused Tucker to become the way he was. It is always helpful for owners to understand the roots of a problem if they are going to invest time trying to correct it. It makes more sense this way than sending folk off to engage in mindless retraining exercises. Kassie sat patiently as I reasoned about the possible causes of Tucker's excessive reactivity. The first possibility, I pointed out, was that he might have inherited this trait from his parents. This would not be good news from the point of view of retraining because we would be going against the flow of his natural disposition. That genetics plays a role in the expression of reactivity was demonstrated beyond a shadow of a doubt in the 1950s by scientists John Scott and John Fuller. Scott and Fuller studied five breeds, rating parameters such as dogs' posture, operant behavior, heart rate, lip licking, vocalization, panting, tail wagging, resistance to movement, biting, elimination, and latency to leave the experimental situation as indicators of reactivity. They found that their terriers, beagles, and basenjis were far more reactive than their cocker spaniels and shelties at all ages tested. Whether these breeds would rate the same way today is doubtful, bearing in mind changes that have occurred because of line breeding. Some cockers, and many shelties I have encountered recently, would definitely not be classified as of "low reactivity." The details aside for now, though, what Scott and Fuller showed was that reactivity, including the emotional response to human beings, was partly an inherited trait. This was a useful finding that, in some instances, lets owners who feel that they have caused their dog's behavior problem off the hook. It also has relevance in the selection of a new puppy. If you don't want a highly reactive dog, do yourself a favor and avoid breeds and lines that exhibit this type of behavior. Reactivity is not always an undesirable trait, though. Some people actually want a live wire of a dog with tons of energy, one that will practically wake the dead if a burglar arrives or will race around the fields from dawn until dusk. The type of puppy you select should depend on your own personal wants and needs.

Tucker's parents were not too bad in terms of reactivity. The sire was a stoic, but Tucker's mom could be a little overenthusiastic at times. Certainly their behavior did not fully explain what we saw in Tucker and there wasn't more to add in what little we were able to find out about his grandparents' generation. We had to look elsewhere to explain his aberrant behavior. Investigating his nurtural experiences was the logical next step. Environmental experiences are intimately involved in the development of all the canine behaviors and temperaments, including reactivity. Kassie admitted that Tucker had been raised as a working dog, not as a pet. His proud Kentuckian breeder was more concerned with his good looks and hunting potential than the secondary issue of his temperament. When Kassie went to the breeder's home to see Tucker for the first time, she found the pups in small crates not much bigger than cat carriers. The pups peered out of their wire prisons like battery chickens on death row. It turns out they had been weaned at the usual age, around six weeks of age, and had been cage-raised ever since (though admittedly they were allowed out to run around at times). Tucker was fourteen weeks old when Kassie first saw him—just beyond the sensitive period of development. In his case the "moving finger" of environmental influences had already "writ" and moved on. Kassie was inheriting seeds of trouble that had already been sown.

Puppies that are isolated from their parents and peers during an early period of their development frequently grow up to be psychologically disturbed. This reasonably well-known syndrome is called kennelitis. The type of disturbance that affected dogs display depends on the breed concerned. Complete isolation, even more extreme than what occurred in Tucker's case, impairs puppies' ability to learn, and they often react to humans and other dogs with fear. They can also become hyperactive and difficult to train. There are some breed differences in the response to isolation, because beagles raised this way become fearful, whereas Scottish terriers become hyperactive. No one knows how bluetick coonhounds respond in this paradigm but, learning from Tucker, we can guess.

Partial isolation, similar to what happened to Tucker, is also detrimental to the development of a stable personality, learning ability, and sociability. The changes seen here are along the same lines as those seen with total isolation, only less marked, and are proportional to the degree of isolation. Even one week of isolation at an early age produces documentable changes in pups' electroencephalogram recordings, so clearly it doesn't take long to cause a problem. I thought Tucker's early experiences may well have figured into his problem and I told Kassie so. Her sad look told me that she wouldn't make the same mistake again, and I felt that, with luck, she would speak out against such mistreatment of pups in the future.

As far as Tucker's treatment was concerned, I outlined several background issues that I thought Kassie should address to give us a level playing field for subsequent behavior modification. The first item to deal with was exercise. My favorite saying, "A tired dog is a good dog," was rotating in the back of my mind as I advised Kassie to step up Tucker's exercise to at least thirty minutes of hard, aerobic, running-type activity every day, preferably first thing in the morning for an effect that would last all day. Exercise generates ample supplies of the neurotransmitter serotonin, which has a general mood-stabilizing and calming effect on personality. I have firsthand experience of this effect as, in the old days, I used to be something of a "gym rat."

Sometimes I would walk into the gym a little tense and edgy after a grueling day at the office. An hour later I would emerge with my jacket slung over my shoulder and a smile on my face, at peace with my world. It's amazing what a little serotonin can do.

There wasn't too much for me to change as far as Tucker's diet was concerned, as Kassie already had him on a low-protein diet, but I suggested that it might be worth trying an all-natural, artificial-preservative-free equivalent. The idea was to see if eliminating chemical additives, such as BHA and ethoxyquin, would have any effect on his behavior. The jury is still out on the efficacy of this measure, but some trainers swear by it. I once approached a pet-food company to see if they would fund a study of this question but was told that no one in the industry wanted to know the answer. Their reasoning was that pet foods need such stabilizers to have an acceptable shelf life, and that artificial preservatives were there to stay even if they were shown to aggravate behavior problems. I could see their point . . . I think.

Kassie's lack of success in training Tucker was a great concern for her. I learned that she had been employing "conventional training" with a choke chain, using leash corrections to control unwanted behaviors. Whatever one thinks of this style of training, there is one cardinal rule of behavior-modification therapy: If something is not working, stop doing it. So we did. I advised Kassie to switch to using a head halter to control Tucker during training sessions and to try click-and-treat training with whatever reward worked best for him. (It turned out that freeze-dried liver was his favorite food.) In addition, I advised Kassie not to pay attention to Tucker when he went ballistic but to do exactly the opposite and leave the room. The idea was to eliminate any attention-seeking components from the behavior, though I didn't think this would have a dramatic effect on Tucker because, according to the neighbors, he did a fair amount of barking when Kassie was not around. In addition to the above measures I suggested medicating Tucker to calm him and take the edge off him. I could see Kassie was open to this suggestion so I launched into a discussion of antidepressants and their serotonin-enhancing, mood-stabilizing effects. I felt that increasing brain serotonin was the right approach for Tucker, and Kassie eventually honed in on Anafranil as her first choice, considering the expense of the Cadillac treatment, Prozac.

The weeks passed by as I awaited follow-up information with enthusiasm. Could we really turn around Tucker's wild behavior? Would the spell be broken? The answer at first was no but eventually it was yes. The Anafranil didn't really get the job done too well and at one point Kassie was getting quite despondent. Then I persuaded her to switch to a more selective serotonin-enhancing drug, not Prozac itself, but Zoloft. The result was smiles all around. Tucker calmed right down and became "normal" and even Kassie herself, I thought, appeared more relaxed and relieved.

Some dogs with reactivity problems present slightly differently. One all-too-common complaint, the tip of the iceberg, so to speak, is that of a dog that barks too much. A puli I treated through our Petfax counseling service provides a good example of this variation. The inquiry came from a breeder, who had recently reacquired the dog. By way of background, this intact female puli, called Tofu, had already had a heck of a life in her nineteen months of existence. The breeder had sold her at about nine weeks old to a young married couple who promised to give her a good home. As it turned out, they didn't really live up to this promise. The first problem was that they moved from a house to a town-based condo shortly before they acquired Tofu, and Tofu spent all day in a crate while the woman was at work. When she came back home in the evening she took Tofu for a walk and winged a ball around for her for a while but then, after dinner, it was back to the crate for poor Tofu, for the night . . . hardly an ideal existence for any dog. But things got worse. The woman's job took her away from home for days at a time and while she was away her husband often didn't get up in the morning to take Tofu for a walk. He spent virtually no time with Tofu during his wife's absences. Tofu was young and alone, spending over twenty hours a day in a crate. This went on for over a year until the woman called the breeder, informed her that her marriage was about to break up, and asked what she should do about Tofu. The breeder immediately took Tofu back, shocked at what had transpired.

But the damage had been done. The breeder found out that Tofu was now a basket case—quite unlike any other puli she had ever dealt with in over twenty years of puli breeding and showing. Her own label for Tofu's behavior was *hyperactive*, which wasn't too far from the mark, but Tofu was peaceful at times; for example, at night when she was crated. First thing in the morning, however, when she heard someone moving around she would react explosively, barking and throwing herself around in her crate for as long as it took for someone to let her out. And there was no escaping her demands. As soon as she was let out of the crate, Tofu would race around crazed, looking for her tennis ball, and she would bark and spin in circles in a state of near hysteria until she found it. The moment she had the ball, she would pester whoever was around to throw it for her, becoming unbearable until her demands were met. But even if the breeder acceded to her demands, that wasn't the end of the problem. Tofu would retrieve the thrown ball untiringly and, if ignored, even for a few seconds, would leap at the breeder's head and spring off her body, barking the whole time. The only escape was to exit the scene entirely.

Another problem was that if Tofu couldn't locate the ball when she was outside she would attack the first thing that moved—except people, that is, but the breeder's other dogs were constantly at risk. Tofu was extremely aggressive when she didn't have the ball in her mouth, and in this situation would fight with almost any other dog, seemingly out of frustration. It was a real problem to know what to do with her during the day. She couldn't be put out in the dog runs or she would bark continuously to be let out, yet she would practically blow a fuse if she was kenneled and saw someone moving outside, barking "as if possessed" and spitting saliva everywhere. ("She sounds like a charmer, doesn't she," the owner commented dryly.)

As an interim measure Tofu's breeder put her out in a field with a male dog that she generally did not attack. In the house, Tofu could not be petted without becoming extremely demanding and flinging herself against the individual, as she always wanted more petting. She would bark and spin when she saw her food dish coming and had no patience for anything that required waiting. This type of intolerance, coupled with her exceptional perseverance, made her quite a handful. To survive living with Tofu you had to, as it were, walk on eggs to avoid the next eruption. It really wasn't much fun.

A variation on the general theme of reactivity that Tofu was showing was her developing aggression. Not only would she attack other dogs when she was worked up but, at the time of the consultation, she

had just begun to show aggression to people under certain circumstances. The first time this happened was at the Westminster Kennel
Club show, when a stranger tried to move her from one pen to another.
On this occasion she became extremely excited, almost frenzied, and
bit the person on the arm. The breeder was called to leash her, as Tofu
wouldn't let anyone else near her. There was little doubt in my mind
that Tofu was also displaying elements of both dominance and fear, but
I felt that *high reactivity* described her general state of mind most
aptly.

The treatment I recommended for Tofu was similar to that I advised for Tucker. It centered around optimizing her environment, increasing her exercise, and adjusting her diet. In addition, I
recommended treating Tofu with medication designed to calm her and
slow her whirlwind behavior to a more manageable and tolerable level.
In Tofu's case I elected to treat her with the antidepressant drug Elavil
because I wanted the benefit of serotonin *and* norepinephrine enhancement. The influence of the former, I reasoned, would calm her
and stabilize her mood, whereas the latter measure might produce a
paradoxical calming effect in a dog as "hyper" as Tofu. Tofu's owner
called me back several weeks later with a long-term follow-up report of
how she was doing. The word was good. No, it was better than good, it
was excellent. Tofu had settled right down and was behaving virtually
normally. We weren't sure which component of the treatment had produced this dramatic change, but I suspect the medication had a lot to
do with it.

It is not hard to fathom the historical factors that contributed to
Tofu's condition. In my opinion, the blame rested squarely on the
shoulders of Tofu's first owners. They should never have had a dog in
the first place since they had neither the time nor patience to take care
of one properly. There wasn't much evidence for genetics underlying
Tofu's behavior, though her mom was stubborn and, according to the
breeder, had a "very strong fight-or-flight reflex." But genetics can
play a role in some cases, as mentioned above.

The question is, which factor is more influential in creating hyperactivity? Genetics or the environment? Nature or nurture? I would say
the environment has the most influence in the majority of cases. In
support of an environmental contribution to the hyperreactivity are

the isolation experiments and numerous anecdotal experiences of breeders, trainers, and behaviorists. Tucker's and Tofu's cases both demonstrate the detrimental effects of adverse experiences. Optimal puppy-raising strategies, including appropriate socialization in the first three months of life, are absolutely critical to the proper development of well-integrated and content adult dogs. I often discover "dysfunctional" early experiences underlying behavior problems, especially those problems related to reactivity, anxiety, and fearfulness. This is not to say that genetic influences are unimportant. It's far better to have everything going for you as you select and train the right dog for you, but a decent puppyhood can go a long way toward counterbalancing the more subtle influences of genetic variation. There's no way of escaping from such a conclusion, or from one's overall responsibilities as a dog owner, and too many excuses are made for shoddy treatment, which is particularly deleterious for the young'ns.

SEXUAL BEHAVIOR

There is no more profound difference between dogs of the same breed than that imposed by their biological sex. Full, red-blooded males are usually larger, stronger, more aggressive, more likely to roam, to mark objects with urine, and to mount (hump) other dogs than their female counterparts. As none of these characteristics is particularly appealing to the average dog owner, the practice of castrating (neutering) males at puberty, or a little before, has become a fairly routine veterinary procedure with wide acceptance. There are, of course, other important reasons for having male dogs neutered, including certain medical benefits (no possibility of testicular tumors, lower incidence of prostatic disease, and reduced risk of various problems in the "nether regions"), as well as for "birth control," as many of my clients phrase it.

Unfortunately, the effect of neutering in suppressing male behaviors is not universal. It often only reduces the frequency of the behavior rather than eliminating it entirely. It has been well documented that certain male-typical behaviors respond better to neutering than others. Roaming, for example, is reduced and virtually eliminated in some ninety percent of dogs, whereas aggression between dogs, urine marking, and mounting are only decreased about sixty percent of the time. This is particularly curious when one considers that the blood level of the male hormone, testosterone, falls to near zero within hours of the surgery in all cases, yet the behavioral effects of neutering are variable and may take weeks or months to become apparent.

The behavior of unneutered bitches is not half so bothersome as that of males, but there are good reasons to consider neutering ("spaying") them aside from the recurrent annoyance of heat periods, when the bitch becomes attractive to male dogs. Heat periods are hard to ignore because all the dogs from miles around detect the pheromonal odors blowing in the wind and come a callin', eyes rolling and tongues sticking out of the sides of their mouths. Unless you are extremely vigilant, the chances are that one of them will slip through the net and, with a bit of aiding and abetting from your now-willing bitch, sixty-three days later it's puppies. True enough, most bitches only come into season a couple of times a year . . . but the heat periods do last about three weeks each time, so they can be something of a penance for the owner. To avoid this otherwise cyclical change, most owners have their bitches neutered unless they are considering them for breeding. Prevention of unwanted puppies, pseudopregnancy, and pyometra (a uterine infection), plus a reduced risk of mammary cancer, are all good reasons to have a bitch neutered. And the beauty of neutering a bitch, as opposed to a male dog, is that the behavioral effects are absolute. Following spaying, bitches do not come into heat, are not particularly attractive to male dogs, and can never become pregnant. It's an open-and-shut case.

Why is it that males behave like males and females like females? And why do males sometimes continue to display male characteristics after neutering? To find the answer to this we have to delve into genetics and development. Genetics determines the sex and therefore the physical appearance and sexual behavior of animals. The course is set at the instant of conception when the newly formed egg has either the XY or XX combination of chromosomes. The XY combination goes on to develop along male lines, and at a certain stage, the rudimentary sex glands develop into testes. Later, a surge of testosterone is released from the embryonic testes causing "masculinization" of specific brain regions of the fetus. A male is thus born a male, with a male brain and, albeit dilute, masculine tendencies even without the prevailing influence of testosterone. A neutered male will return to testosterone-free maleness and will always be a male, never an "it." The neutered male will also be capable of certain male-typical behaviors, though not usually with as much conviction or dedication as a full red-blooded male. I sometimes use the analogy of a light with a dimmer switch to describe the behavioral qualities of an emasculated dog. Following castration the switch is turned down, but not off, and the result is not darkness but a dim glow.

The XX chromosomal arrangement in females is a sort of default situation. In embryos so configured, without the effect of testosterone, the brain develops along feminine lines to have brain centers that control mating and birthing behavior. These centers can be activated later in life under various hormonal influences.

A perhaps not-so-surprising fact about sex-linked behaviors in animals, including us, is that they are not unique to a particular sex, but rather are more prevalent or exaggerated in one sex than the other. Bitches also display aggression, roam, urine mark, and may mount male dogs and other bitches. To make the point even more dramatically, males are capable of nesting, nurturing, maternal-style aggression, and can even lactate. In "M—Maternal Behavior," I describe a neutered male that displayed an assortment of such female behaviors. The point is that the potential for supposedly sexually dimorphic behaviors exists in both sexes.

Of course, nature does not control everything when it comes to sexual behaviors. Environmental experience and learning are extremely important, too. Not only will social isolation of pups prevent the playful interactions that help shape normal social behaviors in youngsters, but also the absence of appropriate outlets may cause sexual behaviors to develop aberrantly. Humping of pillows and cushions, or people's legs, is one of the most common examples of a misdirected sexual behavior in male dogs deprived of female company during a sensitive period of development. The odds are that a "humper" will be a male and that the behavior will begin as hormone levels rise at the onset of puberty, specifically around four or five months of age. Humpers tend to be more pushy and aggressive than their nonhumping subordinates. Although humping is clearly a sexual behavior (dogs aren't trying to dominate cushions), horny little tykes of this persuasion often use the humping behavior as an assertive, preaggressive behavior intended to symbolize mastery or control.

Male sexual behavior and dominance are apparently inseparably linked, even in people. The journal *Nature* recently devoted a column to the subject, jibing about the present rash of embarrassing extramarital affairs of prominent politicians. The article, acknowledging that politicians are socially dominant individuals, bemoaned the fact that a biological tendency for promiscuity was an inevitable accompaniment of the leadership package. It went on to describe how the traits of sexuality and dominance might be segregated, using highly specific antagonist drugs to attenuate these characteristics independently. If this were indeed feasible, the author argued, it might be possible to engineer politicians with no interest at all in bimbos; or, as a corollary, to create socially irresponsible, promiscuous individuals reminiscent of the hippies of yesteryear. The article smacked of Lewis Carroll's *Alice's Adventures in Wonderland,* where one pill makes you small and one pill makes you tall, or perhaps George Orwell's *1984.*

Just in case you are in any doubt about the interaction of sexuality and dominance, let me tell you about Benji, the beagle from hell, who was both dominant and aggressive, and who used humping to signal his mastery over his lady owner. Benji was a "field-strain" beagle bred specifically for hunting. As a pup, he had nipped excessively and growled at his owners with minimal provocation. Unlike Benji, his kindly owners, a young married couple, were quiet, polite, and unassuming. As Benji became older, he started to engage in various unattractive behaviors, including constant face licking, snapping in dominance-type situations—such as in the context of protection of food, valued objects (like Kleenex tissues), and his bed—and, you guessed it, humping. His humping was directed exclusively toward the wife. Benji was castrated when he was eight months old to try to get this humping under control, but the response was underwhelming. When the couple first consulted me, Benji was one year old and was getting worse by the month.

I diagnosed classical dominance aggression as Benji's main behavior problem, but it wasn't his aggression that was of most concern to his harrowed owners, it was the often inseparable counterpart of humping. Apparently, the situation was tolerable until the woman's husband left for work. Presumably his more dominant influence was sufficient to keep the little rascal in check while he was home, but after he was gone the problems began. As soon as the door clicked shut Benji would assume a new, challenging attitude. He would stare at the woman constantly, like one of those annoying paintings where the eyes of the subject follow you around the room, and once he was in this mode, the woman knew she had to watch her step. Occasionally, however, she would forget about her ever-watchful demon and would bend down to open a cupboard or pick something up from the floor. Faced with such an opportunity, Benji would come flying out of nowhere like Zorro and attach himself to her back, oscillating with the velocity of a shuttle on an electric sewing machine. The woman was mortified. She would sob and shake after such an assault and her life turned into a series of horrid nightmares. Something had to be done. The ball was in my court.

It was with great satisfaction that I recommended a dominance-control program for Benji. From that day onward he had to work for everything he wanted from his owners. As the famous Smith Barney commercial spokesman says, "At Smith Barney we make money the old-fashioned way—we earn it." That was pretty much the way it was to be for Benji and his needs from then on. His owners were somewhat surprised when I pointed out that they actually did control everything he needed: his food, toys, petting, access to places, and freedom, to name but a few. They had never really thought about his reliance on them before. I advised them to have him sit, or still better, lie down, to receive any and all perks from them and recommended a hard-nosed approach to his management. It was him or them, simple as that. I told them that if they didn't control him that he would try to control them. In addition, as a training aid, I supplied them with a head halter with a ten-foot-long training lead so that they could control him from a distance if he didn't obey a command.

The weeks ticked by and Benji did indeed begin to behave much better, but not quite perfectly. Then the coup de grâce came unwittingly when the couple went on a trip without Benji, who was boarded at a kennel. You know what they say about familiarity breeding contempt; well, that seems to have been a factor here. The two weeks Benji had in solitary must have given him time to chew things over and gain respect, because when the couple returned from their trip their problems relating to Benji's dominance, including humping, were resolved. They found him practically penitent on their return, and rather than allowing themselves to indulge him in the golden period of being reunited, they enforced the dominance program even more strictly. Benji never looked back after this, although the couple always had to remain on the alert for returning dominance. Dominant dogs, once experienced in their ways, always have the potential to revert, so some components of the program must remain in force indefinitely.

As invasive as Benji was, his intrusions were not a patch on Lucifer's lascivious ways. Lucifer, a five-year-old unneutered male mastiff crossbreed, humped everything that moved and many things that didn't. He lived in a home with his master, his master's lady friend, and her eight-year-old daughter. One day while his master was away fishing, and the girl's mother was mowing the lawn, the young girl decided to change into her swimming suit in the living room. After she had removed her clothes, but before she had time to don the suit, Lucifer mounted her from behind, thrusting wildly and, as fate would have it, managed momentary penetration of her vagina. The girl screamed and became hysterical, but her mother continued mowing, deafened by the sound of the machine and oblivious to her daughter's cries. Eventually the girl composed herself enough to run outside and attract her mother's attention. The mother, horrified by what she was told, downed tools immediately and drove her daughter to the doctor's office.

The penetration was confirmed at the doctor's office but the staff were suspicious of foul play and called the local authorities. Within hours, the girl was taken into custody and questioned extensively about the event. She stuck to her story despite psychologists' attempts to pin the blame elsewhere. Men, not dogs, are the usual culprits in such assaults. The police confirmed the woman's boyfriend's alibi to make sure he could not have been around at the time. He was fishing. Slowly it dawned on the doctors and officials that what appeared to have happened might have happened. As a final check, a forensic specialist working for the police called me to verify that the assault was technically possible. I had to agree that it was. The girl was released from protective custody and returned to her home. Lucifer was neutered and found another home. The whole unfortunate event, barring the mental scars that undoubtedly remain, was over.

The great pity about this whole scenario was that the man had refused to have his dog neutered, even though he didn't intend to use him for breeding, and despite the fact that Lucifer spent his whole life humping people's legs and cushions. I come across this antineutering sentiment a lot in men. It seems to be a macho thing involving deep-seated anthropomorphic sentiment. When it is explained to women that neutering a male dog is the best thing to do they usually accept the advice pragmatically and in the spirit in which it is offered. Men, however, draw air through their teeth and look heavenward, shaking their heads in incredulity as if experiencing some psychological pain. I wish they understood that neutering is a relatively innocuous procedure that will produce a more content and less troublesome pet. Following anesthesia for neuter surgery, dogs simply roll onto their chests and begin thinking about their next meal. Not being self-conscious, they do not have the same psychological consequences that would affect men in the same situation. They just carry on regardless with altered priorities and expectations. Neutering does not quell all desire, though, as I just discussed. Many neutered dogs continue to mount and penetrate bitches for years after being neutered, if not for the rest of their lives. The frequency of sexual behavior should be less, however, whether it takes the form of mounting bitches or cushions. I wish Lucifer's owner had been more open to this treatment and a little less macho in his attitude. To have had Lucifer castrated would not have guaranteed against the events of that afternoon, but it would have made them a lot less likely.

So you see, an unneutered dog's life can revolve around sexual concerns for much of the time. And it would be a surprise if this weren't the case. The whole purpose of an animal's existence is to reproduce to propagate its own species. When you think about it, we all live and breathe, fight and die, to generate and support our kin. It's nature's way. To this end we are equipped with the requisite anatomy, physiology, and drives to facilitate reproduction and nurturing. In dogs, wanderlust is the burning desire to seek and find a potential mate. Urine marking advertises the dog's presence, and intermale aggression epitomizes competitive aspects of social and, ultimately, reproductive success that ensure survival of the fittest. Mounting and intromission represent fulfillment of the procreative aspects of the reproductive cycle and are sufficiently rewarding to ensure that the procedure is repeated many times, both in the short and long term. For a bitch, following the pleasure of mating, the warm glow of pregnancy, and the pain of parturition, the real work of motherhood begins. The male may have little else to do but dream of the next time he strikes it lucky, missing the real point of his wanderings, risky battles, and moments of passion. Even to us humans, with our full knowledge of the cycle of life, the whole process still seems somewhat circular as we and our dogs both live to multiply and multiply to live.

TEMPERAMENT TESTING

Wouldn't it be wonderful if prospective owners, having selected the breed of their dreams, could then choose a pup that would develop into an even-tempered adult with a personality to suit their needs and with no annoying behavioral traits? A friend for life. Some say it can be done but others disagree. The name of the game is puppy temperament testing. Most trainers are proponents of this time-honored art, and the naysayers, you guessed it, are the scientists.

Let me just explain for a second the actual process of temperament testing of pups, though it does vary a bit from tester to tester. First, it is conventionally conducted on the mystical forty-ninth day of the pup's life. I don't mean to decry the significance of the forty-ninth day. There is published work to support the development of fear reactions around this time, hence the testers' obsession with it. Seven-week-old pups are manipulated, approached, led, and startled to produce a character appraisal, which supposedly will determine their personalities and predict their future behavioral tendencies.

Specific tests include cradling pups on their backs in the tester's arms and holding them high in the air under their armpits to test for dominance. If pups struggle, their failure to accept the situation is supposed to portend the development of dominance, whereas if they lie still and hang limply during these tests, they are dubbed submissive and thus more likely to conform to life's little impositions. Sociability is evaluated by monitoring pups' responses to approach by a stranger. Balking or submissive behavior in this situation is ominous of problems of a fearful nature with respect to future interactions with people. The "following test," in which the tester walks away from an isolated pup to see if it will follow, supposedly tests pups' attachment to humans and, by implication, their willingness to please. Finally, startle tests, such as throwing a set of car keys on the ground behind the pup, are designed to evaluate noise sensitivity, reactivity, and innate fearfulness.

Whether such simple tests, performed once at such a young age, can predict the future development of dogs' adult personalities is the subject of a continuing debate. I was once in a think tank, consisting of top trainers and behaviorists, to evaluate current methods for the selection and training of dogs (with service dogs in mind, particularly). The thorny subject of puppy temperament testing came up in discussion and the assembled throng was immediately polarized into two opposite factions—the trainer group, with their extensive practical experience, who vehemently supported temperament testing as a useful predictor; and the behaviorist/scientist faction, stating that temperament testing had never been conclusively proved to work.

Both groups had good reasons for their stance—but one group was wrong. The trainers argued that they had successfully characterized scads of wriggling, willful puppies as dominant and successfully placed them in appropriate homes with people who were "good with dogs" or strong leader types. The behaviorists countered that there had been no "control" group placements of potentially dominant dogs with less-well-equipped owners so no conclusions could be drawn. With only one placement group, if a dominant pup went on to develop dominance, the trainers' character assessment would be validated. If it did not, the trainer could take credit for correctly taming a potentially dominant dog. The behaviorists were fast to point out that this was a no-lose predictive situation for temperament-testing supporters. The trainers replied that people without experience in temperament testing (the behaviorists) could not really hope to appreciate the predictive value of the tests. Touché.

Temperament testing is performed all over the country by people who believe that it works for prospective owners and breeders who pay good money to have it done. Perhaps there is a grain or two of truth that comes out of it. On the down side, there is a lot that can happen to a pup in the six or more weeks of sensitive-period learning that remain following testing at seven weeks. A lot of good and bad messages that may greatly alter a pup's outlook on the world and reaction to it can be sent and received during this time. A pup's activity level at seven weeks has been shown to be a better predictor of future behavior than handling tests, but even this assessment is far from a sure thing during a period of such rapid change. The obvious solution is to test pups more than once—at, say, seven weeks and twelve weeks of age—and to include evaluation of activity-level as well as handling responses in the assessment. The aggregate score of such testing, perhaps weighted to favor the twelve-week rating, would probably provide a more accurate predicator of future temperament and behavior than a seven-week score alone.

There is a problem with a second, later testing at twelve weeks, though. Pups have often been adopted by this time and are with their new families. Not many people would want to believe any bad news about their youngster at this cute stage, and still fewer would act on it. I can just imagine what children would say if they had owned a new pup for a month and then someone was to say, "Sorry, kids, but she must go back to the breeder. She's tested fearful and hyperactive and might turn out to be a real handful." If parents followed through on such an edict their name would be mud. So we may be stuck with one-time seven- or eight-week testing or none at all. Some would say better none at all, but I don't really agree with this view, whatever other pundits may say. I don't think every twist and turn of a pup's personality can be determined at seven weeks, but I think that useful information can be gleaned as long as the results of testing are interpreted with caution and tempered with common sense.

A child psychologist turned puppy temperament researcher, Peggy Shunick, whom I advised on a master's-degree project here at Tufts, had previously conducted some modified puppy temperament testing at her former seat of learning, the University of Montana. She had not tried to evaluate all aspects of temperament testing in her studies but had focused on scientific (measured) assessments of forwardness, active approach, and exploration, versus shyness. The more forward type of puppies, she predicted, might possess the potential for dominance-related aggression, whereas the others would be more likely to be submissive or fearful. She divided a group of more forward pups into two subgroups and followed their progress in two different management paradigms. Owners of pups in the first subgroup were instructed to interact with the pups as they saw fit, nurturing them and supporting them as necessary. Owners in the other subgroup were required to engage in two simple behavioral measures; to crate-train their pups and to feed them only after they had obeyed a command (such as sitting or lying down when instructed). It didn't surprise me to learn that the former subgroup went on to develop dominance aggression whereas pups in the latter subgroup turned out to be respectful and nonaggressive. This experiment demonstrated the validity of predictive tests for dominance as well as the influence of owner interactions in shaping a dog's behavior.

Although puppy temperament testing is an important matter, puppies are not the only ones being adopted. What are the odds of accurately predicting the behavior of an adult dog you want to adopt? It's a good question, but again one where the answer needs some qualification. Basically, it should be a much easier task to evaluate a finished product than one in a state of metamorphosis, but when is the product finished?

Albert Einstein said of human beings that their personalities are largely formed by the time they are around eighteen years of age. After that, he thought, the veneer could be changed but the underlying character would remain the same. You could say, "What did he know? He was a physicist, not a psychologist" . . . but let's face it, the man had brains. Eighteen years of age for a person, awhile after puberty and nuzzling into young adulthood, corresponds to an age of about eighteen months in a dog. If Einstein was correct (and I permit myself to extrapolate a bit), a dog's character should be pretty much formed by this age. If we accept this, the only question remaining is, can you determine anything about that dog's character that might predict how it will behave? Most dog experts say yes, and I would agree with them in this assessment, but the operative word is *expert*. I don't think most would-be dog owners would know a potentially dominant or fearful dog from a hole in the ground. I have come to believe this because of the things my clients tell me when I ask how they chose their dog. Some picked their dog because it ran at them like a long-lost friend and jumped all over them, licking them and barking at them. This is a more dominant type of dog that has the potential for additional aggressive behavior if not properly managed. Others chose a dog because they felt sorry for it. They picked a dog that might, for example, have been sulking in the corner of a kennel, looking miserable and oppressed. This is the more anxious and fearful type of dog with the potential for anxious behaviors.

I have often said that if people wish to choose a problem-free dog they should select a dog in between these two extremes. But one owner corrected me for this point of view. She said that to ignore a dog because it is trembling in the back of a kennel was to pass up on a needy dog that could someday become your best friend. She had a point. On reconsidering I thought there might also be a place for the bouncy "Tiggers" of the world, too. They may be just the ticket for bucking up some lonely person whose quality of life might be greatly enhanced by their effervescent presence. I felt a bit ashamed of my formerly glib statements about how to avoid problem behaviors and now stand corrected. You should choose with your heart as well as your head.

Dutch researchers calculated the predictability of several behavior problems that occur in dogs adopted from shelters. Most behavior problems, but not dominance aggression, were predictable to some extent based on temperament testing. Separation anxiety had the highest predictability . . . one hundred percent. Dogs with separation anxiety are some of the neediest dogs in shelters. They are dogs who, dare I say it, love too much. Although they make very fine and extremely affectionate pets, problems arise when you have to leave them alone. But then again, not everyone spends hours away from home every day. Some people are virtually housebound. Successful adoption of these and other dogs depends on the owner's circumstances, needs, and expectations as well as on the dog's personality.

The results of temperament testing are not the be-all and end-all for pups or adult dogs. In adopting a new puppy I would pay attention to its breed, the behavioral characteristics of both parents (and grand-parents, if possible), and the way in which the pup was raised, as well as to its temperament. In the latter context, I would use standard tests of activity, reactivity, and sociability, as described above. I would then factor in my own situation, making the final decision with input from all my family members. After all, the dog I choose would have to be right for them, too. Lastly, if I adopted a pup, I would make absolutely sure that the youngster had continuing socialization experiences dur-ing what remained of the sensitive period and into the juvenile stage of its development. This whole process sounds a little involved, and I suppose it is, but such considerations are necessary and well worth-while if viewed in the context of a fourteen- (or so) year investment in a prospective family pet. In adopting a shelter dog I would avoid dogs aggressive to children, even though this flaw can sometimes be ad-dressed, and would search for a dog that would integrate well with my family in other ways, too. Temperament testing, or at least my impres-sion of the dog's personality, would be an integral part of such decision making, and I have faith that I would be able to make an assessment that would contribute meaningfully toward a truly successful adoption.

URINATION PROBLEMS

There are many reasons why dogs soil within the home, many of which are simple to correct. First let's take a look at normal elimination behavior, as the voiding of urine and feces is sometimes termed, before we get on to considering aberrations of it. As most folk may already know, puppies, like children, do not have any conscious control of their bladders or bowels when they are first born. Their moms are the ones who stimulate them to evacuate by strategic licking and who struggle to keep them and the nest clean. This all changes around the three-week mark as rapidly developing youngsters start to wobble away from the nest, gradually acquiring more control over when and where they eliminate their waste. Immaculate control of urination, however, including the ability to hold urine for several hours at a time, is not achieved until pups are much older. A simple rule of thumb is that they can hold urine for the number of hours corresponding to their age in months, plus one. Wanting a pup to be housebroken at the earliest opportunity is one of new owners' primary goals, but they have to know what is reasonable to expect, otherwise they will set impossible goals for their pup.

One good thing working in everyone's favor is that puppies, when they have achieved some measure of control over their bodily functions, have a natural inclination to keep their home, their den, clean. This tendency probably arose over the eons as it conferred some survival benefit. For example, it is possible that dogs that were fastidious about keeping their dens clean (of feces, anyway) may have had a lower parasite load, making them more thrifty individuals. Whatever the explanation, pups do go out of their way to avoid soiling close to the areas where they eat and sleep, and this instinct can be used to advantage in housebreaking.

The usual advice to a new owner who is acquiring a six-to-eight-week-old pup is to paper-train it by confining it in a large pen or in the bathroom with newspaper or an absorbent pad of some sort at one end and its food and bed at the other. Pretty soon the pup will confine its urination and defecation endeavors to the paper location, and when this is happening dependably the confinement can be discontinued. Paper-training seems to work quite well for the majority of pups of around two to three months of age but is less useful for older pups, and may even send them the wrong message. It could signal, for example, that it is okay to urinate inside the home, slowing down overall progress in housebreaking. For this reason, it is probably best to shift pups from paper-training, a diaper equivalent, to urinating at outside locations at or around three months of age. If you're starting with a more mature pup, train him to urinate and defecate outside right from the start.

The question now is how to proceed with this training, or in the case of an older dog that has experienced a lapse in housebreaking, how to get it back on track. And the answer is, with understanding and patience—NO punishment for "mistakes." Konrad Lorenz had it pegged right in his book *Man Meets Dog* when he quoted (regarding training of any sort):

> Art and science aren't enough,
> Patience is the basic stuff

With regard to housebreaking, two opposite persuasions should be invoked; one, an attractive force, providing all the opportunity and incentive the dog needs to persuade it to eliminate in a selected area away from the home; the other, a detractive force, achieved by removing all in-home incentive for house soiling. On the attractive side, a suitable area to which the pup (or dog) is taken several times per day should be selected. The best location is one where the dog had previously shown some inclination to urinate, but if a new area is selected it can be made attractive by baiting it with a sample of the dog's urine on newspaper.

The pup should be brought to this area on lead first thing in the morning, fifteen to twenty minutes after its breakfast, in midmorning, after lunch, in mid- and late afternoon, after dinner, and last thing at night. In addition, it is a good idea to take the pup out when it wakes up after a nap and after it has been playing or chewing a toy. These are all key times when the drive to eliminate is high.

For older dogs, a slightly less hectic, but nevertheless regular, schedule should be adopted. On bringing the recalcitrant pup to the chosen area it should be walked up and down, not allowing it to become distracted by anything other than its own attempts to eliminate. It may be helpful to use some repetitive phrase such as "Hurry up" or "Come along" that will in time be associated with the whole ritual—for that's what we are trying to develop. As the pup squats to urinate or defecate, its owner should remain stationary until the triumphant moment, at which point he or she must immediately sing out the dog's praises, pet it, and offer it a tasty (therefore memorable) food treat. The immediacy and delectability of the reward is vital to the success of the process.

It is not a good practice to go straight back to the house after a dog has "performed." This may have the opposite effect of reward if the dog likes to be outside and can cause smart dogs to postpone eliminating in the hopes of extending their time outdoors. When time permits it is best to tarry for a while after the dog has performed to avoid this negative association. Some owners reward their dogs for "going to the bathroom" outside only when they get back inside. Who knows how many other events will have taken place during the homeward trek, including reentering the house? If there is more than a short delay between elimination and the positive reinforcement, it is unlikely that the dog will appreciate the full significance of the reward.

Now that all this is clear, it is easy to understand why simply turning a dog out in the yard in the hopes that it will train itself is not always successful. Maybe some particularly fastidious dogs may get it right when left to their own devices and desires, but when a house-breaking problem develops it is in the owner's best interest to invest time and energy in the retraining process as outlined. Outside, pups in training can enjoy fresh air, obtain sweet relief, and garner warm praise as their just dessert. The whole experience becomes well worth waiting for.

When things go well, pups will start holding on to their urine and feces as they are supposed to within a few short days. Things don't always go well, however, even if the owner does everything right. Some dogs are just hard to train. Trainability, stemming from a willingness to please, was touched on earlier, but to embellish on it a bit regarding housebreaking, females are generally quicker studies than the males, and toys, terriers, and hounds are harder to train than herding and working dogs. Nevertheless, all dogs are potentially trainable unless they have been improperly raised and forced to soil the nest through neglect. The latter situation can produce some extremely recalcitrant characters whose rehabilitation can be a real project.

Now the question that arises is what to do if the pup refuses to urinate while outside. The solution to this is confinement—not as a punishment, but to prevent the pup from urinating in the house. Most pups, when confined in a suitably small space, will hold on to their urine (and feces) rather than stand and deliver and be forced to wallow in the consequences. Confinement should be by means of a crate, or can be in a small gated-off area. The pup should remain there for ten or fifteen minutes before being taken out again. The process is repeated as many times as necessary until outdoor success is achieved. A bowl of chicken soup early in the proceedings will help to hurry things along. What goes in must come out. When a mission is successful, the pup can be allowed a greater degree of freedom on its return to the house. It may, for example, be allowed to run around the whole kitchen area, but to let it out of sight at an early stage of the proceedings is asking for trouble until the dog learns the house rules.

Regarding the confinement technique: If a pup has not been trained to accept a crate and becomes distressed when restrained in this way, a crate may not be suitable for the training process unless the pup is first desensitized to it. This can be achieved but adds another step to the training process. When fear of the crate is a factor, it may be better to try some other method of confinement. The gated-off-recess idea may work, but if it doesn't the pup may have to be secured to a stout table leg by means of a short (four-foot) lead. Alternatively, umbilical-cord training can be employed, in which the pup is anchored to the owner's belt by the lead. The principle behind all these techniques is to prevent the pup from being able to eliminate and then get clear of the mess. The success of the technique relies upon a pup's natural instinct to keep itself clean.

Occasionally an owner will come across a pup that, by some unfortunate quirk of experience, has been forced to soil where it stands. Perhaps it has been confined in a small cage in a pet store or transport cage and has either had to overcome its natural instinct for cleanliness or burst. Such pups are much more difficult to train because there isn't always a "safe" place in which they can be confined. In such cases, I inquire about areas of the home in which the dog has never before urinated and then advise the owners to confine the dog in one of those places at night and following unproductive trips to the backyard. This plan seems to work fairly well, and because of it I have very few problem urinaters that I haven't been able to cure. I have even managed to train some chronic house soilers that were never trained when they were young, didn't respect the sanctity of the crate, and had used the floor as their bathroom for many years. I regard retraining dogs like this as something of a challenge. If I were the dog's owner, though, I would never have got into the situation in the first place. Why would anyone leave it for years before addressing such a problem? It doesn't make sense . . . but it happens.

One question I am often asked is, "But what do I do if I find a mess on the floor or catch him in the act of squatting to urinate? Should I punish him?" There are actually two questions here, the first referring to delayed punishment and the second to immediate punishment. As many of you may already know, delayed punishment does no good and may make matters worse by making your dog anxious. Dogs do not associate something they did hours before with a punishment that you administer long after the fact. The practice of dragging a dog over to a urine-soiled spot and rubbing its nose in it can actually be counterproductive. The second part of the question refers to immediate punishment. This *will* reduce the frequency of the behavior in your presence, but the dog now learns not to urinate in front of you, making subsequent attempts to persuade the dog to urinate outside much less likely to be successful. You can almost imagine what the dog would be thinking in this situation: "I'm not urinating in front of that psycho. Last time I tried that he became practically apoplectic. I'll wait until later when he's not around . . . that way things will be a lot more pleasant."

So you shouldn't punish the dog for messing on the floor. Actually, you should really punish yourself for letting it happen. It wouldn't have happened if you had kept him confined or kept an eye on him, as you were supposed to. What you *should* do is learn the premonitory signs of when your dog is about to urinate (sniffing, circling, and so on), and then, at the critical point, right as he squats, make a loud noise by banging on a table or shaking a "shake can" (an empty soda can with pennies inside). The purpose of this distraction, which, hopefully, will not be associated with your presence, is to startle the dog and shut down his sphincters, causing him to abort the mission. The desired effect should be the same as if a fire alarm were to go off in a busy public toilet—the interruption of all flow. Right after you have made the clatter, you appear—smiling, lead in hand—to take your dog out for a stroll in the garden (where the shake cans are always silent).

Another integral part of the housetraining involves discouraging urination (and defecation) within the home by removing all traces of previous soiling episodes. The simplest and most effective method is that of odor neutralization. This is achieved not by scrubbing the soiled area with detergents or trying to drown odors with fragrances, but by using odor-elimination strategies directed toward removing the components of urine that cause the smell. Odors of untreated urine marks will attract a dog back to the spot as surely as a heat-seeking missile is drawn to a source of heat.

The only way I know to accomplish odor neutralization effectively is by using a commercially produced enzymatic or bacteria-containing product. There are several available and when they are in good shape they work well, but they have to have been stored correctly to retain their potency. If they have sat on a shelf for years or been exposed to bright sunlight you might as well apply water to the spot. When intact, however, these products remove odor-causing chemicals from a urine-soiled surface with the same efficiency that an enzymatic laundry detergent demonstrates in removing biological stains from clothing. Odors just melt away. But beware, the offending surface should not be cleaned with harsh chemicals prior to odor neutralization, as some chemicals will inactivate the biological ingredients.

As a final cleaning hint, ammoniacal products are even worse than useless and should be avoided like the plague. Ammonia smells like urine, because urea breaks down to form ammonia, so it may even act as an irresistible lure for recovering urinoholics.

Consider the case of Murkie, a six-and-a-half-year-old castrated male Pomeranian. Coincident with a death in the family, Murkie began urinating in the house three months prior to his owner consulting with me. The form the behavior took was squatting to urinate on rugs right in front of the owner and it seemed to occur mostly when there was some kind of commotion going on. His owner tried letting him outside several times a day but when Murkie came back in he was just as likely to engage in his obnoxious little ritual. Ancillary historical data suggested that Murkie was mildly dominant, mainly over food and personal space, and that he showed some signs of separation anxiety.

His owner had already taken the first and most vital step in dealing with problems of this nature. He had taken Murkie to the vet for a full physical examination and urine tests. Murkie was found to be in excellent health on physical examination and the urine tests were unremarkable. Many behaviorists have been caught trying to treat what seems like a breakdown of housetraining by behavioral methods, only to find out later in the course of treatment that the dog has a mild bladder infection that is contributing to the problem. Unless medical causes of inappropriate urination are ruled out first, especially in a mature dog that has suddenly started to urinate around the house, purely behavioral therapy will fail.

Another "rule-out" when it comes to a male that is urinating inappropriately is hormonally driven urine marking in the form of leg lifting (see later)—but that wasn't Murkie's problem either; he was neutered, and anyway, he was squatting. A remote consideration was that he might have been urinating as a result of separation anxiety, but Murkie went out of his way to urinate in front of his owner and rarely had an accident when alone. This raised the possibility that submissive urination might be involved. Murkie, however, was more dominant than fearful and, in any case, was too old and the wrong sex for submissive urination to be a serious consideration. I moved toward a diagnosis of a simple house-soiling problem caused by, or somehow linked to, the death in the family; perhaps related to the attendant changes in routine that must have occurred. The only thing seemingly against this diagnosis was Murkie's high-profile, in-your-face pattern of urination right the middle of the rug and the fact that the behavior was exacerbated by environmental stress.

Ultimately I sat on the fence regarding Murkie's diagnosis, explaining to Mr. Murkie (as I will call him) that his dog showed some signs of a breach of housetraining *and* others of an anxiety-related urine-marking behavior. The anxiety, I postulated, could have been a direct result of the family loss as Murkie was closely attached to the dear departed. Alternatively, it could have been a reflection of lack of attention or somehow acquired through observation of the behavior of the grief-stricken occupants of the house. To cover all bases I suggested retraining Murkie to use an outside location for urination, thorough cleanup of soiled areas with an odor neutralizer, and pharmacologic therapy. I selected the antidepressant Elavil for the retraining process. The combination treatment may have been overkill, but it worked. Murkie's little problem, which may have been a combination of two problems, as is often the case, was resolved within a couple of weeks. His medication was tapered off a couple of months later and he never looked back.

Another cause of inappropriate urination involves older dogs, who begin soiling within the house for reasons of cognitive decline. I will not dwell on this topic here because I devoted some time to this "cognitive dysfunction syndrome" (aka canine Alzheimer's) in the section "G—Geriatric Behavior Problems." Nevertheless, this possibility must be borne in mind when dealing with house-soiling problems in dogs approaching or over ten years of age. One of the ways it can present is nocturnal incontinence, although in the final stages affected dogs may walk around the house with urine or feces practically falling out of them. I know at least one owner who resorted to diapers for his dog, but there is now an effective treatment, L-deprenyl (trade name Anapryl), which can reverse some of the behavioral changes of aging—in the early stages, anyway—and buy older dogs a little more time.

Leg Lifting

"What is it that men do standing up, women do sitting down, and dogs do on three legs?" I read recently on the outside of a greeting card. The answer inside the card was "Shake hands." So well known is the three-legged urination stance adopted by many (but not all) dogs that jokes about it are rife, from vaudeville to present-day movies. I took my kids to see the movie *Mr. Magoo* recently. In this film, Magoo's English bulldog is depicted standing on its hind legs behind a louvered screen, supposedly urinating against an enameled image of a fire hydrant. All the children in the movie theater roared with laughter at this scene, the significance of the unusual canine-urination posture not lost on them. Dogs' predilection for cocking their legs on fire hydrants and lampposts is practically legend. But what more do folks know about leg lifting, other than the fact that it occurs? Why do dogs do it? Which dogs do it? What does it mean? Can it be a behavioral problem (for owners), and if so, how can this problem be redirected or otherwise controlled?

Nothing I have read has addressed the fundamental issue of how dogs discover that they should lift a leg to urinate in the first place. When you understand that leg lifting is almost exclusively a male phenomenon, and considering the male anatomy, it makes sense that they might attempt it to avoid urinating on themselves—that is, for logistical reasons similar to those determining human urination postures—but there are other drives favoring leg lifting, too. Leg lifting in males starts at around four or five months, an age of enlightenment as hormones start to course through the veins and youngsters realize for the first time which way in this world is up. I imagine that around this time one or two prime thinker males in the litter get fed up with standing in a pool of urine when they relieve themselves and find that cocking a leg makes a lot more sense. Their littermates may then copy them, if they don't figure it out for themselves, including some tomboy females.

But urine carries a potent chemical signal in the form of pheromones, a signal that is subtly different for males and females and provides information about a dog's sexual status and identity. The male signal seems to shout "Kilroy was here" and is the olfactory equivalent of Tim (the Tool Man) Taylor's all-male yodel, whereas the female signal passively indicates sexual receptivity. Think how thrilling it must be for a male pup to discover that he can stay dry *and* deliver a powerful signal of his adolescent doghood all over the neighbor's rose bushes at the same time. It's a twofer deal that is too good to pass up. In fact, it's so good a deal that most dogs don't want to have all that fun at once and carefully ration their urine supply to ensure that they can "mark" around their entire territory. This requires some practice and considerable concentration but, once mastered, brings hours of one-upmanship pleasure.

As a matter of form, dogs that are urine marking by leg lifting deposit urine in prominent locations along the periphery of their territory (especially in zones where conflict occurs). They do this partly to refresh their own fading urine marks, and partly in an attempt to "overmark" their competitors' urine. They also overmark the urine of neighborhood bitches, as if to advertise their interest and stake a claim. When intermale competition focuses on a strategically situated hydrant, tree, or lamppost, the proverbial pissing contest ensues. Each dog tries to eclipse the pheromonal odor of its competitors by issuing the most recent and comprehensive urine mark. Sometimes a dog's attempts to cover an adversary's mark require special effort; a leg cocked extra high, for example. For small dogs, the limits of coverage come all too soon when conventional leg-lifting practices are employed, and some utilize the ingenious gymnastic measure of standing on their front legs to raise their nether regions higher into the air. This handstand posture assures them the most complete coverage they are capable of without climbing on a chair. The whole practice is really quite an art to dogs, though an enigma to us two-legged observers in the kingdom of the olfactorily blind.

No one really gets bent out of shape by the fact that males lift a leg to urinate. It's urine marking *in the home* that causes the real headaches. By definition, urine marking involves the frequent disposition of small volumes of urine in strategic locations. When these locations are outside, everything is copacetic as far as owners are concerned, but when urine marking occurs within the home, most of them quickly lose patience with the situation.

Let's ponder this problem for a while because the causation and treatment of in-home leg lifting can be quite complex. First, there's a hormonally driven variety of in-home urine marking that occurs only in unneutered dogs. Urine marking of this type is just as troubling as any other kind of indoor urine marking, but the treatment, castration, usually provides a simple and expedient solution. Male identification signals in urine are fabricated under the influence of the male hormone, testosterone. In the absence of testosterone, following castration, dogs seem to lose the piquancy of their male odor and may be viewed by their peers as being of neutral, noncontesting sociosexual status. I believe that neutered dogs realize they have lost a little je ne sais quois following "the snip," including the ability to leave a meaningful mark. This lack of aromatic potency could be the explanation for the fact that some sixty to seventy percent of dogs show a dramatic decrease in urine marking within the first few weeks of castration.

More troubling and obdurate is urine marking that occurs (or persists) in neutered dogs. We cannot attribute this behavior to hormones, yet the motivation can still be sexual because it is sometimes triggered or enhanced by a neighboring bitch coming into heat. The mechanism of maleness persisting after neutering is discussed more fully in the section on sexual behavior. Let it suffice to say at this point that a male brain is hard-wired in utero and many other male behaviors often persist after neutering, including the extreme ones of mounting and even penetrating bitches. Residual maleness, coupled with the fact that old habits die hard, may be responsible for this apparent paradox—though some dogs may still just not want to get their feet wet.

For bitches in heat, estrogen increases urine marking by squatting, thanks to a mechanism similar to the one that inspires their male counterparts to run around lifting their legs. This sudden increase in the frequency of urine marking in bitches around estrus is part of their sexual-advertisement display. I have never been presented with a case of urine marking within the home resulting from this cause, but I stand prepared. The solution would be to neuter the bitch, though this would not be acceptable to the owner of a brood bitch. In any case, the problem would be of a temporary nature, occurring only during the heat period, though it would most likely return at the next heat some six to twelve months later. Treatment with synthetic progesterone would shut the problem down, but the possible side effects of these agents in an unneutered bitch are unacceptable and amount to a contraindication.

Another reason for neutered dogs to engage in urine marking relates to dominance, as urine marking can be a defiant gesture. When the hierarchical structure of a dog's pack (including human family members) is destabilized, some would-be dominant dogs employ urine marking to identify objects and territory they wish to claim as their own. The culprits often show other signs of dominant behavior, such as food guarding or space guarding, and may be having contretemps with other dogs in the household. Such dogs respond well to the reestablishment of law and order within the family pack, with the owners doing the policing. A dominance-control program (see Appendix) is what is needed here. Such a program will often curtail dominance-related urine marking by bossy dogs as well as controlling ongoing aggression.

Leg lifting (or urine marking by squatting) can stem from anxiety or conflict. Many species of animal signal their distress about environmental issues by increasing the frequency of urine marking to underline their presence and validity. In this situation, they behave as if they are insecure and have an increased need for acknowledgment. Factors that precipitate this kind of marking include sudden alteration in the family pack caused by the arrival of a new baby, unwelcome visitors, and environmental upheavals (as in the case of Murkie, earlier in this section).

Sudden-onset urine marking for reasons such as these is a call for recognition, a rebellion of sorts. But it's not only males that react in this way: Females also may register their disapproval by means of such uriniferous graffiti. Bitches do not usually leg lift to deliver their message of disapproval, but squat in their usual way to deposit small amounts of urine on selected horizontal surfaces. One example of female marking that I was consulted about involved a female Lhasa apso that started to urine mark in the home following the arrival of a new baby one warm and clingy July day. Interestingly, this dog also used fecal marking, a much less frequently used marking strategy, to symbolize the summer of its discontent. Successful treatment of this problem involved a thorough cleanup of soiled areas with a proprietary odor neutralizer, desensitization of the dog to the presence of the baby (a process that would probably have occurred naturally over time), and symptomatic pharmacotherapy with the antianxiety drug BuSpar. Interestingly, conventional veterinary wisdom has suggested that antidepressants, such as Elavil and Tofranil, may be effective in curtailing in-home urine marking that is not amenable to behavioral therapy alone. The rationale for this treatment, however, was lacking. As antidepressants tend to calm nervous and apprehensive dogs, it seems likely that most otherwise treatment resistant cases of urine marking responding to this line of therapy must, in retrospect, have arisen as a result of some kind of psychological pressure. Since BuSpar's action is in many ways similar to that of antidepressants, it is not surprising that it, too, can sometimes be deployed successfully in such situations.

So there you have it in a nutshell; from the fire hydrant to the psychologist's couch in three easy steps. Seriously, though, leg lifting is more complex than it may at first appear, especially to us unenlightened humans, with its motivation ranging from simple delineation of territory to dominance struggles, antagonism, and anxiety. As usual in the treatment of behavior problems, it is imperative to know what forces are operating in a particular case if therapy is to be applied successfully. To this end, a thorough behavioral history, vis-à-vis a detailed analysis of the problem, is of paramount importance and should precede any attempts to alter the behavior—though neutering intact dogs is usually a good first step and is often indicated for other behavioral and social reasons as well. Finally, we should all remember that urine marking by leg lifting or squatting is a *normal* canine behavior—a signaling system that simply demonstrates a dog's natural reaction to surrounding circumstances and events. It is one of those species-typical behaviors, like barking, digging, and chasing small varmints, that, though sometimes aggravating for owners, does not represent a problem per se for the dog. I think it is important to bear this in mind before getting too frustrated with our pets' behavior. After all, we are the ones that brought them in to live with us and they're only doing what comes naturally.

Inappropriate urination behavior is the most common issue reported by owners who are solicited about problem behaviors their dog may be showing. On its own it accounts for some twenty percent of all problems reported to behaviorists. Not only are elimination problems prevalent but they portend serious consequences for the offenders. About twenty percent of dogs brought to shelters have house soiling reported as at least part of the reason for the dog's surrender. Owners can be very forgiving about a number of canine transgressions, sometimes their patience stuns me, but inappropriate urination is not one of those behaviors that lends itself to the owners' forebearance and understanding. To live in a house reeking of urine gets tiresome pretty quickly, and if someone doesn't give frustrated owners of "problem eliminators" the right advice fairly early on, the dog can rapidly find itself in a Russian roulette-type adoption situation in which (according to published figures) the gun has three chambers and two of them are loaded. For a behaviorist, the words *inappropriate elimination* should and in fact do command our undivided attention lest we fail the dog and the client. The consequences are too serious to consider this problem any other way.

VETERINARY CAUSES
OF BEHAVIOR PROBLEMS

Sometimes I wonder how anyone can advise about behavior problems without first having some knowledge of the medical processes that may underlie them. I was watching a television program on dog training one day when I heard a not-so-knowledgeable trainer advise the owner of a mature dog that was urinating around the house to crate it and deny it water to train it out of this supposed bad habit. "Cripes," I thought, "with that advice this guy's going to kill thousands of dogs, who, because of medical problems (like diabetes and kidney disease), need greater-than-normal water intake to maintain a consistent internal environment."

A few months later I was invited to join this trainer on a TV show to discuss treatment of separation anxiety and obsessive-compulsive disorder in dogs. Hoping for the best but prepared for the worst, I lined up a couple of cases and looked forward to a healthy debate that would enlighten dog owners about these problems. Meanwhile, the trainer contacted one of the clients, the owner of the dog with separation anxiety, and told her that it was her fault her dog was acting out. He told her that the problem had arisen because she hadn't trained the dog properly and verbally scourged her for using a crate. Not content with this assault, he contradicted my provisional diagnosis of separation anxiety and generally made a fool of himself.

I saw the dog a couple of days later and was able to confirm the diagnosis irrefutably: separation anxiety—textbook variety. During the owner's visit with me, I tried to pour oil on what were now troubled waters, but the effect of the trainer's criticisms made her feel so terrible that she would not permit the filming of her dog. The TV producer was informed about the trainer's inappropriate behavior and choked him off, but I doubt that the producer's words made much impression. The final straw came when this Gaston-like trainer told the owner of the dog with obsessive-compulsive disorder that it didn't need a behaviorist, just a good (choke-chain-style) trainer. As any human OCD sufferer, psychologist, or psychiatrist appreciates, boot camp is not what helps in such a disorder. When I heard this latest gaff I was left in no doubt as to this trainer's lack of knowledge as well as professionalism and I threw in the towel. In deference to trainers in general, most of them would really appreciate the opportunity to learn more about the animals they work with, but not this guy. As the old boardroom saying goes, "Where you stand on an issue depends on where you sit." But then again, whatever your position, there is no excuse for having a closed mind.

For those of you with open minds, here's a brief synopsis of how medical conditions can affect behavior. First, let's take a look at a few neurological conditions, starting out with partial seizures (sometimes referred to as petit mal) and then working through various other innate and acquired conditions.

Partial Seizures

The prevalence of partial seizures has not been widely appreciated until recently because of their discrepant presentations, similarity to "normal" behaviors, and because of difficulties in their validation. In fact, they are quite common and cause a plethora of abnormal behavioral signs, ranging from episodes of extreme aggression and fearfulness to apparently-compulsive eating and grooming disorders. The precise manifestation in any particular case depends on the area of the brain affected. Most agree that the limbic system and hypothalamus are most commonly affected. Seizure-prone breeds, such as poodles, retrievers, bull terriers, and German shepherds, are the ones most commonly affected, and puberty (around six to twelve months) or young adulthood (one to two years of age) are the times when the condition usually surfaces. Perhaps it is stress associated with the pressures of growing up that triggers these seizures in the first place. No one knows for sure.

A few basic rules apply to the diagnosis of behavioral seizures, though none is absolute. First, it is important to be on the lookout for so-called pre-ictal (preseizural) mood changes that herald the seizures. These can vary from slight "spaciness" and staring at walls or spots on the floor to growling and seclusion. Next, the behavior that erupts during this state of altered mood is often excessive, inappropriate, and out of context and may be accompanied by signs of "autonomic" arousal, such as dilatation of the pupils and salivation. Finally, following a seizural bout, whatever form that takes, some dogs show post-ictal signs such as tiredness, detachedness, and lack of response to behavioral cues. This is the classical picture of a behavioral seizure, although there are many variations on the theme.

The main features that lead a clinician to diagnose these behaviors is their weirdness and impropriety. Confirmation of the clinical diagnosis is by electroencephalography (EEG) when abnormal (epileptiform) spikes are seen. EEG testing, however, is not always definitive. False-negative results are the neurologist's bane. Sometimes circumstantial evidence plus a positive response to anticonvulsants, such as pheno-barbital, is the only way to confirm behavioral seizures. Even so, some dogs with a suspicious history do not respond to anticonvulsants, leaving the final diagnosis up in the air.

One of the most infamous and dreaded presentations of behavioral seizures is so-called rage syndrome. Rage is a rare condition of extreme aggression affecting primarily springer and cocker spaniels, bull terriers, and retrievers (to name but a few susceptible breeds). Classical features are that the aggression is triggered by trivial, sometimes almost undiscernible stimuli and that the dog's aggressive reaction is excessive for the situation in which it occurs. Sufferers frequently show

signs of dominance aggression, too, confusing the diagnosis and leading some behaviorists to believe that the behavior represents an extreme of dominance rather than a seizural condition per se. Some
behaviorists sit on the fence with this condition, calling it idiopathic
aggression—which means literally "aggression of unknown cause" (not
very helpful). However, since I have come across dogs with classic
behavioral signs of rage plus EEG signs of seizure activity, and have
had success in treating some of these dogs with phenobarbital, I remain convinced in the existence of the syndrome.

One dog with rage that I treated had me confused about its diagnosis initially, because of the dominance crossover to which I just referred. The dog, a three-year-old neutered male English springer
spaniel called Sir Chatham Bar, started to act aggressively when he
was two years old. In these early days of Sir Chatham's problem behavior, aggressive incidents took the form of growling or biting his owners
and were provoked by touching or approaching his food while he was
eating it, by petting him, or by threatening him with a newspaper.
These are classic signs of dominance aggression. Luckily, Sir Chatham's owners, Bill and Sharon Miller, were devoted to his welfare and
were committed to doing whatever could be done to get him back on
the right track. I found a lot of things that needed to be adjusted in Sir
Chatham's life, including providing him with more opportunities for
exercise and entertainment and adjusting his diet. Then, to address the
aggression problem more directly, I advised Bill and Sharon to avoid
situations likely to promote conflict and to alter their interactions with
Sir Chatham by means of the Nothing in Life Is Free program.

I followed Sir Chatham's progress, or rather, lack thereof, with
great interest. Bill and Sharon were super at staying in touch and sent
me faxes every couple of weeks detailing Sir Chatham's behavior and
asking for fine-tuning advice. I was left in no doubt that they were
religiously following the behavior-modification program, but Sir Chatham's behavior worsened. I tried Prozac for a while but that didn't help
either. Bearing in mind the relatively late onset of Sir Chatham's aggression, his breed, and escalating aggression in the face of a well-run
dominance program, I was getting more and more suspicious that his
behavior could reflect a seizural problem.

His aggression was becoming increasingly irrational and extreme. As he approached three and a half years of age, he refused to allow anyone to attach a lead to his collar, so the Millers had to leave his lead on at all times and pray that it would not become detached. The lead was taken off once during a visit to the vet's office and it took the Millers a couple of days to find Sir Chatham in a frame of mind that permitted them to reattach it. He had also started to guard the house, becoming extremely aggressive to all visitors . . . and to Bill when he came back from work. Bill could not come into his own home unless Sharon first picked up the lead and restrained Sir Chatham. Even so, the snarling and lunging that occurred were beyond a joke. Once Bill was inside, Sir Chatham would settle down, but coming home, for Bill, was like running the gauntlet.

It got to the point that neither Bill nor Sharon could pet Sir Chatham at all, they had to stay well clear of his food bowl, getting him out of the house (or even worse, back in) was risking life and limb, and their mealtimes became something to survive. When he wasn't in an aggressive frame of mind (which wasn't very often), Sir Chatham would show signs of nervousness and anxiety, often whining, pacing, and seeking attention. It was a strange dichotomy, much more marked than the typical moodiness of a purely dominant dog. He was a true Jekyll and Hyde.

One day, against my advice and his better judgment, Bill decided to give Sir Chatham a cube of cheese from a leftover salad. As he offered the cheese to Sir Chatham, the dog's eyes glazed over and he lunged at Bill, biting him badly in the hand. But it didn't stop there. Although Bill threw the cheese down, Sir Chatham continued to advance on Bill, growling and baring his teeth. Bill fled the table and backed up toward a wall. Sir Chatham kept coming, apparently intent on inflicting yet more injuries on Bill. Sharon heard the commotion and came running, somehow managing to pick up Sir Chatham's lead and dragging him off at great personal risk. The type of aggression that Sir Chatham showed is not typical of dominance aggression, which is usually over in a couple of seconds once the dog has got its own way. Afterward, dominant dogs usually seem remorseful or unaware of what has occurred. Sir Chatham did not respond in this way. He was seething, festering in a state of rage, and was not going to desist from attempting to injure Bill until he was physically prevented from doing so. Luckily for Bill, Sharon had saved his bacon.

Then came the clinical-diagnostic coup de grâce: A few days later Sir Chatham had a peculiar turn that could only be explained as a seizure. It occurred at six o'clock in the morning, when Bill heard a strange bumping sound coming from the direction of Sir Chatham's bed. He got up to see what was going on and found Sir Chatham trying to walk toward him shakily, apparently having difficulty standing. It wasn't long before Sir Chatham fell on the floor with a startled look on his face, and lay there quite still, unable to move, his back legs shaking violently. The whole episode only lasted a couple of minutes, after which he seemed to regain his focus and things were back to normal— until five hours later, that is. At eleven o'clock that morning, rather atypically, Sir Chatham had fallen asleep on the kitchen floor. While he was asleep, Sharon noticed that all four of his legs began to tremble and shake for about two minutes. As Bill and Sharon related these incidents to me, my worst suspicions were confirmed. I painted a rather grim picture of what the future held in store for them and Sir Chatham. Nevertheless, the Millers were determined to persevere with him and asked me to perform an EEG, which I duly did. The classical epileptic spiking pattern was immediately evident and I returned the neurologist's verdict to the Millers immediately. They wanted to know if there was any hope for Sir Chatham. I told them that there was but that it was only a really long shot. They opted to take their chances.

For several weeks I tried progressively increasing doses of phenobarbital and Prozac as shotgun therapy to reduce Sir Chatham's aggression. By this time the Millers were so scared of him that they asked me to keep him in the hospital for reasons of personal safety. In the hospital, he lunged at and tried to bite anyone who came anywhere near him. He was so bad that some days he could not even be taken out to go to the bathroom and had to have his kennel hosed down with him in it. He had turned into the Hannibal Lector of the canine world and was totally unapproachable.

Bill and Sharon came to visit him regularly and brought him food treats and some of his favorite toys. As they crouched outside the kennel whispering sweet nothings to him, he snarled and growled at them like a dog possessed, occasionally lunging at the bars of the kennel, startling the Millers and causing them to jump back. It was as if he didn't recognize them, or anyone else, for that matter. He was a dangerous dog.

Eventually, reluctantly, and with tears running down their faces, the Millers asked me to put Sir Chatham to sleep. This I did, and they loaded his body into a dog-sized pine coffin that Bill had made and that they had brought with them in the back of their station wagon. I stood in the parking lot and watched them slowly pull away as they headed off to a gravesite they had selected on the Cape. It was a tragic moment. I vowed at that time to continue to try to find out more about this terrible affliction and to try to devise some treatments that work.

Sir Chatham's aggression could well be described as compulsive. Several more conventional compulsive disorders rest on the dividing line between pure compulsions and partial seizurelike conditions. Among these sit-on-the-fence conditions are fly snapping (directed toward imaginary flies), shadow or light chasing, and "compulsive" spinning or tail chasing. There are several papers in the literature that describe fly catching as a sequel of seizure activity, and I have published a couple of papers myself documenting EEG changes of seizure-like activity in tail-chasing bull terriers. But these behaviors are also described as compulsive. The fact is that these two apparently discordant diagnoses are not necessarily exclusive and there may be some relationship or overlap between them. In support of this concept, there are some groups of human obsessive-compulsive behavior sufferers who have a high incidence of epileptiform activity on their EEGs. Epileptiform spikes indicate the release of small bursts of neurochemicals that predispose an animal, person, or dog to various aberrant and excessive behaviors, the nature of which depend on the site of the release. Though not ubiquitous, the occurrence of epileptiform activity in some patients with compulsive behavior provides a link between partial seizures and compulsions, one that explains what we see, what we get, and what we measure.

Congenital Problems

Aside from epileptiform seizure activity, other congenital or inherited central-nervous disorders of dogs that can cause weird behaviors include hydrocephalus and lissencephaly. Hydrocephalus, otherwise known as water on the brain, is quite common in brachycephalic (short-snouted) dogs but also occurs occasionally in mesocephalic (middle-nose-length) dogs. It is often asymptomatic, causing no problems at all for a dog throughout its life, but that isn't always the case, and central-nervous signs, such as depression and visual problems, can occur. Lissencephaly is a really strange developmental problem that occurs mainly in Lhasa apsos. In this condition, which manifests itself as mental retardation and incontinence, the normal corrugations of the cerebral cortex are practically absent, giving the forebrain a smooth, glisteny appearance on postmortem. Trying to train a dog with this problem is pointless. Unfortunately, no other treatment works either for these poor dogs.

Trauma

Head trauma can cause dramatic changes in personality. I have known this since I was a boy because of an incident that occurred to one of the workmen at my dad's factory. The man, a precision engineering grinder by trade, fell off his motorbike one day on his way to work and smashed his head on a lamppost. He was hospitalized for weeks following the accident but eventually returned to work. And when he did, he was a changed man. Before the accident this man was always angry, impatient, and aggressive (that might have had something to do with why he fell off the bike in the first place), but after his convalescence he was as mild-mannered as a monk. It was a night-and-day change—in this case, for the better.

Not all central nervous system trauma has a placating effect; in fact, the opposite change is also quite possible. A dog story illustrates this point. The dog in question, an amiable six-year-old dachshund, was struck on the head by his owner's estranged husband one day in a fit of jealousy. Immediately after that the dog developed grand-mal seizures and started to display what appeared to be fits of rage. To my mind there was no doubt that the aggression was seizure-related, but this was one case where the EEG let me down. There were no epileptiform spikes visible on the tracing, and the diagnosis of seizure-linked rage remained presumptive. I treated this dog with phenobarbital, and to the best of my recollection, the seizures did decrease in frequency and the rage attacks were somewhat quelled as well.

Trauma or diseases causing pain can also alter a dog's disposition, particularly when it comes to aggressiveness. I remember my wife (also a veterinarian) telling me about a dog she went to see that was lying on the road after it had been struck by a car. She carefully warned all the people standing around not to touch the dog because, whatever it was like before, it was now primed to bite. Cautiously, the folks helped her gently lift the dog onto a makeshift stretcher so that it could be safely transported into a house nearby. Just as they were about to ascend the front steps the stretcher wobbled and it appeared that the dog was about to fall. My wife reached to stabilize the dog and was bitten quite severely in the hand. She returned home that evening with her white coat wrapped around her hand and wearing a hangdog look. I knew something was wrong. She unwrapped her hand to display a dental map of puncture wounds still oozing blood and proceeded to tell me the story. Luckily she was vaccinated against rabies (as was the dog) and there was no nerve or tendon damage, so all that was necessary was some topical treatment and a ten-day course of antibiotics. A fortunate escape indeed. This experience firmly fixed in both of our minds the sometimes alarmingly immediate connection between theory and practice.

Infectious Diseases

No discussion of medical causes of behavioral problems would be complete without mention of infectious causes of altered behavior. The viral condition of rabies must top the list of considerations because of its severe effects and the public-health risk. Whenever a dog bites a person or acts peculiarly, the possibility of rabies, no matter how remote, should always be borne in mind. Quarantine of the dog or euthanasia followed by postmortem are the two alternatives stipulated by law in such cases. Luckily, vaccination provides very effective protection if a dog is bitten by a rabid wild animal, but vaccination, like safety netting, does not completely eliminate the possibility of breakthroughs. If a vaccinated dog that has been exposed to wildlife suddenly starts to behave oddly it's time to isolate the dog and call your vet.

Several other infectious diseases that affect the nervous system, including canine distemper and toxoplasmosis, can also alter behavior, but a full description of them is not really called for here. Let it suffice to say that odd behavior often arises from odd causes and that there are established diagnostic paths to follow to rule these diagnoses in or out.

Other Central Nervous System Causes of Altered Behavior

Noninfectious conditions affecting the central nervous system, such as tumors, cysts, and intoxications, can manifest as behavior problems, too. If a twelve-year-old boxer starts to pace and circle in one direction and presses its head on walls, the chances are that it has a brain tumor. Under these circumstances, the dog should be properly examined by a veterinarian to confirm the diagnosis. It would be an error to label this dog's behavior as compulsive without such a check. Treatment of brain tumors is sometimes possible these days depending on the type of tumor, its exact location, and stage of development.

In the process of examining a dog with a neurological problem, such as circling or head pressing, most veterinarians run a screen to check the blood-lead level. Although circumstances sometimes dictate against this test (no lead paint or fixtures in the house), where the logistical possibility of lead poisoning exists it is prudent to run this check. Lead poisoning can cause a number of different neurological signs and, without evidence to the contrary, can be a spoiler for virtually any neurological diagnosis. Check lead. It pays.

Metabolic Problems

A number of metabolic conditions, ranging from kidney disease to liver problems, can surface as behavior problems. Liver disorders are the most notable in this respect. One particular problem, which often presents early in life, is well worth bearing in mind if a young dog starts acting peculiarly, especially if the strange behavior occurs right after a meal. I refer to congenital vascular shunts, in which blood from the intestine bypasses the liver: so-called portosystemic shunts. What happens in these cases is that ammonia absorbed from the intestines is not detoxified in the liver as normal, but is transferred directly to the circulation. An insidious autointoxication ensues, with central-nervous signs of this "poisoning from within" becoming apparent. As with other forms of liver disease, signs of the condition range from depression to circling and seizures, but no one manifestation is diagnostic.

One case seen here at Tufts was misdiagnosed when it was first brought to our hospital. The dog was about four or five years old at the time, and was showing signs of lethargy, irritability, and aggression. The vet who initially saw this dog advised the owners to work on a dominance-control program, but they called back a few weeks later stating that there had been no improvement. Two things struck me as odd about this case. The first was that the behavior change had occurred suddenly at four years of age, and the second was that behavior modification was ineffective. I suggested to the owners that they should make an appointment with our medical service, which they promptly did. The clinician who saw this dog ran a battery of tests. Most suspicious was the finding that the dog's bile acids were elevated, indicating some kind of liver problem.

The dog's condition deteriorated significantly in the following weeks despite dietary and other measures designed to improve the situation, and finally the owners requested euthanasia for their dog. On postmortem it was found that the dog had a portosystemic shunt, and in retrospect it was apparent that this was the cause of all its problems, both behavioral and medical. Earlier diagnosis, which would have been difficult, would not have helped the dog in this case. The signs the dog was showing on its first visit were mild, nonspecific, and were not related to feeding. Some diagnoses are just not that easy. That's life.

Hormonal Disturbances

Some other important medically related behavioral problems in dogs are associated with hormonal deficiency or excess. Of the possible causes, hypothyroidism must rate as the most likely, being the number one genetic concern in six of the seven AKC breed groups. Simply by virtue of prevalence, you would expect problems related to hypothyroidism to surface more frequently than other conditions of hormonal imbalance. The relatively new realization is that hypothyroidism isn't an all-or-none type of condition. Dogs aren't simply hypothyroid or "normal"; there are shades of gray in between. For example, a youngish dog of almost any breed that registers a 1.25 on a scale of one to four for total serum thyroxine (T4) may have a value "within normal limits," but not one that is optimal for form or function. The other new finding is that suboptimal thyroid hormone levels do not necessarily produce sluggishness and lethargy, like the classical hypothyroidism, but may produce a paradoxical response of increasing a dog's anxiety level. This may lead to a multitude of behavioral sequelae, including increased aggression, inexplicable fearfulness, and even some compulsive behaviors.

I first encountered this syndrome in a family of show Afghans from New Mexico. The dogs were reported to be stable in temperament until they reached about nine to eighteen months of age. At this time several of the dogs suddenly developed extreme fearfulness, particularly in a show-ring situation. In the process of turning over all stones to determine the cause of these dogs' fears, the owner had her vet run blood tests for just about everything under the sun, including thyroid hormone levels. It turned out that thyroid function was below par in all of the fearful dogs. I only became involved later in the story as a remote reference, agreeing that hypothyroidism could be to blame. And it probably was, because the dogs responded well to thyroid hormone replacement therapy, regaining their former composure.

This got me thinking. About this time I read an interesting communication in the *AKC Gazette,* written by a knowledgeable, open-minded, and well-educated trainer, Margaret Gibbs, from Illinois. Gibbs, too, had a concept of this hypothyroid syndrome and supported it with reference to a particular case. I then learned that another vet, Dr. Jean Dodds from Irvine, California, was at least as consumed as I was with the emerging syndrome of subclinical hypothyroidism. To cut a long story short, I started to work with Jean Dodds, using her laboratory to run my samples and her expertise to help interpret our results. The evidence began to accumulate, including dramatic examples of dogs that made almost incredible recoveries.

One such dog was a German shepherd called Lizzy. Lizzy's owner had been all over the place trying to get her dog's aggressive behavior under wraps. The problem was that Lizzy seemed anxious and didn't like other dogs or strangers. Her response to either was one of violent aggression. Because of her great strength, Lizzy was difficult to control, and her powerful jaws made her something of a liability, particularly on walks. When Lizzy was brought to see me I ran thyroid tests based on her clinical signs and her breed (German shepherds rank number seven in the all-time hit parade for hypothyroidism). The results came back that her thyroid hormone levels were in fact lowish, being in the bottom twenty-fifth percentile of the normal range. I decided to boost her levels by treating her with synthetic thyroid hormone for four to six weeks to see if that would improve things. A few weeks later I had a follow-up letter from the owner, which read as follows:

> . . . five days after starting the medication I took Liz on her first posttreatment walk in the company of other dogs. Anxiously I watched her encounter with each new dog. By the end of the walk I was tearful with joy and relief: Her behavior had totally changed. When she encountered bitchy females, she now put her ears back and her tail down and moved out of their way; she responded to invitations to play by playing; she approached a four-month-old puppy and invited it to play; she allowed another dog to play tug-of-war with the other end of her stick; she tolerated the excitement of two or three other dogs joining in the chase with her. Alleluia!

Actually, as well as providing this dramatic insight into her dog's changed behavior, this owner also had some good thoughts to add to the mix. She said that a psychiatrist friend of hers had reported that hypothyroidism is a not-unusual cause of paranoid aggression in humans and went on to interpret her own dog's behavior as paranoid, "if you define paranoid as the tendency to see ordinary, nonthreatening stimuli as having a threatening social meaning; for example, noises on the telephone mean that the FBI is tapping your line, persons who accidentally bump into you are trying to kill you." Liz, she felt, misinterpreted social signals, her perception so skewed that any social signal not known through long experience to be unequivocally friendly was seen as dangerous. Moreover, Liz's perception of the world seemed resistant to change; she didn't learn from ordinary experience, a characteristic often associated with paranoia. Whatever the final analysis, it seems that subthreshold or subclinical hypothyroidism is a syndrome that should be taken seriously. Certainly, the potential advantages of correcting dogs' thyroid hormone levels into the "optimal" range (the upper end of the scale) far outweigh the risks involved, which are minimal, if not nonexistent.

Needless to say, thyroid hormone problems are not the only hormonal challenges dogs face that can alter their behavior, but are probably the most prevalent. Excess secretion of various reproductive hormones may be the next most common cause of behavioral problems. The feminizing effects of a Sertoli-cell (testicular) tumor in males springs to mind, but adrenal tumors can produce confusing effects, too. Earlier I mentioned a rather uncommon hormonal disturbance in a neutered male dog that was acting like a pseudopregnant female. This dog had the hormone prolactin present in its blood at three times the normal level. A pituitary tumor was probably lurking behind the scenes in this case. Since the pituitary gland is the conductor of the endocrine orchestra and secretes many different hormones, tumors of this gland can produce a myriad of behavioral and physiological changes whose causation is not always easy to pinpoint.

Allergies

Some allergies create behavior problems, too. Allergic dermatitis resulting in a lick-granuloma-like syndrome may be the most common example of this (remember, lick granuloma proper is a compulsive behavior). I was once at a symposium when a veterinary dermatologist stood up and said that it was his opinion that *all* cases of canine acral lick dermatitis (lick granuloma) were caused by allergy. Taken aback at this extreme view, I called the president of the American Association of Veterinary Dermatology when I got home and asked him his opinion. He was much closer to my viewpoint, saying that he thought that some fifty percent of cases were allergic in origin and fifty percent were "psychogenic" (that is, the real McCoy). Anyway, this controversy in a teapot points out that just because a dog is licking its wrist excessively doesn't always mean that it has a psychogenic condition, but it doesn't confirm allergy as the cause, either.

Allergy may also feature in some dietary causes of behavior problems. This whole area is a little gray, but if you believe hearsay, allergy to a particular constituent of the diet may increase irritability and thus aggressivity. I have some anecdotes of my own to support this, but the scientific jury is still out on the matter. What *is* known about diet is that the protein level may make a difference in behavioral reactivity. In one study we conducted, low-protein diets appeared to decrease aggression resulting from territorial anxiety and fear. I am currently attempting to replicate this earlier finding and extend it to other behavioral conditions, such as dominance and hyperactivity aggression. The results of these studies are pending.

Whatever I may or may not have accomplished in trying to explain my view of the relevance of medical conditions to behavioral-problem recognition and management, I hope I have made the point that not every problem is trainable. Training may be an integral part of most behavior-modification programs, but medical causes of disturbed behavior must be weeded out first and dealt with appropriately. That may be all that is necessary to resolve the problem in some cases. For nonmedical folk, trainers included, it is probably as well to have a veterinarian examine every dog that shows a sudden change in its behavior, every one that displays an inexplicable aggression, every one that spins, head presses, or stares. In addition, dogs that display excess timidity or nervousness for no good reason, and those that display altered appetite or thirst in conjunction with a behavior problem, should all receive a thorough veterinary examination. Last but not least, dogs that exhibit an apparent breakdown in housetraining should be professionally checked before being subjected to the rigors of a retraining program. And water should never, ever be withheld except under the direction of a veterinarian.

WHINING

If only they could speak—wouldn't that be something? Dogs, after all, appear to understand so much of what's going on that it would be wonderful to hear what their views are on a few subjects. It doesn't seem likely that we'd be engaged in some philosophical exchange of ideas with them if they could talk, because they probably only have the mentality of a three-to-four-year-old child, but at least we could confirm what we suspect—that they have feelings such as loyalty, animosity, jealousy, guilt, and so on, just like us. But when you think about it, they can and do communicate in their own way; to some extent, at least, we are able to appreciate what they want and how they feel. What owner doesn't know when his dog is anticipating food or needing attention, or when his dog is unhappy about a situation, excited, or frustrated. Part of dogs' communication system involves body language, but there's another component to their communicative ability: their vocal skills. Although dogs are always thought of as plain old barkers (and barkers they certainly can be; see "B—Barking"), when the situation dictates, they use another, more subtle form of audible communication that can deliver a message almost as expressively as words. I refer to the ancient art of whining.

Of course, people whine, too, but it's a slightly different kind of whining. For humans, whining is a way of complaining about something. It's hardly a compliment to say that someone is a whiner because, in human terms, whining is regarded as a form of venting rather than a serious attempt to get something accomplished. With dogs, whining is a more basic communication, being a vital means by which pups transmit to the bitch their need for care and attention during the first few weeks of life. This etepimeletic (care-soliciting) vocal communication has an effect on the mother dog like a baby's cries on a human mom. The pups' squeaky whines send an almost irresistible biological message to the mother dog (and humans, too), coaxing nurturing support of the warmth- and food-providing variety. Pups whine when they are cold or hungry or just plain in need of attention. Whining also functions as a distress call when a pup becomes separated from its mom or the litter, although the bitch usually appears to spy the wanderer off base before she hears it.

Most pups grow out of habitual whining shortly after weaning, reserving this heartfelt communication for situations in which they are desperately trying to transmit some pressing need, seemingly willing it to materialize. Others, however, abuse the communication, learning from their owners' rapid responses that whining is a good way to make things happen quickly, building on their past experience eventually to become only slightly less invasive than their whining human counterparts. Such dogs whine when their owners are occupied . . . to get their attention. They whine when they want to go out. They whine when they want food. They whine when they want a toy, or to be petted.

Whining can turn out to be a real problem for some owners. I saw one fairly intense whiner in the behavior clinic a couple of days ago. It was a four-year-old neutered male greyhound recycled from the track that had been brought to me because of a separation-anxiety problem. I kid you not, this slightly pushy but needy dog whined without respite the whole way through the appointment. His master, who clearly spoiled him rotten, was the object of the constant whining. The dog couldn't stand the fact that his owner had to take time out to talk to the doctor and whined and pawed at him incessantly. We could barely hear each other talk over the racket. However troublesome this dog's whining was, I reminded myself of the years of inattention the poor creature had suffered in years gone by, and made mental allowances for this fact. At one point I did ask the owner to reattach the dog's lead, put his dog into a "down" position, and step on his lead, but the dog was a real wriggler and constantly escaped from his owner's control. I always figure that whining of this type and intensity is communicating anxiety and uncertainty, in this case saying, "Pay attention. I need to get out of here, right now." It's as if the dog was willing something to happen and knew that the noise would eventually get his owner's attention.

To prevent whining for attention it is important not to reward what you don't plan to endure and cater to in the future. Attention withdrawal, if practical, discourages whining. But remember, following attention withdrawal, things often get worse before they get better so you need tolerance as well as patience. A slightly more proactive approach to dealing with the problem whiner is to give the dog something to do rather than having it freewheeling in uncertainty and anticipation. This is what I was attempting to do with the greyhound when I had the owner put it in a down-stay. Okay, so it didn't work that time, but usually when you give an anxious, whining dog a job to do, it takes the dog so much concentration to follow the command—particularly if it's (benignly) enforced—that it forgets to whine. This trick, which is definitely preferable to yelling "no," "stop it," "cut that out," never ceases to amaze the owners of pacing, whining dogs in our clinic.

Another situation in which some dogs whine for attention is if they have separation anxiety and they have become physically separated from their owners. Under these circumstances the whining takes on an even more plaintive tone, seemingly transmitting the message "Don't leave me. Please come back." It is heartrending to hear such pitiful sounds. I once showed a video of a dog with separation anxiety to a crowd of some five hundred people at the Smithsonian Institution in Washington, D.C. The audience watched with bated breath as the dog, Mandy the beagle, wandered around by the front door for a few minutes after her mistress had left. Then, when Mandy started to whimper and whine, the whole audience emitted clearly audible, almost synchronized *ooohs* and *aaaahs* of empathy, understanding exactly what poor Mandy was going through. Of course, when she jumped up on a chair and pressed her nose to a window to see if she could catch sight of her departed mistress, it practically brought the house down. This wasn't a case of theatrics on Mandy's part because she didn't know anyone was watching—it was genuine concern for her own welfare, bordering on misery.

There are a couple of other types of whining that are variations on the original theme. The first is not so much to be pitied as enjoyed. It is excited whining; the whining of anticipation of some cherished end point. You can picture a dog whining excitedly as it waits for a Frisbee to be thrown. The dog knows it's going to happen. It just can't wait. How like a child. It's a hurry-up-and-wait whine, which displays all the energy and excitement of anticipation. If the end point is inextricably delayed, the dog's whining will continue but it may gradually transform into the whining of frustration; a slightly different tone to those attuned to this sound. Other frustrated I-want-it-now scenarios when dogs whine excitedly and pathetically occur because of balked attempts to realize a predatory goal—for example, to catch a squirrel that has climbed a tree to safety or to nab a small varmint that has gone to earth before the dog's very eyes. Note that this type of whining, like the barking that sometimes accompanies it, is not really designed to get attention so much as it is an outlet, an expression of inner tension and frustration. A variation on this theme is whining in the car at every prey facsimile that passes tantalizingly close before disappearing out of sight.

One last type of whining, analogous to some of the others in terms of motivation, and auditorially similar, too, is the whining that accompanies pain. As a now-retired veterinary anesthesiologist, I have seen (or rather heard) my share of this whining in my day. There is no doubt in my mind that this whining is at least partly etepimeletic rather than a release of tension or an expression of frustration. A dog recovering from some painful surgery, for example, will usually whine piteously in the postoperative period. Some centers treat these dogs with analgesic drugs, on the reasonable assumption that they are in pain. I cannot fault this practice and would encourage the liberal, prophylactic, and presumptive use of postoperative analgesic techniques. However, I have frequently observed that it is human attention rather than analgesic drugs that silences postoperative whining most efficiently. My in-terpretation is that these recovering dogs feel miserable, lonely, lost, and are possibly also in pain. A little TLC (tender loving care) seems to go a long way toward making them feel much better and then the whining ceases. In this situation, I like to say an ounce of attention is worth at least ten milligrams of morphine.

While on the subject of postoperative whining, it may be worth mentioning that many dogs whine as they are "masked" to sleep with a volatile (inhalational) anesthetic. There is no pain associated with this process, so this whining is often regarded as being a sign of "disinhibi-tion" (occurring for the same reason that drunken men sing). It could, alternatively, represent a cry for help as the dog slips from conscious-ness, or may indicate a dreamlike stage of anesthesia in which a veri-table Pandora's box of uncontrollable images and sensations flood through the dog's mind, as occurs in rapid eye movement sleep. After all, we are fairly certain that dogs dream while sleeping, and whining is an occasional accompaniment of dogs' nocturnal sojourns. Now, whether the dream is of days of yore and of maternal bliss, a day at the vet's, or a squirrel up a tree, is impossible to determine at present. But even these mysteries may be resolvable in the future for those with the time, facilities, and the interest, thanks to newer brain-scanning tech-niques. Of course, anyone exploring such avenues of research would have to prioritize his studies carefully, as resources are very scarce. He would probably have to start by studying more mundane forms of communication first, saving the best whines until last, so to speak.

X-FILES

Sadie, a Scottish terrier with classical separation anxiety, was brought to Tufts to be part of a clinical trial. As I attempted to elicit all kinds of relevant information about Sadie's background and behavior when left alone, her owner interrupted me with a wry smile on her face.

"Dr. Dodman," she said, "I have to tell you, Sadie is really a most unusual and puzzling dog. I left her in her crate one day and came home to find that she had escaped. There's nothing out of the ordinary about that except that the crate door was still closed, and my pocketbook, which I had left hanging on the door, was inside the crate. The pocketbook was shredded to pieces and its contents were laid out in a perfectly straight line on the opposite side of the crate. I stress that the door of her crate was tightly closed, locked shut, and no one had been in the house while I was away. When I returned home Sadie ran up to me and greeted me in her usual exuberant way. I looked at the locked crate door, looked at Sadie, and then I just scratched my head."

My jaw fell when I heard this story and I blinked a couple of times before admitting that I had no clue as to how this might have happened. It was at this point Sadie's owner broke down and confessed that she had finally figured out what had gone on in her absence. Apparently the crate was quite close to the door on which the pocketbook was hanging. The owner's theory was that Sadie had managed to flex the metal door of the crate sufficiently wide to be able to reach out and grab the pocketbook, pulling it back inside the crate with her. Then, as is the wont of many separation-anxiety-prone dogs, she dissipated her frustrations by tearing the object into shreds and (for reasons yet undetermined) proceeded to line up the contents of the pocketbook on the opposite side of the crate. Perhaps she was a stickler for symmetry, as some more compulsive dogs seem to be. The pocketbook episode over, Sadie must have then concentrated her efforts on escape from the crate, which she eventually managed by springing the metal door. Ostensibly, the door had flexed wide enough to allow her to escape and had then sprung back into its original position, giving the impression that it was still locked tight. As unlikely as this scenario sounds, it is the only one that accounts for the observations—though *Star Trek* fans might favor an alternative explanation: "Beam me up, Scottie."

Extraordinary stories of dogs' behavior and capabilities abound, some confirmed and some only poorly substantiated, but a sufficient mass of unanswered questions remains to warrant some intriguing speculation. I call all these mystery files X-files whether the enigma is eventually resolved or not. Officially, the term *X-file* should be reserved for unsolved problems (an overflow from the burgeoning file *U* for "unanswered"), though my liberal interpretation permits the inclusion of cases for which some reasonable explanation eventually emerges.

Consider the case of Shawnee, the sharp shar-pei. Sharp, that is, because Shawnee apparently could understand English sentences, answering questions by barking once (affirmative) or twice (negative) to communicate his desires. His owner had "known" about his linguistic skills for quite some time. She would ask him, "Do you want to watch *Jerry Springer* today?" Shawnee might bark twice (smart dog). "How about *Leeza*?" Shawnee might bark twice. "Well, how about *The Oprah Winfrey Show*?" Shawnee would then bark once, his preference firmly established. One day, Shawnee's owner was in a bar ordering drinks when she noticed that he would bark the number of drinks that were ordered. I wasn't there but I imagine it went like this.

Owner to bartender: "I'll have three more beers, please."
Shawnee in the background: "Arf, arf, arf."
Owner to bartender: "Two more for the road, please?"
Shawnee: "Arf, arf" (meaning either "No, don't do it—you shouldn't drink and drive" or "Two beers coming up").

Anyway, impressed with his new skills, his owner tried him out with a few more numerical games. It started out pretty simply. For example, his owner would hold up one finger and say, "Shawnee, how many fingers am I holding up?"

Shawnee's answer might be "Arf" (meaning "yes" or "one").

Owner: "Good boy, Shawnee. What a good dog. You're so smart."

The skill level was advanced . . . to having Shawnee read the number on a playing card (did I mention that he read, too?).

Owner holds up the four of hearts. "What number, Shawnee?"
Shawnee: "Arf, arf, arf, arf."
Owner: "All right, Shawnee. You good dog." (She pets Shawnee.)

This was all so exciting that Shawnee's owner decided to put on a couple of shows for friends, and then classes of schoolchildren, with the mathematical problems becoming even more complex over time. Eventually the media picked up on the phenomenon and a local news show swooped in to document the action at an elementary-school gathering.

On the day of the big show, tensions were running high—except in Shawnee's case, of course. He appeared to be enjoying the attention. He got off to a slow start, making a few elementary mistakes but finally, once his full attention had been grabbed by upping the ante with food treats (smoked turkey), he put on a near-flawless performance.

Owner to Shawnee: "What is nine minus four?"

Shawnee to owner: "Arf, arf, arf, arf, arf."

The owner stands up straight and claps. The children cheer.

Reporter to Shawnee: "What is the square root of four, plus one."

Shawnee to reporter: "Arf, arf, arf."

Reporter to Shawnee: "What channel is this?" (He shows Shawnee the side of the camera with the number 8 on it.)

Shawnee: "Arf, arf, arf."

Reporter: "No, that's wrong, Shawnee." (He inspects the camera but then notices that there is also a large number 3 on the side of the camera describing the model number, and gives Shawnee another shot at the correct answer. You guessed it . . . eight barks.)

Finally, just in case the owner was sending any covert signals to Shawnee, she was sent out of the room for the ultimate test.

"This is it, Shawnee . . . the big one," the reporter said. A hush fell over the room.

"What is nine minus five plus three?"

Shawnee: "Arf, arf, arf, arf, arf . . . arf . . . arf."

The crowd goes wild.

Reporter to camera: "This is one sharp shar-pei."

And he was right. Shawnee had learned to play the game, to read the body-language signals of the quizmaster or the response of the assembled throng ("he always does much better in front of a crowd") and to bark until the requisite response occurred. This phenomenon, known as the Clever Hans effect, was first described last century in an Arabian horse, Clever Hans, who people thought could solve math problems. His trainer would pose a mathematical question to Hans, who would strike out the correct answer with his hooves. As it turned out, the trainer or other person posing the questions was unwittingly sending body-language signals to Hans, who, it was discovered, could not solve the problems unless someone in the room knew the correct answer. So subtle were the cues Hans was picking up that even if the person with the correct answer stood motionless and expressionless it didn't fool him. I don't think the actual cues were ever determined in the end, but at least part of the mystery was solved.

Undoubtedly a similar situation prevailed in Shawnee's case. And who knows what signs he was reading? Perhaps it was the questioner's facial expression, a change in the size of his or her pupils, or the slumping of the person's shoulders when Shawnee attained the correct number of barks; perhaps it was the buzz from the crowd. Whatever it was, it was something other than his mathematical ability. There's no way he spoke English sentences (dogs have no language center), he couldn't read (same reason), and couldn't add or subtract, never mind figure out square roots. But he sure had a lot of people fooled and kept himself well supplied with smoked turkey. Now, that *is* smart. His owner still believes that he really does read numbers and does math . . . but she also thinks he is the reincarnation of a famous American Indian chief because he barked once at the chief's name when she read a list of American Indian names to him.

I heard another amazing story that highlights dogs' sensitivities and intuition while I was on a plane coming back from a meeting. A dog owner in the seat next to mine told me about a dog she once owned. The dog in question must have had a tad of separation anxiety because it normally shadowed the woman wherever she went and moped when she got ready to leave. The most distressing time for this dog came when the woman prepared to go away on a long trip. It was her custom to get out her case a few days before she was due to leave and to slowly assemble and pack her gear. Like many other dogs, hers had learned that the suitcase heralded her impending departure and would begin to sulk and act depressed at the sight of it. To the woman, this predeparture misery seemed only to add to, or perhaps even compound, the suffering that the dog would have to endure anyway, so she devised a scheme to hide her intentions from the dog until the last possible moment. She decided that in the future she would keep the door of her room shut while packing so that the dog could not catch sight of her case or accumulating gear.

Three days before her next trip she took out the case behind closed doors and began her covert activities. The plan seemed to be working. The dog remained calm during the entire predeparture period and the woman was delighted that she had solved the problem. But, on the actual day she was due to leave, as she lugged the packed case from her room, her dog did something that it had never done before. It went directly to her red pickup truck and sat there staring at it, whining. The pickup truck was the vehicle the woman always used when taking the dog anywhere—she had another vehicle she used when she was going somewhere alone. The message to her couldn't have been clearer: "Please take me with you." The dog clearly anticipated her departure and came up with a way of signaling its desires to her.

Not all X-files are cute or enchanting. Some of them are downright disturbing, perplexing, or even bloodcurdling. Among these not-so-cute stories are a number of unusual reports of attacks of dogs directed toward people. Just to give you some idea of the spectrum of disasters that can occur, I will mention one particularly unpleasant mystery involving the supposed aggression of a pack of terriers toward an elderly woman who was left alone with them. The result of this attack, by whoever or whatever was responsible, was that the woman was maimed, her left arm severely injured and her hair ripped out, and then she was killed. Following the assault her body was stuffed under a couch. As it turned out, the woman had lived in mortal fear of her son's terrier pack and insisted that they be contained in the kitchen every time she was left alone with them. When the police inspected the scene of the crime, they found that the barrier was down and the dogs were wandering around the house aimlessly. It appeared that the dogs were responsible for the attack. As a feasibility study, the police decided to reconstruct the crime using a mannequin. Accordingly, a life-sized female doll, complete with wig, was suspended from the ceiling and the dogs were released from their retreat in the kitchen. They proceeded to attack and dismember the mannequin, grabbing it by the left arm, ripping off the wig, and then stuffing the mutilated doll under the sofa. The events of this reconstruction so accurately mirrored what was supposed to have happened that the police closed the investigation, convinced that this was a case of death by misfortune. It would be hard to disagree.

Some less disturbing X-files pertain to dogs' fearfulness. One such case involved a dog belonging to my neighbor, Ken Sherman. The dog, a large-eared Chihuahua-dachshund crossbreed called Mr. Spock (and affectionately known as the Bat) was having what appeared to be panic attacks. The way these attacks appeared left much to the imagination. Suddenly, for no apparent reason, Mr. Spock would start pacing, panting, and salivating in apparent terror for his life. Ken, a client of my wife's and an ardent animal lover, could not bear to see his dog whip itself into this frenzy several times a day, so he contacted my wife to see what could be done about the problem. My wife was at a loss to explain the behavior herself and decided that a formal consultation between Ken and me was the best way to go. Accordingly, Mr. Spock was brought to the veterinary hospital.

Ken and I sat down for a detailed analysis of the problem at hand. Fortunately for me, but unfortunately for Mr. Spock, he had a panic attack in front of my very eyes during the consultation, so I was able to see exactly what Ken was talking about . . . but the mystery of what was causing Spock's panic remained an enigma at the time. I remember saying to Ken that I thought that a sound phobia was most likely involved, though I couldn't for the life of me figure out what sound was involved. We discussed the possibility that trucks on the nearby Massachusetts Turnpike might be alarming him or that sonic booms or quarry blasting could be to blame. None of these explanations seemed to fit with Ken's observations, but at least my line of questioning gave him something to ponder. At a loss for definitive treatment, I prescribed antianxiety medication for Spock to make him feel calmer about whatever was causing his phobia, and I asked Ken to call me back after a few days to let me know how things were going.

Ken called me a couple of weeks later to say that Spock was better on the medication, though the attacks continued and the precise cause of the problem was still obscure. The very next day, however, Ken struck oil with the sudden realization of what was behind Spock's panic attacks. It was his neighbor's power equipment: the lawnmower, a power saw, a grinder, an electric drill, and so on. Ken figured this out when he noticed that one of Spock's attacks coincided exactly with his neighbor pulling the cord to start his lawnmower. Apparently Ken's neighbor was a do-it-yourselfer who had a power tool for every purpose under heaven. This was extremely bad news for a dog like Spock. Every time the neighbor activated some piece of machinery, Spock went into a flat spin and started his pacing and panting routine.

Just as you need to know where you're going if you want to get there, you need to know what is causing a behavior problem if you are to be able to treat it properly. The revelation that power equipment caused Spock's anxiety enabled Ken to take some preventive action regarding the dog's exposure to the sound of his neighbor's activities. He started by confining Spock to the quieter side of the house when the neighbor was busy and informed his neighbor of Spock's dilemma. A little bit of coordination between Ken and his neighbor went a long, long way toward reducing the number and intensity of Spock's negative experiences. In addition to avoidance strategies, I advised Ken about systematic desensitization to make things easier on Spock in the future. I don't know how effective this was because Ken still calls on occasion requesting additional medication for Spock. I do know, however, that Spock is no longer anxious on a daily basis and sometimes enjoys several months of freedom from attacks.

Dogs' extraordinary sensory abilities can sometimes be quite valuable to their owners, even though an owner cannot always fathom which sense it is that the dog is using. For example, dogs are able to detect the onset of seizures in seizure-prone people some minutes before the people themselves realize what is going on. Also, dogs, like cats, seem able to sense minor earthquakes that are imperceptible to us. Reactions can range from attention seeking to frank nervousness. Although the precipitating cause of one of these "premonitions" eventually comes to light (in the form of the seizure or the earthquake itself), there are other instances when dogs react peculiarly but the cause of the altered behavior is never determined with certainty.

A number of owners have reported to me that their dog appears to be reacting to things that aren't there. The dog may suddenly start staring at a particular part of the room or begin reacting nervously or fearfully (like Spock) when there is apparently nothing extraordinary going on. The temptation, of course, is to explain these phenomena as "seeing ghosts," but the real explanation lies either in the occurrence of some bona fide physical event that is beyond our perception or, alternatively, some disturbing experience of internal origin. Partial seizures, incorrectly termed *petit mal*, account for at least some of these anomalous behaviors. Known seizure-prone breeds sometimes stare fixedly at a point on the floor or the wall or go into some kind of trance for minutes at a time. Bull terriers are famous for this. One common bull terrier behavior of standing motionless beneath a plant or the branches of a bush or tree is likely of preseizural significance. The presence of the arboreal canopy over the dog seems to initiate this peculiar trancelike behavior that some say is normal for the breed. Normal for the breed it may be, but normal it is not. It's just another one of a series of behavioral enigmas still in need of a proper explanation.

And now for some really weird stuff. One of my most interesting patients was a dog that sucked in air until its stomach swelled up like a meterological balloon. I never did determine whether seizure activity or true obsessive-compulsive disorder was at the heart of this behavior, though antiobsessional drug treatment was at least partly effective. The dog, a two-and-a-half-year-old spayed female golden retriever called Shelby, engaged in this peculiar air-sucking activity at any time of day, often while she was loafing around the house, being trained, being groomed, or at bedtime. The way it appeared was that Shelby would lower her head toward her chest and start gulping air silently. After a while, she would become noticeably larger around the girth and would reach a point of maximum inflation and apparent satiation. Shelby's owner took aerial photographs to document the swelling for me. The pictures were quite remarkable. The "before" pictures showed the sylphlike, youthful figure of the dog but the "after" shots depicted Shelby pumped up and pear-shaped. To her owner's great displeasure, Shelby would then discharge the accumulated gas from either end until she resumed her original shape. The procedure was repeated on average about three times daily.

Treatmentwise, I initially ruled out attention-seeking behavior as a cause of the problem by having Shelby's owner ignore her whenever she engaged in the behavior. But there was no effect, not even when I advised that a bridging stimulus (a duck call) be used to increase the potency of the technique. The next treatment I tried was with an antiobsessional drug, Prozac. Although I was quite pleased with the results of this treatment, a sixty- or seventy-percent decrease in the behavior, Shelby's owner was underwhelmed, wanting and expecting a one-hundred-percent cure. I could not achieve this for her so she discontinued the medication and we parted company on somewhat cool terms.

I never did find out exactly why Shelby sucked air, though I suspected an anxiety-driven compulsive behavior etiology. I have looked out for similar cases since that time, but have not encountered any—in dogs, anyway. Horses that suck wind are a dime a dozen, and I did come across one institutionalized, mentally handicapped elderly person that indulged, but that is the extent of my experience. Until I learn more, Shelby will definitely remain in an X-file.

One of the most ethereal findings that I have encountered involves dogs that seem to know when their time has come. One owner reported that her elderly dog, her best friend who had walked a beaten path with her every day, suddenly decided to veer off the straight and narrow into the woods for no apparent reason. The owner found herself being dragged along by this normally well-behaved dog and it was only with some considerable coercion that she managed to steer her faithful friend back on course. She wondered what was going on.

"Why this sudden change in his behavior?" she thought. Her answer came all too soon. When she got back home she put her old friend in his outdoor kennel as usual and went inside the house to make a few phone calls. About an hour later she went out to check on him and found that he was dead. She felt terrible. "He must have known what was happening and I didn't understand," she scolded herself. Postmortem revealed no obvious cause of death (the dog did not have a bloated stomach, hemorrhaging internal organs, or signs of acute heart failure). He had died presumably from some subtle but insidious age-related organ failure. The odd thing was that this dog had been sick before, but had never attempted to hide away as he did this last time. He seemed to know that his number was up. This was the big one.

Dogs' apparent knowledge of the shape of things to come is a curious phenomenon. I can understand a dog acting painfully when in pain, disoriented when internal functions have gone awry, or being anxious about some impending disaster—but walking out of someone's life to die at exactly the right time is hard to explain. An operant behavior like sloping off in the woods implies a greater appreciation of what's going on than we currently credit to our dogs. I may be waxing anthropomorphic, but it seems to me that dogs know when their last moments have arrived. Like us, though, they can have no appreciation of what, if anything, comes next—the ultimate X-file for dog and owner alike.

YAWNING

Yawning is one of the most poorly understood canine behaviors of all— but that's hardly surprising because it is really quite a complicated concern. One thing we may think we know about yawning is that it occurs as a result of tiredness. To an extent this is true, but the whole story is much more involved than that and nature has added some bizarre extemporizations on this theme. For years I've sat in the behavior office and watched scores of nervous dogs and clients yawn their way through appointments. "How come they're acting as if they're about to take a nap when they're out in a public place, on edge, and on display?" I always think. Students in a lecture room are big on yawning, too. Show me sixty students struggling to fathom a critical lecture and I'll show you a yawner. But note, neither stressed dogs, bored owners, nor pressured students yawn once they are out of the high-tension situation. Afterward they will all be chipper and completely nonyawny. What's going on?

Some say that yawning is not simply a function of tiredness but that it also involves stress. It explains why nervous dogs and owners yawn in front of me in the consulting room and it also explains why students yawn in the lecture room. But can it explain the dog (or person) that yawns and stretches on awakening at home in the morning? I believe it can but you have to redefine stress to encompass this apparently stress-free variety of yawning. Here's a definition that works. "Yawning (and stretching) serves to increase an animal's attention when sleep is pressing in the face of perceived danger or some demanding social circumstance."

Translated, this means that the basic requirements for yawning are: *(a)* tiredness and *(b)* a circumstance in which a tired animal (or person) knows that sleep is unsafe, inappropriate, or undesirable.

So the dogs in the consulting room yawn because they perceive threat in the situation and are struggling to stay awake amid the droning voices. In the case of owners and students, the pressure is more social and intellectual than physical (as it is with the early-morning and late-night yawners). Yawning and stretching are mechanisms designed to elevate us from a situation of welling sleep into alert consciousness. If the pressure to perform is eliminated, the need to yawn is abolished. Either sleep will prevail or normal awake function will be resumed.

So what is it, exactly, that the process of yawning and stretching does to activate us when this wake-sleep conflict occurs? The answer is, it ventilates and activates the airways and the musculoskeletal system, respectively. The flushing of the airways carries oxygen into the lungs and removes carbon dioxide, while stretching extends joints and tenses muscles, increasing nerve impulses to the brain and increasing alertness. In the morning, yawning represents a serious, though reflexive, attempt to get going, a biological kick start, and in the evening it represents an internal tussle between tiredness and the refusal to surrender to it. What better way, in either case, than to ventilate and activate.

One really odd fact about yawning is that it and penile erection seem to go hand in glove. Reference to the rodent literature demonstrates that these two behaviors are mediated similarly and in some cases simultaneously. A controversy exists about the precise mechanism of these twinned behaviors, whether it is pre- or postsynaptic and the exact role of neurochemicals such as dopamine, opioids, serotonin, acetylcholine, and oxytocin. But what is known is that these various neurotransmitters operate together to facilitate the behaviors in complicated and sometimes antagonistic ways. The biological reason for the association of yawning and penile erection has always puzzled me. Do male rats and stud dogs feel tired and yawn before they mate, or do creatures that yawn while tired suddenly find themselves sexually aroused? I don't really know the answer to this but can only assume that the subtle "pick-me-up" function of yawning has become paired with erection because it has some biological survival value. It certainly wouldn't be appropriate to fall asleep when the opportunity to mate presents itself, but there is some sense in having an animal wake up fighting sleep with an erection pointing the way to reproductive success!

One last word about yawning. It's infectious. The mere sight (or sound) of another animal yawning is enough to trigger the behavior in a susceptible recipient. Apparently, yawns function as a releaser of what is called a fixed-action pattern of motor discharges—thus creating another yawn. A fixed-action pattern is a series of neurologically encoded instructions that, when activated, run their course (note how difficult it is to interrupt a yawn). Behaviors encoded this rigidly always have immense survival value to the species. If all yawning indicated was being tired, it wouldn't confer any particular advantage to the yawner. Perhaps its usefulness derives from the fact that it activates a whole group of animals into alertness when danger is pressing, with possible lifesaving consequences. Think about this the next time your dog yawns. It will tell you a whole lot more about how it's perceiving the world around it, as well as whether it needs a nap.

ZOONOSIS

The term *zoonosis* refers to diseases that are potentially transmissible from animals to man, and some diseases are, despite what my (otherwise wonderful) physician brother-in-law Peter used to say. A dog aficionado, Peter claimed that dogs could not pass on any diseases to people, seemingly unaware of "old-chestnut" interspecies diseases such as leptospirosis, salmonellosis, visceral larva migrans, and so on. It is not the prerogative of this text to dwell on the pathology of the various types of zoonoses; for the record, however, let it be known that leptospirosis can be so severe that the bottom falls out of your world, whereas in salmonellosis the reverse is true—the world falls out of your bottom. The Russian-roulette-style visceral larva migrans refers to the unpleasant results of roundworm larvae migrating around the human body and sometimes coming to rest in awkward places. Narrowing ourselves to zoonotic diseases that have something to do with dogs' behavior, however, we only need to consider infectious diseases transmitted by biting—although physical injury to people caused by savage biting attacks is a form of zoonosis too, if you stretch the definition a bit.

Biting is a sequel of aggression, which, in a circuitous way, leads us back to the beginning of this book. Aggression and its consequences are thus the alpha and omega of this behavioral treatise and it behooves us to be reasonably well-versed about both. Aggression, which is the number one behavior problem of dogs, reflects one of the most deleterious aspects of our association with this otherwise resplendent species affectionately known as man's best friend. Although the physical consequences of aggression can be severe, other equally sinister long-term complications may result, including serious systemic infections and psychological trauma. Dog bites are epidemic in the U.S., and children are most frequently on the receiving end. Acknowledging the magnitude of this problem (some four million bites reported per year), the American Kennel Club, in the latest version of its handbook, attempted to label certain breeds as "not good with children," but their efforts backfired because of widespread complaints of injustice from breeders and breed fanciers. You know what they say—"You can't please all of the people all of the time." The AKC list was a bit funky, labeling Yorkies and toy poodles as potentially dangerous while omitting mention of known aggressive breeds such as the various types of bull terrier and springer spaniels, but it provided a starting point for discussion and could have been modified later. A weakness of the AKC's approach was that the list failed to acknowledge multiple other factors involved in aggression, not the least of which are faulty line breeding, inappropriate management, and a lack of proper training. But at least, with the list, the AKC was officially acknowledging the dog-bite problem and attempting to do something about it. This would have represented a huge step forward—though the organization was forced to recall thirty thousand copies of the book to appease the distraught masses.

Most people that receive a serious bite from a dog go to an emergency clinic. In fact, dog bites account for about one percent of all emergency-room visits. At the clinic, victims are given antibiotics and a rabies shot to deal with the very problems we are about to consider here. I have known some folks who have declined (or have not been offered) antibiotic therapy following a dog-bite wound and they have lived to regret their decision. Though "cleaner" than the cat's mouth (and our own), the dog's oral cavity is inhabited by a variety of bacteria that, when inoculated by way of a bite puncture wound, can lead to serious infections. One of the most common pathogens is *Pasteurella multocida,* which normally causes acute swelling and pain within twenty-four hours of a bite.

Of course, whatever "germ" is inoculated, the consequences of untreated infection will be more severe in people who, for some reason, have an impaired immune system. Immune suppression and immune deficiency are more common today than ever before because of the widespread use of corticosteroids, the progressively more frequent deployment of immunosuppressive agents in the treatment of cancer and, last but not least, the AIDS epidemic. Immunosuppressed people and their doctors should take note when the potential for zoonotic disease occurs, including bite wounds. One veterinarian I know had her spleen unnecessarily removed during an exploratory abdominal surgery. As far as the spleen is concerned, you don't know what you've got till it's gone. One of the aspects of its function you might miss the most would be its immunologic role. Such was the case with Dr. Jean Kay, an "asplenic" veterinarian, who was told that a normally innocuous bacterium of the dog's mouth now presented a mortal threat to her should she become inoculated with it via a cut on her hand, accidental ingestion of dogs' saliva, or through a bite wound. Needless to say, this changed her modus operandi when it came to small-animal practice: Though gloved, masked, and gowned, she soldiered on with her house calls.

And then, of course, there's rabies, which is now reaching epidemic proportions in the nation's wildlife. Luckily most pets are vaccinated for rabies, but vaccination against any disease is never one-hundred-percent protective, and strange encounters "of the third kind" should still be taken seriously if a potentially rabies-infected creature is involved. My wife, Linda, had just such an encounter in her veterinary practice when one of her clients called her one Friday to report that her dog had come home with a dead bat in its mouth. Salient points to bear in mind here are that some five percent of all bats in Massachusetts are infected with rabies (representing something of a harbor of the infection) and that a dog, in the process of catching a bat in its mouth, might well sustain some minor scratches or punctures of its oral mucous membranes. Cognizant of this potential, Linda advised the clients to allow her to reinforce the dog's rabies-antibody titer with a booster vaccination. This was duly done. Early the next week she had another distress call from these folks to say that they thought their dog might have swallowed something, as it was gagging and was seemingly uncomfortable around the mouth. She went out to see them and found the dog salivating profusely and opening and closing its mouth. Good clinician that she is, and concerned about the dog's welfare, she carefully examined its mouth, inspecting every nook and cranny. There was nothing visible that would account for the dog's strange gagging behavior and salivation . . . but then a scary thought slowly dawned on her. "What if it's rabies? I've just had my ungloved hands inside this dog's mouth and I have some small cuts on my hand from cat scratches."

As unlikely a diagnosis as rabies was, she could not ignore the fact that the dog had a history of potential rabies exposure, had started to salivate profusely, and she had just put her cut hands inside its mouth. Off to the hospital she went and had her own rabies titer boosted, just to be on the safe side. As it turned out (and as you may have suspected), all was well and the mystery cause of the salivation did eventually become apparent. A few days after the salivation started, the dog developed a huge saliva-filled cyst under its tongue; it was a so-called salivary mucocele (or ranula). This benign occurrence is not uncommon in dogs, though the precise cause is often undetermined. Mucoceles arise as a result of a leaky salivary duct so that saliva accumulates within the tissues. In this case, because of the circumstantial evidence and the timing of events, it seems likely that the damage to the dog's salivary duct was sustained during the tussle with the bat. The premise that the dog had direct exposure to the rabies virus via a bat bite was thus much more likely and, because of the site of the bite, the dog's clinical signs were (artifactually) more convincing.

I don't mean to cause a scare among the dog-owning public, but these days it is important to keep heads up with regard to potential rabies infection in wild and domestic animals. Altered behavior is the primary sign in each. The change in behavior is succinctly summed up by the expression "Mad dogs and friendly foxes." In a prodromal (early-symptom) phase, normally friendly and affectionate pets become fearful and hyperreactive, hiding away and avoiding company. Wild animals, on the other hand, lose their fear of people and approach them with uncharacteristic abandon. They are also found in unusual locations, places where they normally would not venture, and nocturnal animals can be seen wandering around in broad daylight. Such animals, if they are hurt, obviously should not be approached by untrained people. Rather, the correct public authority should be alerted. Unfortunately, our dogs will never exert such caution and will go out of their way to "razz" an overconfident, drunkenly wandering, potentially rabid skunk (or some such creature), and that's where the trouble starts. All I can say is thank heavens for vaccination, because although not infallible, the immunity provided is exceptionally good and no doubt keeps vaccinated pets and us as safe as we presently are.

Following the bizarre prodromal phase of rabies comes the excitative phase, in which dogs react excessively to every little perturbance in their time-space continuum. Dogs in this stage snap and bite at everything that moves and stationary inanimate objects, too. Biting at wooden and metal fixtures is not an uncommon manifestation, mirroring what is seen during partial epileptic seizures in "rage syndrome." Apparent hallucinations, indicated by dogs "seeing" and reacting to "imaginary" things, are also features of this stage of rabies, as is rage syndrome.

Salivation occurs during the final, "paralytic" phase of rabies as the nerves that facilitate swallowing are put out of action. This phase precedes respiratory failure and death as the nerves of respiration are affected. The dog my wife saw did not display any prodromal or excitatory signs of rabies. This could have been interpreted as evidence that rabies was not the cause of this dog's problem, but the absence of precursory stages is not a guarantee in itself that rabies is not involved. Some affected animals do not show signs of being affected until the paralytic phase sets in. Such cases, in which the clinical signs are muted, are referred to as having "dumb" rabies. This pattern is the rule, rather than the exception, for large-animal species affected with rabies.

In conclusion, whatever moms may think, it doesn't present much of a health hazard to have the family dog lick a child's face till it is positively dripping with saliva. Whether this behavior should be permitted for other reasons relating to developing dominance and the potential for aggression, however, is doubtful, and the safe answer here is "probably not." If dogs are regularly vaccinated, kept free of roundworms, and properly raised and looked after, they present virtually no public-health hazard. With pets that are not cared for properly, including feral or "formerly owned" dogs, however, it is a slightly different story. The bottom line is that with dogs that we know are owned and cared for, we (and our children) are far less likely to "catch something" by consorting with them than with our own species. My brother-in-law wasn't so far off base after all.

EPILOGUE

Neighbors of mine, Dave and Sue Cosello, recently acquired one of the most adorable pups I have seen in a while. I first saw this cutie when I went around to pick up my daughter Keisha, who had been swimming in their pool all afternoon. The pup was a nine-week-old female yellow Lab, soft as a duster, with big seal-like eyes and winning ways. Unspoiled by human hand, this youngster had arrived from the breeder's home that very afternoon and was cavorting around on the grass beside the pool, learning the restrictions of a collar and lead for the first time. I was "off duty" but couldn't resist a couple of questions about the pup's background. "Did you visit with the pup's parents?" and "How was she kept at the breeders?" were two questions I felt compelled to ask. I was delighted with the answers that came back favorably for the pup (and therefore the Cosellos) on both counts. The bitch and sire were confident, friendly individuals and the breeder had raised the litters in the warmth and comfort of her kitchen as extended family. Genetics and early environmental experiences were on the pup's side. I found myself observing her more closely to see if I could determine what the future held in store.

"May I?" I asked as I picked the pup up and cradled her on her back in my arms. She lay there motionless, gazing trustingly into my eyes. Then I lowered her to the ground, kneeled down, and backed away, making a clicking sound with my mouth. The pup advanced toward me, tail wagging, and started to chew my shoelaces. I clapped loudly to see if she would startle but she just looked up to see what was going on. "Not overly dominant, socially appropriate, a bit mouthy, not sound-sensitive, not a bad deal," I thought. Admittedly, what I had just done was not the most extensive temperament testing that could have been performed, but I liked what I saw.

The only troubling thing this pup did was to nip Sue's leg with her needle teeth. I saw Sue trying to get the pup under control and then heard her cry out "Ouch." I thought she had been stung by a deerfly and was even more convinced of this when I saw a trickle of blood on the back of her leg, but no, it was the pup trying to get a point across. This type of behavior clearly could not be allowed to continue. When I got home I found that my daughter's arms were scratched and bruised because of the pup's rough ways. It wasn't that the pup was being malicious, just overly mouthy. Her modus operandi was to grab things first and ask questions afterward. I told Sue to start setting limits, to say "no" loudly and withdraw from the pup when it nipped her to make quite sure that the pup learned that this behavior was not acceptable. I also told her to use simple, preferably one-word commands when instructing the pup to do anything, followed by immediate reward for a job well done.

A week passed and Dave and Sue had occasion to visit my house, this time to collect their daughter, Ashley, who had been playing with Keisha. The pup, now named Lucy, was in their truck. What a difference a week makes, particularly at this age. She had grown accustomed to the lead and was already sitting on command and paying much more attention to Sue's instructions. Lucy wasn't cowed, but she wasn't forward, either. The Cosellos were handling things just right and were reaping the rewards.

Lucy still had all the character and energy she had demonstrated at our first meeting, but that energy was becoming channeled along constructive lines. I was delighted with her progress. The "no" command had soaked in well, making life more manageable for the family, and there had been no further nipping incidents. That morning the pup had followed Dave on every stripe of his lawn-mowing and had subsequently collapsed in a tired but happy heap to sleep off the morning's entertainment. What a terrific pup she was shaping up to be. Despite precautions to the contrary, she had already taken the plunge into the pool, where she swam like a fish. Luckily, folks were around to haul her out. What a rascal. I could only project good things for this pup's future and couldn't help but contrast her positive early experiences with some of the dysfunctional starts I hear of in the behavior clinic.

When you consider that a good dog is a fourteen- (or more) year project, it makes good sense to provide the best possible environment for its upbringing and to go out of your way to establish clear channels of communication and appropriate early-socialization experiences. It's like money in the bank. All efforts in this direction are rewarded with compound interest and even dividends.

Rescued dogs can make fine pets, too, although they are a different story and often something of a black box with regard to their antecedent behavior. The way they have to be incorporated into a family structure varies too. Some dogs require kid-glove treatment whereas others need subtle reminders of their place in the home. With both rescued dogs and new pups, owner attitudes can make or break the deal. If all goes well with a new pup or an adopted dog, owners can find they have a marvelous pet, faithful family friend, and all-around good canine citizen. The alternative outcome, which doesn't bear thinking about, often results in the dog winding up back in the pound.

A good dog is a terrific addition to any family. Caring for it can teach children and adults to appreciate another living creature and to develop loving bonds that enrich the quality of life. Understanding your dog properly is the key to a healthy relationship. I encourage readers to refer to appropriate sections of this book when faced with difficulties and attempt to work them out, with or without the help of an expert. Although this book deals with the treatment of behavioral problems that already exist, it also contains a lot of information about the prevention of behavior problems. Along these lines I have discussed breed differences (which should influence selection), appropriate rearing practices, and I have stressed the provision of adequate exercise, entertainment, and other behavioral outlets for *all* domestic dogs. If these matters are attended to conscientiously, owners as well as their dogs will benefit. A well behaved dog is a joy to own and its very conformity signals its contentedness with its lot.

APPENDIX

BEHAVIOR-MODIFICATION TECHNIQUES

Although you *can* teach an old dog new tricks, it goes without saying that early socialization and some effort to inculcate puppies with a basic command-response sequence as a method of interspecies communication are both of paramount importance in raising the dog of your dreams (as opposed to your nightmares). A dog that is genetically well-balanced, fearful of nothing, and understanding of and obedient to commands will never present a behavioral problem for anyone. And you can cut most dogs a little slack in the latter department. Obedience, yes, but an automaton, no. After all, most of us want a lovable pet, not a little canine soldier that is compelled to obey our every command. But sometimes the early advantage is lost and dysfunction or willfulness arises. This is the time for an abrupt turnaround—a reinstallation of confidence or respect as necessity dictates. These procedures are the yin and yang of behavior-modification therapy, complemented by clear communication, limit setting, and the provision of a happy and healthful lifestyle for the dog in accordance with breed requirements.

For the Fearful Dog:

(A) Counterconditioning
Counterconditioning involves teaching a dog that a mildly fear-inducing stimulus or situation leads to a contrary sensation of relaxation, pleasure, or reward. Sometimes counterconditioning can be used on its own to reverse minor fears and anxieties. For example, if a dog is introduced to a fear-inducing stranger who always arrives bearing gifts (say, food treats),

the person's arrival (heralded by the doorbell) will, in time, elicit an appetitive response rather than one of fear and apprehension. Pavlov's experiments demonstrated primary conditioning, when the sound of a bell (a neutral stimulus) heralded to dogs the arrival of food and caused them to salivate. Counterconditioning reverses the response to a previously conditioned stimulus by changing a preformed perception and facilitating the development of an alternate response. Food treats are often employed to alter a dog's perceptions in this way. Operant counterconditioning is a similar technique in which the dog is trained to lie down and relax in the presence of a stimulus that previously elicited a fearful reaction. Of course, it is not always possible to accomplish this goal, unless the intensity of the fear-inducing stimulus can first be controlled so that it can be presented at a tolerable level.

(B) Systematic Desensitization

When fears are too strong to be overcome by counterconditioning alone, a graded approach (systematic desensitization) to confronting the dog with his nemesis must be employed. For example, if a fearful dog is too frightened to be able to think about receiving food or relaxing in the face of a particular fear-inducing stimulus, a systematic and incremental introduction to the fear-inducing stimulus is indicated. Systematic desensitization is almost always employed along with simultaneous counterconditioning, though it can also be conducted on its own. Simply allow the dog to settle at each level that the stimulus is presented without attempting to readjust the dog's perspective.

The principles of systematic desensitization are as follows:
1. Identify accurately what is causing the dog's fear.
2. Prevent the dog from experiencing fear of that stimulus by preventing exposure to it.
3. Reintroduce the dog to the fear-inducing stimulus in a graded fashion—usually using the dog's distance from the fear-inducing stimulus as the variable factor.
4. Reward the dog with praise, petting, or food treats (counterconditioning) for remaining nonfearful and relaxed in the presence of the fear-inducing stimulus.

5. Incrementally reduce the dog's distance from the fear-inducing stimulus as the dog's reaction permits.
6. Take time and be prepared for setbacks.

One mistake that some trainers make is to advise rapid desensitization. For example, if your dog is frightened of children, they say, "Take him to the Little League game," or if it is frightened of strangers the word is "Bring him to a shopping mall and plant him by the entrance so that he will be exposed harmlessly to hundreds of people. That way he will desensitize to people's presence." Neither of these two techniques is systematic desensitization, which involves an approach more like peeling off the layers of an onion. Sudden and continued exposure to a fear-inducing stimulus (flooding) is a technique that is rarely indicated or successful in anything but the mildest fears. In more severe fears it is positively inhumane and its execution is not only ineffective, but also counterproductive.

For Separation Anxiety:

Although systematic desensitization with counterconditioning can be used to treat separation anxiety ("the planned-departure technique"), the very first requirement of this program—never to leave your dog alone during the entire retraining period (which can be weeks or months)—is often a major stumbling block. Not only that, but also the retraining procedure is both tedious and time consuming and requires considerable owner compliance. My experience with this program is that owners do not do well with it and thus the results of retraining are not good. Instead, I use a program called independence training. The principle of this retraining method is to teach the dog to "stand on its own four feet" when the owner is present, with the express intention that the dog's newfound confidence will spill over into times when the owner is away. Essential components of this program are as follows:

1. Benign obedience training should be instituted to instill confidence in the dog. The exercises should be geared toward distancing the dog from its owner; that is, having the dog sit or lie down while the owner moves progressively farther away (as opposed to

recall techniques that involve teaching the dog to come to the owner). To have the dog sit and stay while the owner leaves the room for a few minutes would be a huge positive step on this ladder of improvement.

2. Owners should be the ones to initiate all interactions with their dog (not the other way round) and they should discourage their dog from following them around. If a dog with separation anxiety trails around after its owner, the owner should gently take the dog by the collar or training lead and escort it to a nearby rest area; say, a dog bed. Here the dog should be instructed to lie down and stay and should then be warmly praised for obeying. The bond between dogs with separation anxiety and their owners must be loosened in this way if treatment is to be successful.

3. Dogs with separation anxiety should be discouraged from draping themselves across their owner's lap while the owner is watching television or sitting on the couch reading. This is done in a way similar to that suggested in Step 2 above.

4. Unfortunately, from the owner's perspective, dogs with separation anxiety should not be allowed to sleep in bed with the owner. To be in the same bedroom at night is fine, but the dog should be required to lie on a blanket on the floor or on a dog bed. Initially it may test the owner's patience to make this happen. Several attempts to get the dog to stay may be necessary before it gets the message that the owner really means what he is saying. Success should be rewarded as before. For refractory cases it may be necessary to tie the dog to a fixture in the room by means of a four-foot lead. Alternatively, for dogs familiar with crates, these may be used to prevent unwanted excursions.

5. Play tug-of-war games with the dog and let the dog win. This builds confidence. If the dog starts to growl, the owner may have gone too far and it is time to back off with this approach.

6. The dog should be ignored for fifteen minutes before an owner leaves and for fifteen minutes following his or her return. This evens out the emotional roller-coaster ride that these dogs otherwise experience with overly emotional departures and exuberant greetings from owners when they come home.

7. Counterconditioning is used with this technique. The way this is

done is to put down a "sustained-acting food treat" fifteen minutes before departing in the hope that the dog will associate this treat with the owner's departure. I heard of one dog that actually seemed to look forward to the owner going out after this practice was initiated. Treats to use include hollow bones stuffed with peanut butter or soft cheese, drilled-out nylon bones or hollow rubber chew toys (such as Kong toys) similarly enhanced, or a suitably large real bone (uncooked), though this can be messy.

8. In addition to all of the above, the dog should receive plenty of exercise and suitable rations for its level of activity.

9. Medication is usually used in conjunction with the above technique and is generally helpful. Traditionally, antidepressants like Elavil and Anafranil have been used but recently Prozac has shown itself to be a real winner for the treatment of separation anxiety. Critical to the success of medication is the correct dose, given for an appropriate period of time (at least four to six weeks in the case of an antidepressant).

For the Dominant Dog:

Dominance-Control Program

(aka Nothing in Life Is Free, Working for a Living, or No Free Lunch)

This nonconfrontational program was designed specifically for use with dominant-aggressive dogs but it can also help restructure a stronger, healthier leadership role for the owner of an anxious or fearful dog. With regard to the principles implicit in this program, the mnemonic phrases bracketed above say it all. The basic requirement is the owner's mind-set that the dog must, initially at least and to some extent for time immemorial, earn every valued asset. This attitude will, in time, cultivate the dog's dependence, respect, and reliance, and thus the owner's control and influence.

There is one essential prerequisite for the program—a modicum of training. The dog must understand and obey at least one or two commands prior to starting the program, though its repertoire can and should be increased subsequently (see "O—Obedience Training"). It is not imperative that a dog entering this program obey every command at first, just as long as the owner is sure that it understands some directives issued and is in a position to obey should it so choose. As a backdrop to the program, owners are asked to reinforce any obedience training they have learned by rehearsing it with the dog for a few minutes each day and utilizing commands whenever possible to accomplish various ends. This said, the stage is set. Here is what I call the twelve-step program of rehabilitation (or, in the abridged version, leaving out diet and exercise advice, the ten commandments).

1. Avoid Confrontation

The golden rule of a nonconfrontational program is *no confrontation*. To facilitate this approach, I ask owners to complete a list of circumstances that elicit aggression from their dog, including those that induce growling, lip lifts, snaps, and bites, and I then run through the individual situations advising the owner how to circumvent each. As benevolent as this sounds, it is no soft shoe approach. Avoiding aggression is an essential component of nonconfrontational programs, and if not engaged it will undermine other measures applied. It is useless to work on such a program while simultaneously attempting to apply coercive training methods, as the two approaches are, like water and oil, immiscible.

The axiom to keep in mind while engaging a nonconfrontational approach is that if you live by the sword, you die by the sword, or more basically, aggression begets aggression. It's the same reason you shouldn't allow your kids to watch the Power Rangers. Naturally, there is a level of aggression you can apply that will silence any dominant dog, but that approach is not for me or my clients. As my new resident, Dr. Gerry Flannigan, recently explained it to one client, "You *can* get the better of a dog by fighting with it, but you must be prepared to fight to the death." I think he made his point, because the client declined this approach.

Following the sort of measures I advise means that if your dog tries to guard a rawhide chew from you, it doesn't get them anymore. Problem solved. If possessiveness of stolen bathroom tissues is an issue, thwart the dog's access to the tissues by putting them in a cupboard (and while you're at it, keep the wastebasket behind closed doors). If by chance the dog still gets hold of a tissue somehow, let him have it. Who cares? He won't choke on it. Chasing a dog with a stolen object is a sure way to get more of the same pilfering behavior. If you really need to get a stolen object back, say, your credit card, then distract the dog by issuing a command and providing a more enthralling alternative. For example, get the dog's lead, make for the door, and command, "Rover. Come here. Good boy." (And don't forget to praise Rover for coming.) This latter approach is not bribery, it's distraction. Bribery does not work and may even aggravate the behavior.

There are many other measures that may be necessary in an individual case. If your dog growls when you pet it on the head, it is trying to tell you something. So don't do it. Pet him under the chin instead—but only when he has done something to deserve it. And if your dog snaps at you when you groom him, bathe him, or clip his nails, take him to the groomer to be coiffed and be done with it. Groomers have their own way and, whatever it is, it will not affect your relationship with your dog. It's only what *you* do that makes any difference to that relationship, not what anyone else does. The list of wheezes goes on and on. Get imaginative. Just to give you a little confidence in the method, as I mentioned in the section on aggression, avoiding all aggressive incidents for a period of two weeks will seriously deter dominance. It's as if dominance aggression feeds on itself. If you reduce input, the behavior simply fades away.

2. Feeding

Since food is such a valued commodity within the pack, it is imperative to make the dominant dog realize that you control this asset. It must learn that it is powerless over food and that you are its higher power. Food must no longer appear like manna from heaven but only (and obviously) from you. Right from the get-go of this program your dog must earn all food from you (including food treats) by responding positively to some command from a family member. As I've said, there is no free lunch.

Initially owners can cut their dogs some slack in terms of the speed and quality of its response—just as long as there is some reasonable attempt to conform to the instruction given. For example, if the command "Sit" is given before putting down the dog's food and it obeys, however slowly, dinner is served. If the dog does not sit, however, the food is withdrawn, not for five minutes only but until the next mealtime. There's nothing like the increased motivation provided by hunger to facilitate the desired response. As time goes by, owners should insist on speedier and more precise responses from their dog. Let's say that initially the dog sits within three seconds of the command being given and is fed. Once this level of response is achieved reliably, the time allocation for the response should be reduced to two seconds, then one second, and ultimately an immediate response is required. Insistence on a speedy and accurate response from the dog is not a fool's errand. It teaches the dog to respect an owner's authority.

To help my clients understand the importance of this seemingly trivial feeding regimen, I often refer to what I call my waiter analogy. (No disrespect to waiters intended.) It goes something like this: If you are in a restaurant and a waiter brings you food you have ordered and puts it in front of you, that manner of serving does nothing to increase your respect for that waiter. It's what you expect and what you normally get. If, however, the waiter says, "Get down on your knees in front of me or I will not serve you," that would certainly attract your attention. You might mutter under your breath and go to leave the restaurant in disgust . . . but if the waiter had locked the door and refused to let you out (and had the power to enforce this measure), you would eventually have to sit down again. You might then refuse to eat rather than kneel in front of a waiter . . . but how long could you hold out? Twelve hours? Twenty-four? One thing is for sure, you wouldn't allow yourself to starve to death for petty principles. If the waiter held his line, a breaking point would eventually come when your hunger was so overwhelming that the food in front of you would become irresistible. At this stage you kneel down and are rewarded for conforming as demanded by receiving the food. The waiter would have firmly made his point and could then afford to smile, issue a few platitudes, and even offer you a drink (you might need it).

Now, this would be a pretty jerky thing for a waiter to do, and I'm not suggesting to any waiters reading this that they should try it, but like it or not, under these circumstances you would have to view the waiter in a whole new light—with a lot more respect and a sudden realization of your dependence on him (or her). I have known some very willful dogs that hold out for three days before they will obey a command to receive food, but most fold a lot earlier than this. They will all submit to their owners' authority in the long run; they have to, and it is important for owners to realize this. After all, it's a battle of wills, your against theirs.

In most instances when I implement such measures, I point out that it's imperative that the owner win the mental tussle, either for reasons of their personal safety or because success of the program is a life and death matter for the dog. The only caveat in applying the no-free-lunch approach comes with large, deep-chested dogs that are prone to bloat. It is inadvisable to allow these dogs to pig out after any period of fasting or food deprivation, as under these circumstances they may develop bloat. For such dogs, the rules are the same except that only small meals are offered after a period of fasting rebellion. This way, when the dog finally concedes, it will not be able to gorge itself into oblivion with potentially disasterous consequences. Such dogs may come up hungry after their initial token meal, but they can be fed another small meal an hour or so later, and so on until they are reasonably well satiated.

Dogs that have conformed to the feeding strategy outlined are allowed fifteen minutes to eat, after which any surplus food should be picked up— but not in the dog's presence, to avoid a confrontation. The running-buffet phenomenon is now a thing of the past. You can almost picture a dog's surprise in the early stages of this program when it rounds a corner to find a normally well-supplied food bowl empty or absent. I imagine the dog's reaction is similar to Kramer's in the *Seinfeld* show when he is confronted by the unexpected. There's nothing like a change in the ground rules to make a dog pay more attention to what's going on around it, and in its new awareness it will learn that you are the supreme being that supplies all good things. After all, "The Lord giveth and the Lord taketh away."

3. Petting

The tactile stimulus of petting, and the acknowledgment that goes with it, is a powerful reward for most dogs and as such should be rationed in the same way as food. But petting is a two-edged sword because it can become an annoyance for the dog if it is improperly performed, rendered by the wrong person, at the wrong time, or if it is continued beyond a certain welcome period. In the latter instances, petting may actually stimulate aggression. Petting dogs on top of the head, for example, especially by patting, is one of the most common reasons for being bitten.

To be pleasurable and nonthreatening, petting should be performed under the chin or chest, using a scratching motion, or along the side of the face by stroking the hair in the same direction that it grows (that is, with the "grain"). In addition, petting sessions should be brief enough to leave the dog wanting more . . . although some really bad players will bite you if you shortchange them, so the appropriate duration of petting is a judgment call. If in doubt, don't pet the dog at all for several weeks until other aspects of the dominance-control program have kicked in.

A further point: If low-ranking humans (in a dominant dog's eyes) try to pet it at an inopportune moment—for example, while the dog is eating, resting, or otherwise engaged—they will find themselves on the receiving end of its ire in fairly short order. Petting should only be engaged at times other than these and preferably when the petter knows that the attention is welcome. But here comes the rub (if you'll excuse the pun): Petting of any description and at any time has to be on *your* terms to send a clear signal of your leadership. No longer can kindly owners, who are at other times on the receiving end of a dominant dog's aggression, submit to their dog's demands for petting. Such demands, transmitted by head butting and pressing, must be circumvented or ignored—though the message that the dog is amenable to petting can be registered. This is the correct time to insist that the dog "says please," asking to be petted by sitting in response to a command in order to receive the petting it desires.

As with the feeding routine, owners must define the ground rules and set limits to send the correct message of authority. No sit, no pet, is the order of the day. This is difficult to do for many folks who have become used to petting their dogs indiscriminately and who actually enjoy this freedom of action. No one said a nonconfrontational program was easy. It involves toughness—just a different kind, a mental one.

The point is that to supply petting for a dog whenever it demands it from you is to undermine your own authority. If you supply petting and other "good things of life" for free, you will never be able to get a dominant dog to obey you when you need it most or to respect you. After all, why should such a dog work for rewards when they are supplied free? If *we* got paid whether we went to work or not the workplace would be a pretty lonely place. Dominant dogs should have to work for a living, too. That's the way for previously insubordinated owners to assume their rightful position as the boss in the home and to command the respect they deserve. Success necessitates taking a hard line.

4. Praise

Depending on the dog in question, praise can be another highly valued asset for which dominant dogs should be required to work. Praising a dog continuously dilutes the value of this otherwise much-appreciated acknowledgment, undermining an owner's unique position as the keeper of the key of approbation. My grandmother used to say of human families, "The one who holds the purse strings rules the house." Praise (and petting) can be thought of as money for a dog and can be used to command the same kind of respect. If you control and ration both praise and petting, your dog will view you in a more authoritative light. As a detail, the timing and tone of the praise is critical. Correct timing of praise involves conferring it when it is due. For example, praise the dog when it is walking calmly next to you on lead (not pulling), waiting for you patiently while you are otherwise occupied, or within half a second of its responding to a command. Regarding the tone of praise, it should be warm and heartfelt. Women praise better than men, who, I'm afraid to say, often mumble it into their beards—"Goo'dug." The latter will hardly be worth working for, making the dog far less apt to behave and less likely to work to earn such meager recognition. The message here is to put some energy into praising a dog when it has done something to deserve it, and for goodness sake, never praise a dominant dog that is growling.

5. Toys

The provision of toys is another privilege for which dominant dogs must work. Again, fair's fair, they can have all the toys they want . . . they just have to work for them. The way to arrange it is as follows: Pick up all toys and put them in an assigned drawer or cabinet and supply toys only when your dog obeys a command. For example, call your dog to the toy drawer to demonstrate its existence. "Hey Benji. C'mere, good boy." (Dog comes, albeit slowly.) You say, while exhibiting a favorite toy, "Sit" (assuming a modicum of basic training). Dog sits. You respond immediately "Good boy, Benji," and supply the cherished object. Benji plays with the toy for a while. When he's done you pick it up and replace it in the drawer, ready for the same charade the next time. The alternative scenario is that Benji doesn't sit when commanded. The result, analogous to the situation regarding feeding, is that the drawer is closed and the toy is not allowed. It's the dog's choice, but *you* hold the key to this pleasure. It's

amazing how quickly dogs learn which way is up. I can have a dog knowing that I have something worth having in a drawer in my office within a
minute or two (or less). After that we both have decisions to make. No
paying, no gain.

6. Games

Now, this is getting repetitive—but it won't hurt to drive the tin tack
home. Games are fun, and as such should be rationed, along with all of
life's other pleasures for the dog. The trouble with dogs and games is that
if you don't make the rules, they do . . . and the next thing that's happening is they're playing with you, instead of the other way around.

Take the game of fetch, for example. The dominant dog will often
bring the ball to you to initiate the game. If you pick up the ball at this
point you have just made mistake number one. You have allowed the dog
to determine when the game starts. Since dominant dogs initiate most
activities within the pack, if you respond, you have just dealt yourself a
card of low denomination. It is important that, similar to the situation with
petting, you realize that the dog wants to play but decide the time and
place yourself a short while later. Just when the dog is fed up with waiting
for you to respond, pick up the ball and issue a command—"C'mon,
Whiskey, let's go"—and stride to the throwing place. Whiskey either
comes or doesn't and by now you know how to respond to either occurrence. If Whiskey comes and you initiate the game, you play by your
rules.

The rules are that the ball is brought back to you and dropped at your
feet. Dominant dogs tend to take over the game and drop the ball short or
refuse to let it go . . . to jerk your chain and gain the upper hand. If you
lumber forward to pick up the ball they may grab it and take another
couple of steps back. "What's-a-matter, too quick for you, eh?" would
describe what they are thinking. It is imperative that you don't end up
falling for this trap, and you don't need to. If things don't go your way, you
simply quit the game with a finish command such as "Finish" or
"Enough." It doesn't matter who has got the ball at that point; you just
walk away if necessary, leaving the dog standing there with the ball in its
mouth, thinking, "What went wrong?" But don't worry, they soon figure it
out. The alternative is to have the dog decide it has had enough and to
walk off leaving you holding the ball, saying, "Whiskey . . . wanna play

s'more? Whiskey, oh Whiskey." (Dog pads off with a slightly bored look and a smirk on its face.) Who's in charge here?

The game of fetch was just one example, but the same general rules should apply to any game you play with a dog that's causing you problems because of its dominance. Basically you have to do what dominant dogs do in the pack. That is, you initiate all activities and you decide when they're over. Anything less just isn't leadership. And one further point, rough games, like slap boxing, wrestling, tickling, and tug-o'-war, are simply verboten. It's another one of those live-by-the-sword, die-by-the-sword type of situations, and men are the worst offenders in promoting aggression this way. They even do it with their own sons. I quote from Tim (the Tool Man) Taylor, "Ourgh, ourgh, ourgh, ourgh, ourgh." So powerful are the effects of these rough games that competition trainers use them to build confidence and "character" in young dogs prior to shaping their behavior to suit. Regular owners aren't so knowledgeable as to know how to turn off this faucet of confidence, so the simple rule is don't mess with it . . . just leave well enough alone.

7. Needs vs Wants

Demanding what they want, and getting it, is another way that dominant dogs exercise control over compliant owners. These willful dogs sometimes rag on unsuspecting owners to get their own way, barking in their owners' faces, interrupting their conversations, and refusing to take no for an answer. Constantly responding to such willfulness can undermine an owner's authority with such dogs, creating an atmosphere favorable for the expression of dominance aggression. Some believe that an owner's thoughtfulness in responding to such demands is interpreted by dominant dogs as a form of weakness, and that the dog subsequently capitalizes on its owner's compliance by assuming the alpha position in the family "pack."

On the other side of the penny, going against a dominant dog's will can lead to aggression against the usurper. A common situation in which dominant dogs bite people occurs when the dog is prevented from achieving some goal by being grasped by the collar or scruff. So what is an owner to do? It seems that you are damned if you do and damned if you don't facilitate their wishes.

Well, that isn't exactly the case. There's a middle ground between facilitation and prevention called ignorance (pronounced "ignore-ance," in this case). Basically, you should not cater to any demanding behavior from the dog, whatever the short-term consequences. It is rare for a dog to attack an owner because the owner isn't doing something it wants, though many such dogs make quite a nuisance of themselves initially if their owners attempt to give them the cold shoulder. The invasiveness gets worse before it gets better. Again, mental toughness is needed to get through this phase of treatment. It goes without saying that, "ignorance" aside, the dog can have anything it wants if it is prepared to work for it, and that all spontaneous good behavior should be rewarded. The value of the "cold-shoulder" component of a dominance-control program is highlighted by the effects of forced attention withdrawal resulting from temporary separation or the less-humane trainer tactic of isolating dominant dogs in a crate for a couple of weeks and totally ignoring them (except for providing for their basic needs). In each case, dominant dogs suddenly become a lot more respectful and well behaved . . . but it is important to provide appropriate leadership if the advantage is to be maintained.

8. Company

Along similar lines to the provision of attention to a dog is the provision of companionship, only this is a more passive type of situation. No one said that dominant dogs weren't fond of their owners; they often are and will seek out their owner's company and close physical contact when the mood so takes them. The typical scene is of a dominant dog taking up residence on an owner's lap and just hanging out there. The proverbial lap dog, if you will.

I always say to these owners, "Think about it—when he's sitting on top of you, who's the king and who's the throne?" Then I see the truth dawn. The analogy usually makes the point.

Larger dogs may simply lean against their owner's feet or position themselves on the couch next to their owner, or some such. You would think that these Norman Rockwell-type images would depict a dog in fine humor . . . and in many ways they do, but some dominant dogs are so enamored of the situation that if the owner goes to leave or move he may find himself on the receiving end of the dog's ire. I came across a dominant dog just the other day that bit his owner if the owner moved when he was lying pressed against his foot. Another typical scenario occurs when dominant dogs are allowed to sleep with their owners. Some of these dogs will growl or even bite if their owners stir during the night. Owners sometimes put this down to the dog having a bad dream, but the truth of the matter is that they're ticked off at the owner disturbing them.

As treatment for this curious aspect of dominant behavior, your company and close physical presence should be rationed in the same way as everything else and only provided as a reward for submissive behavior. In the early stages of a dominance program it may be necessary to ban lap sitting and, in my view, such dogs should never be permitted to sleep in bed with their owners, if for no other reason than it breaks the "high-place rule."

9. High Places

The simple rule for dominant dogs is No High Places, and this means no going on beds or other furniture. When dominant dogs get on eye level with a person, or conversely when a person gets down to their level, their authority is increased and aggressive encounters are more likely. Even David Letterman has his seat four inches higher than his guests to convey mastery and authority. By the same token, preachers use pulpits and public speakers use soap boxes.

Some of the worst accidents I have heard of involving dominant dogs have occurred when owners have inadvertently challenged their dog while they are lying on the floor or when a child approaches a dog that is lying on a bed or couch. The simplest solution is just to "say no to furniture" or, more precisely to say "Off" to dogs that climb up on furniture. Owners who have difficulty in enforcing this rule without forbidden confrontations of collar grabbing should attach a ten-foot-long nylon training lead to their dog so that they can gently pull the dog off the couch from a safe distance should it not respond to the command promptly. But they should not forget to praise the dog the minute it has four feet firmly on the floor, even if they did have a hand in facilitating the response. For really difficult dogs, booby traps that will deter future excursions onto the furniture can be arranged. Upside-down mousetraps provide one method of achieving this, although you can create quite a stir with a black thread and some cans containing pennies ("shake cans").

10. Freedom

Believe it or not, freedom, for dogs, too, is one of life's great privileges, and with privilege comes the need for social responsibility and respect. If all a dog has to do to obtain its freedom is to bark at its owner or paw at a door, where's the respect in that? Freedom is a gift and, for dogs of dominant disposition, one that should only be allowed to those deserving of it, and denied to the unruly. This is not to say that an unruly, dominant dog can never go out, just that its freedom should be curtailed if it refuses to toe the line. For example, if a dominant dog in need of "the program" fails to obey a command to earn its freedom, it should only be taken out under escort and on lead.

Though exercise may be important for such a dog's welfare, it can be supplied by means of brisk walks or jogging on lead with the owner, instead of permitting the rebel to run around unrestrained when it has done nothing to deserve its freedom. The hope is that in time, even hard-liners will conform to house rules by sitting or lying down when instructed, in order to earn the opportunity to cavort chaperon-free. For dominant dogs, however, freedom can never be absolute. It would be irresponsible for the owner of a dominant dog to turn his (or her) dog free in a park or other public place, giving it the opportunity to attack other dogs and passing children as it saw fit. Rather, such dogs' freedom should be limited, being permitted only within a (preferably) largish, fenced-in area where potential targets for aggression, be they other dogs or children, are absent.

11. Exercise

The jury is still out on the benefits of exercise in the treatment of dominance. It can be argued both ways. On one hand, exercise appears to be generally beneficial, but then again, most dominant dogs are more aggressive to their owners in the evening, when they are tired. The latter could be due to daily variations in the brain level of serotonin, a neurochemical involved in regulating aggression, which tends to fall during the day as it is metabolized to melatonin. If fluctuations in the serotonin level are the cause of aggression, exercise should be a good therapy because it elevates and stabilizes brain serotonin, preventing mood swings and reducing aggression.

A minimum of twenty to thirty minutes of aerobic exercise daily is necessary to make exercise a worthwhile therapy, and I leave owners to work out for themselves whether they think it is beneficial for their dog's aggression problem. By the way, in the provision of exercise, the philosophy of "work in exchange for freedom" must be borne in mind. Note that simply walking a mile or two with your dog is not really enough for most young, fit dogs. I used to take my eighty-five-year-old mother for a one-mile walk every day when she was visiting from Britain and neither of us was particularly exhausted at the end of the day.

12. Diet

Here's one other gray zone where the advice you get depends upon who you ask. Again, the jury's out on this one, but until the judgment time many behaviorists and trainers advise low-protein, preservative-free diets for dogs manifesting various types of aggressive behavior, dominance aggression included. We showed that territorial aggression was reduced by feeding low-protein diets but, in the same study, dominance aggression was not significantly affected. More recently we have repeated the diet-study work and found some individual dogs that do seem a bit calmer and less aggressive when fed low-protein rations—but we still have to complete our final analysis. Until that time, like almost everyone else, I advise owners to try switching diets to see if it makes a difference to their dog. After all, the change is almost immediate and there's not much to lose. There are some dogs that develop diarrhea if their diet is changed, and that is a risk, but it can be minimized by switching the diet gradually over three days.

Summary

Thus ends this brief description of the twelve-step program for the control of canine dominance, on the nebulous note of diet. But the program itself is not so nebulous. In fact it is quite concrete and very effective if diligently performed. We have demonstrated that nine of ten owners see positive results after engaging in a dominance-control program with their dogs. The improvement peaks about two months after implementation of the program and many owners see such outstanding results that they report their problems with the dog as solved.

The bottom line is, however, that dogs that have been allowed to develop dominance always have the potential to revert to their old ways should an owner's guard be lowered too far. Some elements of the dominance-control program must be maintained indefinitely. Dominant dogs are always testing the limits to see just how far they can go; challenging to see what they can get away with. How far you can relax your guard depends on the dog in question, but for most dominant dogs at least half of the above measures must remain in place if the improved status quo is to be maintained. And there is no point in just hoping and praying that dominance aggression will go away when the dog gets older. It won't. Only when dominant dogs become geriatric and their mental function deteriorates is there something of a remission in the struggle for power. It takes a special mind-set to maintain the upper hand with these willful dogs in what is an ongoing game of interspecies one-upmanship.

For Compulsive Dogs:

As mentioned in chapter "C—Compulsive Behavior," the provision of a healthy and entertaining environment is critical in the prevention and treatment of dysfunctional repetitive behaviors in dogs. In addition to avoiding reinforcement of these behaviors by poorly timed attention, there are several key areas to address:

1. Provide adequate exercise. As mentioned above, it is aerobic (running) exercise that is really indicated, not just a twice-daily saunter around the block. Provision of exercise of this type means that owners have to invest time and energy—yes, energy—into the care and maintenance of their dogs. What a revelation! Lying on a couch and wishing your dog were happier just doesn't cut it. But you don't actually have to run alongside your dog, even supposing you were fit enough to accomplish this. It is supervision and promotion of exercise that falls into the owners' bailiwick. Whether exercise is provided for the dog by throwing a tennis ball or Frisbee, lunging it on a long line, taking it jogging, or by means of long country excursions, is a matter of personal choice for the owner, one that must necessarily factor in logistical considerations as well as the personality of the dog involved. The lazy man's approach of simply turning the dog out in the backyard is often insufficient, as most dogs do not tire themselves out this way. They may run a bit, rest a bit, and so on, not

really pushing themselves to the maximum. They need you, their personal trainer, to make it all come together.

2. Feed an appropriate diet. Again, the definitive word on what is an appropriate diet has yet to be determined, but we are working on this issue today. Until our results are collated and published it might be worth owners of compulsive dogs attempting a diet trial of their own, by working from first principles. What intuitively makes sense is to switch from "performance" or other high energy product to a food designed for less active dogs. It might also be worth exploring the possible effects of artificial preservatives by feeding an "all natural" ration for a while. I usually advise switching the diet for a trial period of two to four weeks to see if there is any improvement in the dog's behavior. Sometimes I believe that there is, according to what I am told. But owner impressions can be unreliable, particularly since the placebo effect runs at around thirty-five percent, even in veterinary medicine. What this means is that thirty-five percent of owners will report that their dog is considerably improved when no effective treatment has been given. Apparently, the power of suggestion is sufficient, for some wishful owners, to generate these inaccurate perceptions. The only way to eliminate biases is by "blinding" (concealing) the true nature of the treatments given and comparing the results of a treatment group with that of a "control" (unrelated) group.

3. Ensure clear communication with the dog. As mentioned in the section on obedience training, early training of dogs to obey simple one-word commands is important in reducing stress which often underlies compulsive behavior. As comforting as it may be for the owner, constantly blabbering to your dog does little more than confuse it. Gary Larson, as usual, had the situation pegged in his cartoon, *The Far Side*, depicting what a dog really understood of an owner's conversation. Remember the line, "Blah, blah, blah, blah, blah, blah, Ginger." How true that is. I'm not saying that you shouldn't rattle on merrily to your dog. Even though he won't understand much of what you're saying, depending on the tone of your conversation, the white-noise effect could be somewhat soothing. However, real communication is necessary, too. Dogs are capable of understanding over forty word-signs (sounds), such as "sit," "come," "down," et cetera. In terms of verbal communication, short is sweet and more effective, and it helps if the word ends in a consonant so that it has a precise end.

For deaf dogs, American Sign Language can be used with the same effect of opening lines of communication—which in turn reduces stress. One of my star patients, a deaf Dalmatian called Hogan, had mastered forty-three or -four words of sign language at last count, and this communication with his owner, Connie Bombaci, appeared to contribute significantly in his rehabilitation from a compulsive-digging disorder.

4. Provide appropriate environmental enrichment and "occupational therapy." Every dog may have his day but also needs a fulfilling environment and a job to help make that day more meaningful. In the section on independence training I mentioned an array of toys and treats that can be left out to occupy dogs that must be left alone for hours, and a few other tricks to enrich this otherwise tedious portion of their lives. Naturally, the optimum strategy is to spend as much quality time with a dog as it needs, though the hustle and bustle of modern life does not always permit this luxury. Failing your ability to provide a rich and diversified life of interesting or entertaining experiences for your dog, you should consider engaging the services of others who have more time on their hands. Perhaps neighboring schoolchildren might enjoy spending some time with your dog if you are too busy, and maybe a friend or relative would be happy to look after your dog when you are away. Also, puppy day-care can provide an otherwise lonely dog with company and entertainment and is certainly better than the alternative of being left home alone.

The point is that dogs are living creatures and need something to occupy their time, just as we do. Many of the modern-day canine psychoses seem to stem from an inappropriate lifestyle that is boring and unfulfilling. My grandmother again had a saying that described this situation. It went something like this: "Idle hands the devil's work do." A bit melodramatic, perhaps, but it makes the point. It benefits dogs to be gainfully employed in something, to have a job to do. In the process of designing a job for your dog, make sure you incorporate breed-specific needs, such as herding-type activities for collies and retrieving games for sporting dogs. And remember, though not all dogs love trucks, they do all love company.

INDEX

ABOUT THE AUTHOR

NICHOLAS H. DODMAN was born in London, England, in 1946. He graduated from Glasgow University Veterinary School in 1970 and after a spell in practice rejoined his alma mater on faculty in 1972. He is board certified by the American Veterinary Medical Association in both veterinary anesthesiology and veterinary behavior and is a member of the Association of Pet Behavior Counselors. Dr. Dodman is a professor in the Department of Clinical Sciences at the prestigious Tufts University School of Veterinary Medicine, where he heads the Animal Behavior Clinic. He is the bestselling author of *The Dog Who Loved Too Much* and *The Cat Who Cried for Help* and has co-authored two textbooks and over one hundred scientific articles. Original ideas in the fields of behavioral physiology and pharmacology have earned him six United States patents and an international reputation as a prime mover and innovator. His desire to convey scientific information to the public has brought him national celebrity, with appearances on *20/20, Good Morning America*, the *Today* show, *CNN Headline News*, National Public Radio, and *The Oprah Winfrey Show*. A communicator of the first order, Dr. Dodman continues in his quest to spread the good word about the fascinating subject of pet behavior.